Math in Focus®

Singapore Math®
by Marshall Cavendish

Student Edition

Program Consultant
Dr. Fong Ho Kheong

Authors
Dr. Lai Chee Chong
Leong May Kuen
Low Wai Cheng

Course 2A

marshall cavendish
education

U.S. Distributor

Houghton Mifflin Harcourt.
The Learning Company™

Contents

Algebraic Expressions

▶ Activity

© 2020 Marshall Cavendish Education Pte Ltd

Chapter

3 Algebraic Equations and Inequalities

Chapter Opener

 How do you solve algebraic equations and inequalities?

RECALL PRIOR KNOWLEDGE

Solving algebraic equations by balancing • Solving algebraic equations by substitution
• Graphing inequalities on a number line • Writing algebraic inequalities

▶ Activity

Chapter

4 Proportion and Percent of Change

Chapter Opener

What happens to the proportion when variables in direct or inverse proportion change?

RECALL PRIOR KNOWLEDGE

Comparing quantities using a ratio • Recognizing equivalent ratios • Finding rates and unit rates • Identifying and plotting coordinates • Solving percent problems

▶ Activity

Manipulative List

Algebra tiles

Counters

Additional features include:

RECALL PRIOR KNOWLEDGE	**Math Talk**	**MATH SHARING**	**Caution** and **Math Note**
Helps you recall related concepts you learned before, accompanied by practice questions	Invites you to explain your reasoning and communicate your ideas to your classmates and teachers	Encourages you to create strategies, discover methods, and share them with your classmates and teachers using mathematical language	Highlights common errors and misconceptions, as well as provides you with useful hints and reminders
LET'S EXPLORE	**MATH JOURNAL**	**PUT ON YOUR THINKING CAP!**	**CHAPTER WRAP-UP**
Extends your learning through investigative activities	Allows you to reflect on your learning when you write down your thoughts about the mathematical concepts learned	Challenges you to apply the mathematical concepts to solve problems, and also hones your critical thinking skills	Summarizes your learning in a flow chart and helps you to make connections within the chapter
CHAPTER REVIEW	**Assessment Prep**	**PERFORMANCE TASK**	**STEAM**
Provides you with ample practice in the concepts learned	Prepares you for state tests with assessment-type problems	Assesses your learning through problems that allow you to demonstrate your understanding and knowledge	Promotes collaboration with your classmates through interesting projects that allow you to use math in creative ways

Are you ready to experience math the Singapore way? Let's go!

Preface

Welcome!

Math in Focus® is a program that puts you at the center of an exciting learning experience! This experience is all about equipping you with critical thinking skills and mathematical strategies, explaining your thinking to deepen your understanding, and helping you to become a skilled and confident problem solver.

What's in your book?

Each chapter in this book begins with a real-world situation of the math topic you are about to learn.

In each chapter, you will encounter the following features:

THINK introduces a problem for the whole section, to stimulate creative and critical thinking and help you hone your problem-solving skills. You may not be able to answer the problem right away but you can revisit it a few times as you build your knowledge through the section.

ENGAGE consists of tasks that link what you already know with what you will be learning next. The tasks allow you to explore and discuss mathematical concepts with your classmates.

LEARN introduces new mathematical concepts through a Concrete-Pictorial-Abstract (C-P-A) approach, using activities and examples.

Activity comprises learning experiences that promote collaboration with your classmates. These activities allow you to reinforce your learning or uncover new mathematical concepts.

TRY supports and reinforces your learning through guided practice.

INDEPENDENT PRACTICE allows you to work on a variety of problems and apply the concepts and skills you have learned to solve these problems on your own.

Rational Numbers

How far is it?

Have you ever been on a long road trip, perhaps even across state lines? Whether you stayed within your state or traveled to another, you probably noticed a variety of signs along the way. There are always speed-limit signs, of course. Some warn drivers not to travel too slowly. But most warn drivers not to go beyond a maximum driving speed.

Then, there are signs that alert drivers to how far away certain places are, like the next gas station, restaurant, or roadside attraction. There are also small, green signs called mile markers, which indicate the distance from a state line. If you think of a state line as 0 on a number line, then the mile markers are the tick marks on that number line. Emergency-service providers can use the signs to locate accident scenes. Ordinary drivers can use them to estimate the distance to an exit.

In this chapter, you will learn how to represent rational numbers on the number line. You will also learn to add, subtract, multiply, and divide rational numbers as you solve a variety of real-world problems.

Middleville
EXIT 32
Drive Friendly

Mile
23.5

? How is adding, subtracting, multiplying, and dividing rational numbers similar to performing operations with whole numbers?

Name: _____   Date: _____

Recognizing types of numbers

Type of Number	Whole Numbers	Negative Numbers	Fractions	Decimals
Examples	0, 1, 2, 3	−1, −2, −3	$\frac{1}{4}, \frac{3}{5}, \frac{19}{10}$	1.3, 2.71

Graph the numbers in the table on a horizontal number line.

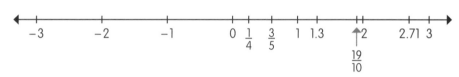

You can also graph the numbers on a vertical number line.

▶ Quick Check

Graph each number on a horizontal number line. Then, order the numbers from least to greatest.

1 $\frac{11}{17}$, $1\frac{3}{5}$, 0.3, 1.6, $\frac{19}{10}$

Comparing decimals

When comparing two decimals, 1.945 and 1.954, you may use a place value chart to determine which decimal is greater.

	Ones		Tenths	Hundredths	Thousandths
1.945	1	•	9	4	5
1.954	1	•	9	5	4

The two decimals have the same values in ones and tenths. So, we compare hundredths. In the hundredths place, 4 < 5. So, 1.954 is greater than 1.945.

You can also use a number line to compare the decimals.

From the number line, you can see that 1.954 lies to the right of 1.945. So, 1.954 > 1.945.

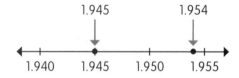

▶ Quick Check

Compare each pair of numbers using <, >, or =. Draw a number line to help you.

2 3.87 ◯ 3.68

3 0.982 ◯ 0.982

4 5.23 ◯ 5.235

Determining absolute values

The absolute value of a number n is denoted by $|n|$.

Examples: $|2| = 2, |-3| = 3$

The absolute value of a number is a measure of its distance from 0.

The distance from -3 to 0 is 3 units.

The distance from 2 to 0 is 2 units.

▶ **Quick Check**

Use the following set of numbers for ⑤ to ⑨.

34, -23, -54, 54, -60

⑤ Find the absolute value of each number.

⑥ Which number is closest to 0?

⑦ Which number is farthest from 0?

⑧ Name two numbers with the same absolute value.

⑨ Which number has the greatest absolute value?

Draw a number line to find the absolute value of each number.

⑩ $|-15|$

⑪ $|6|$

⑫ $|-2.1|$

Compare each pair of numbers using <, >, or =.

⑬ $|-7|$ ◯ $|-72|$

⑭ $|5|$ ◯ $|-5|$

⑮ $|-26|$ ◯ $|7|$

Comparing numbers on a number line

You can use a number line to compare numbers. On a horizontal number line, the lesser number lies to the left of the greater number. On a vertical number line, the lesser number lies below the greater number.

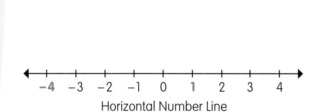

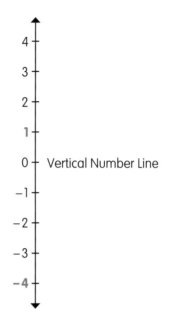

$-4 < 1$, because -4 is to the left of 1 on the horizontal number line, and -4 is below 1 on the vertical number line.

▶ **Quick Check**

Compare each pair of numbers using > or <. Draw a number line to help you.

16. $-3 \bigcirc 5$ 17. $-7 \bigcirc -12$

18. $10 \bigcirc -16$ 19. $-28 \bigcirc 0$

20. $\frac{1}{2} \bigcirc \frac{3}{4}$ 21. $-1\frac{1}{4} \bigcirc 2\frac{2}{3}$

22. $0.15 \bigcirc 0.13$ 23. $-1.23 \bigcirc -1.25$

Using order of operations to simplify numerical expressions

 **STEP 1** Perform operations within parentheses.   **STEP 2** Evaluate exponents.

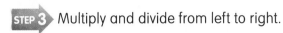 **STEP 3** Multiply and divide from left to right.   **STEP 4** Add and subtract from left to right.

Evaluate $(58 - 16) + 7 \cdot 3$.

$$(58 - 16) + 7 \cdot 3$$
$$= 42 \quad + 7 \cdot 3 \qquad \text{Perform operations in parentheses.}$$
$$= 42 \quad + 21 \qquad \text{Then, multiply.}$$
$$= 63 \qquad\qquad\quad \text{Then, add.}$$

▶ **Quick Check**

Evaluate each expression.

24. $75 - (18 + 2) \cdot 3$

25. $15 \cdot (40 \div 8) + 72$

Expressing improper fractions and mixed numbers in other forms

You can express improper fractions as mixed numbers.

$$\frac{19}{4} = \frac{16}{4} + \frac{3}{4} \qquad \text{Rewrite the fraction as a sum.}$$

$$= 4 + \frac{3}{4} \qquad \text{Write the improper fraction as a whole number.}$$

$$= 4\frac{3}{4} \qquad \text{Then, write the sum as a mixed number.}$$

You can express mixed numbers as improper fractions.

$$2\frac{1}{5} = 2 + \frac{1}{5} \qquad \text{Rewrite the mixed number as a sum.}$$

$$= \frac{10}{5} + \frac{1}{5} \qquad \text{Write the whole number as a fraction.}$$

$$= \frac{11}{5} \qquad \text{Then, write the sum as an improper fraction.}$$

▶ **Quick Check**

Express each improper fraction as a mixed number.

26. $\frac{12}{7}$

27. $\frac{19}{3}$

Express each mixed number as an improper fraction.

28. $4\frac{3}{5}$

29. $6\frac{7}{9}$

Adding and subtracting fractions

You can add and subtract fractions with unlike denominators.

$$5\frac{2}{3} + 1\frac{3}{4} = 5 + \frac{2}{3} + 1 + \frac{3}{4}$$ Rewrite the sum.

$$= 6 + \frac{2}{3} + \frac{3}{4}$$ Add the whole numbers.

$$= 6 + \frac{2 \cdot 4}{3 \cdot 4} + \frac{3 \cdot 3}{4 \cdot 3}$$ Rewrite the fractions as fractions with a common denominator.

$$= 6 + \frac{8}{12} + \frac{9}{12}$$ Simplify the products.

$$= 6 + \frac{17}{12}$$ Add the fractions.

$$= 6 + 1\frac{5}{12}$$ Write the improper fraction as a mixed number.

$$= 7\frac{5}{12}$$ Write the sum as a mixed number.

▶ Quick Check

Add or subtract. Express each answer in simplest form.

30 $\frac{2}{3} + \frac{5}{4}$

31 $\frac{7}{8} - \frac{2}{3}$

32 $1\frac{1}{4} + 3\frac{2}{5}$

Multiplying and dividing fractions

You can multiply two fractions.

▶ **Method 1**

$\dfrac{2}{3} \cdot \dfrac{3}{4} = \dfrac{2 \cdot 3}{3 \cdot 4}$ Multiply the numerators. Multiply the denominators.

$= \dfrac{6}{12}$ Simplify the product.

$= \dfrac{1}{2}$ Write the fraction in simplest form.

▶ **Method 2**

$\dfrac{2}{3} \cdot \dfrac{3}{4} = \dfrac{\cancel{2}^{1}}{3} \cdot \dfrac{3}{\cancel{4}_{2}}$ Divide a numerator and a denominator by the common factor, 2.

$= \dfrac{1}{\cancel{3}_{1}} \cdot \dfrac{\cancel{3}^{1}}{2}$ Divide a numerator and a denominator by the common factor, 3.

$= \dfrac{1 \cdot 1}{1 \cdot 2}$ Multiply the numerators. Multiply the denominators.

$= \dfrac{1}{2}$ Simplify the product.

You can divide a fraction by another fraction.

$\dfrac{3}{4} \div \dfrac{3}{8} = \dfrac{3}{4} \cdot \dfrac{8}{3}$ Rewrite using the reciprocal of the divisor.

$= \dfrac{3}{\cancel{4}_{1}} \cdot \dfrac{\cancel{8}^{2}}{3}$ Divide a numerator and a denominator by the common factor, 4.

$= \dfrac{\cancel{3}^{1}}{1} \cdot \dfrac{2}{\cancel{3}_{1}}$ Divide a numerator and a denominator by the common factor, 3.

$= \dfrac{1 \cdot 2}{1 \cdot 1}$ Multiply the numerators. Multiply the denominators.

$= 2$ Simplify the product.

▶ **Quick Check**

Multiply or divide. Express each answer in simplest form.

33 $\dfrac{2}{9} \cdot \dfrac{3}{4}$

34 $1\dfrac{2}{3} \cdot 5$

35 $\dfrac{5}{8} \div \dfrac{21}{4}$

36 $\dfrac{3}{4} \div 1\dfrac{1}{2}$

Multiplying and dividing decimals

Ignore the decimal as you multiply. Then, decide where to place the decimal point in the product.

$$
\begin{array}{r}
\overset{1}{3}.6\,2 \quad \longleftarrow \quad \text{2 decimal places} \\
\times \quad 0.3 \quad \longleftarrow \quad \underline{+ \text{1 decimal place}} \\
\hline
1\,0\,8\,6 \\
0\,0\,0 \\
\hline
1.0\,8\,6 \quad \longleftarrow \quad \text{3 decimal places}
\end{array}
$$

You can express the division expression as a fraction when you divide by a decimal. Then, multiply the dividend and divisor by the same power of 10.

$$17.8 \div 0.25 = \frac{17.8}{0.25}$$ Write division as a fraction.

$$= \frac{17.8 \cdot 100}{0.25 \cdot 100}$$ Multiply both the numerator and the denominator by 100 to make the denominator a whole number.

$$= \frac{1{,}780}{25}$$ Simplify the product.

$$= 71.2$$ Divide as with whole numbers.

▶ **Quick Check**

Multiply or divide.

37 $15.8 \cdot 2.7$

38 $8.82 \div 0.6$

Representing Rational Numbers on a Number Line

Learning Objectives:
- Find the absolute values of rational numbers.
- Express numbers in $\frac{m}{n}$ form.
- Locate rational numbers on a number line.

> **New Vocabulary**
>
> set of integers   positive integer
> negative integer   negative fraction
> rational number

THINK

Each of the unknown numbers, A, B, C, and D has one of the following values:

$$-3.4 \qquad 5\frac{3}{4} \qquad -\frac{1}{2} \qquad 2.1$$

The following clues are given:

$A > D \qquad |B| > |C|$

D can be expressed as $\frac{21}{10}$.

Find the values of A, B, C, and D. Then, order them from least to greatest.

ENGAGE

Draw a number line.

Graph $\frac{1}{4}$, $-\frac{1}{4}$, 1.65, and -1.65 on your number line.

How did you choose what intervals to use?

What do you observe about the numbers you graphed and their distances from zero?

Share your observations.

LEARN Find the absolute values of fractions, mixed numbers, and decimals

1. Previously, you learned how to graph whole numbers and negative numbers on a number line. The set of whole numbers and their opposites is called the set of integers.

The numbers on the right of 0 are called positive integers. The numbers on the left of 0 are called negative integers. The number 0 itself is neither positive nor negative.

There are gaps between the integers on the number line. These gaps contain fractions.

In the gap between 0 and 1, you can write proper fractions such as $\frac{1}{4}, \frac{1}{2}, \frac{3}{5}$, and $\frac{9}{10}$.

The integer 1 is one unit from 0. So, the fraction $\frac{1}{2}$ must be $\frac{1}{2}$ unit from 0. You can write this distance as $\left|\frac{1}{2}\right|$. The measure of the distance of other fractions from 0 is defined in the same way.

The absolute value of a positive fraction is just the fraction itself.

Examples: $\left|\frac{1}{4}\right| = \frac{1}{4}, \left|\frac{3}{5}\right| = \frac{3}{5}$, and $\left|2\frac{5}{8}\right| = \frac{21}{8}$, because $2\frac{5}{8} = \frac{21}{8}$.

2 Imagine a mirror placed on the number line at the number 0.

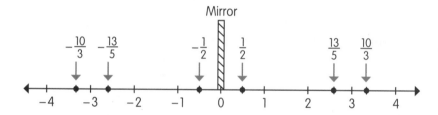

As you look into the mirror, you see the images of the positive integers. These images are the negative integers.

In the same way, fractions such as $\frac{1}{2}, \frac{13}{5}$, and $\frac{10}{3}$ each has an opposite in the mirror.

The negative fractions are $-\frac{1}{2}, -\frac{13}{5}$, and $-\frac{10}{3}$.

In a mirror, the distance of an image from the mirror and the distance of the object from the mirror are equal.

The absolute value of a negative fraction is defined as the distance of the negative fraction from 0. You find the absolute value of negative fractions in the same way as for negative integers.

Examples: $\left| -\frac{10}{3} \right| = \frac{10}{3}$

$\left| -\frac{13}{5} \right| = \frac{13}{5}$

$\left| -1.35 \right| = 1.35$

So, the distance of $-\frac{10}{3}$ from 0 is $\frac{10}{3}$ units. In the same way, $-\frac{13}{5}$ is $\frac{13}{5}$ units from 0, and -1.35 is 1.35 units from 0.

TRY Practice finding the absolute values of fractions, mixed numbers, and decimals

Solve.

1 Find the absolute values of $3\frac{2}{7}$, $-\frac{18}{5}$, and -1.87.

2 Graph the three numbers on a number line and indicate their distances from 0. Which number is farthest from 0?

ENGAGE

a How can you express $-\frac{10}{13}$ in another way?

b What other ways can you express $-2\frac{2}{3}$?

Share your ideas.

LEARN Express integers, fractions, and mixed numbers in $\frac{m}{n}$ form

1 A rational number is a number which can be written as $\frac{m}{n}$, where m and n are integers with $n \neq 0$. The definition of rational numbers comes from the concept of fractions.

Examples: $1\frac{1}{2} = \frac{3}{2}$. So, $1\frac{1}{2}$ is a rational number.

$3 = \frac{3}{1}$. So, 3 is a rational number.

> To express 0 in the form $\frac{m}{n}$, you can write 0 as $\frac{0}{1}$.

For negative fractions, mixed numbers, and whole numbers, the negative integers may be the numerator or denominator.

Examples: $-\frac{2}{9} = \frac{-2}{9} = \frac{2}{-9}$

$-1\frac{1}{2} = \frac{-3}{2} = \frac{3}{-2}$

$-3 = \frac{-3}{1} = \frac{3}{-1}$

TRY Practice expressing integers, fractions, and mixed numbers in $\frac{m}{n}$ form

Write each number as $\frac{m}{n}$ in simplest form, where m and n are integers.

1 $11\frac{1}{6}$

2 48

3 $-5\frac{4}{12}$

4 $-\frac{25}{10}$

ENGAGE

Write a decimal with at least three digits. Use at least two different strategies to find its equivalent fraction. Share your strategies.

LEARN Express decimals in $\frac{m}{n}$ form

1 Write 30.5 as $\frac{m}{n}$, where m and n are integers with $n \neq 0$.

$30.5 = 30\frac{1}{2}$ Write the integer, 30. Write 0.5 as $\frac{1}{2}$.

$\quad\quad = \frac{61}{2}$ Write as an improper fraction.

2 Write -0.186 as $\frac{m}{n}$, where m and n are integers with $n \neq 0$.

$-0.186 = -\frac{186}{1,000}$ 6 is in the thousandths place. Use 1,000 as the denominator.

$\quad\quad\quad = \frac{-93}{500}$ Simplify.

TRY Practice expressing decimals in $\frac{m}{n}$ form

Write each decimal as $\frac{m}{n}$ in simplest form, where m and n are integers with $n \neq 0$.

1 11.5

2 -7.8

3 0.36

4 -0.125

ENGAGE

a Draw a number line and graph $\frac{1}{2}$ and 0.8. On the same number line, graph 0.53 and 1.8.

b Graph $-\frac{1}{2}$, -0.53, $-\frac{4}{5}$, and -1.8 on another number line.

c How can you graph $\frac{1}{2}$, -0.53, $-\frac{4}{5}$, and -1.8 on the same number line? How did you decide what your endpoints should be on the number line? How about your intervals? How did you decide where to graph each point? Explain.

LEARN Locate rational numbers on a number line

1 Locate the rational numbers $\frac{3}{5}$ and -2.4 on a number line.

STEP 1 Find the integers that the rational number lies between.

$\frac{3}{5}$ is a proper fraction so it is located between 0 and 1.
-2.4 is located between -3 and -2.

⚠️ **Caution**

-2.4 can be written as a mixed number, $-2\frac{2}{5}$ or $-2\frac{4}{10}$.
Remember that it is a negative mixed number. Make sure that you do not graph -2.4 by counting to the right of 0.

STEP 2 Graph a number line and label the integers.

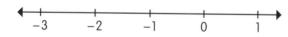

STEP 3 Divide the distance between the integers into equal segments.

Divide the distance between 0 and 1 into 5 equal segments and the distance between -3 and -2 into 10 equal segments.

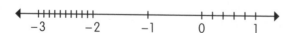

STEP 4 Use the segments to locate $\frac{3}{5}$ and -2.4.

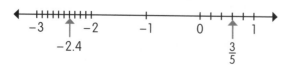

① Locate each of the following rational numbers on a number line.

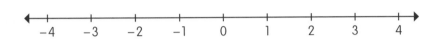

$$-3.6, \quad -\frac{1}{2}, \quad 2.9, \quad 1\frac{1}{4}, \quad 0.25, \quad -\frac{16}{5}, \quad 3.6$$

The rational numbers on the right of 0 are positive.
The rational numbers on the left of 0 are negative.

② **Mathematical Habit 2 Use mathematical reasoning**
Explain how you located each rational number on the number line.

③ **Mathematical Habit 3 Construct viable arguments**
What is another way to locate the rational numbers on the number line? Explain your answer.

TRY Practice locating rational numbers on a number line

Draw a number line to locate each pair of rational numbers.

1 − 1.5 and $\frac{15}{4}$

The negative decimal − 1.5 lies between _____ and _____.

$\frac{15}{4}$ can be written as a mixed number, $3\frac{3}{4}$.

$3\frac{3}{4}$ lies between _____ and _____.

2 $\frac{1}{6}$ and $\frac{15}{3}$

3 − 0.4 and $\frac{11}{5}$

4 $\frac{12}{15}$ and − 1.8

5 $-\frac{5}{15}$ and $-\frac{25}{30}$

INDEPENDENT PRACTICE

Find the absolute value of each fraction. Draw a number line to show how far the fraction is from 0. Write each fraction in simplest form.

1 $\dfrac{7}{10}$

2 $\dfrac{18}{8}$

3 $-\dfrac{5}{13}$

4 $-\dfrac{48}{15}$

Write each integer or fraction as $\dfrac{m}{n}$ in simplest form, where m and n are integers.

5 67

6 -345

7 $\dfrac{25}{80}$

8 $-\dfrac{264}{90}$

9 $-\dfrac{14}{70}$

10 $\dfrac{600}{480}$

Write each mixed number or decimal as $\frac{m}{n}$ in simplest form, where m and n are integers.

11. $7\frac{7}{9}$

12. $-5\frac{1}{10}$

13. $2\frac{5}{12}$

14. $-10\frac{11}{36}$

15. 0.4

16. -0.625

17. 5.80

18. 9.001

19. -10.68

Locate the rational numbers on the number line.

20. $-\frac{1}{4}$, -1.5, 0.8, $\frac{5}{2}$

21. $1\frac{7}{10}$, $-\frac{13}{5}$, 2.25, -0.7

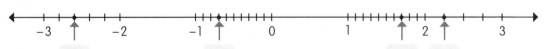

Graph each rational number on a separate number line.

22. $67\frac{1}{8}$

23. $\frac{305}{20}$

24. $\frac{98}{28}$

25. $-\frac{21}{12}$

26. -25.8

27. -45.3

28. A video game gives you 10 minutes to find some treasure. The numbers below show the amount of time left when you have found the treasure for each of eight games. A negative time means you have gone beyond the 10 minutes allotted. Use these data to answer **a** to **h**.

$\frac{23}{8}$, 0, $-7\frac{1}{5}$, 6, $-\frac{17}{4}$, 8, 7.8, -9.1

a Order the times from most to least time left using the symbol >.

b Write the absolute value of each number.

c Which number has the greatest absolute value?

d Order the absolute values from least to greatest. Use the symbol <.

e Graph the original numbers on a number line.

f Which negative number in the list is farthest from 0?

g Which positive number in the list is closest to 10?

h Which time is closest to – 5 minutes?

2 Writing Rational Numbers as Decimals

Learning Objectives:
- Write rational numbers as terminating or repeating decimals using long division.
- Compare rational numbers on the number line.

New Vocabulary
terminating decimal
repeating decimal

THINK

Write two possible rational numbers in the form $\frac{m}{n}$ such that $0.125 < \frac{m}{n} < \frac{2}{9}$.

How do you express your numbers as decimals?

ENGAGE

a   List the factors of 100. Now, make a list of fractions that have a denominator that is a factor of 100. Trade your list of fractions with your partner. Write each of your partner's fractions as a decimal. What method did you use? Share your method.

b   Using a nonfactor of 100, write a fraction and find its corresponding decimal. Share your decimal and discuss what type of decimal it is.

LEARN   Write rational numbers as terminating decimals using long division

1   In a previous course, you learned to write some rational numbers as decimals.

Examples: $\frac{3}{10} = 0.3$, $\frac{21}{100} = 0.21$, and $5\frac{323}{1,000} = 5.323$.

Any rational number may be written in decimal form using long division.

Since $\frac{1}{4}$ means 1 divided by 4, you can write $\frac{1}{4}$ as a decimal using long division.

$$
\begin{array}{r}
0.25 \\
4\overline{)1.00} \\
\underline{8} \\
20 \\
\underline{20} \\
0
\end{array}
$$

Divide 1 by 4.
Add zeros after the decimal point.

The remainder is 0.

So, $\frac{1}{4} = 0.25$.

Math Talk
Any fraction whose denominator has only 2s and 5s in its prime factorization can be written as a terminating decimal. Why?

The fraction $\frac{1}{4}$ is written as 0.25.

Notice that the long division ends with a remainder of zero. A decimal, such as 0.25, is called a terminating decimal, because it has a finite number of nonzero decimal places.

2 Using long division, write the rational number $6\frac{2}{25}$ as a terminating decimal.

$$\begin{array}{r} 0.08 \\ 25\overline{)2.00} \\ 2\ 00 \\ \hline 0 \end{array}$$

Divide 2 by 25.
Add zeros after the decimal point.

The remainder is 0.

You can also write $6\frac{2}{25}$ as the improper fraction, $\frac{152}{25}$. Then, divide 152 by 25. The answer is the same.

So, $6\frac{2}{25} = 6.08$.

TRY Practice writing rational numbers as terminating decimals using long division

Using long division, write each rational number as a terminating decimal.

1 $\frac{7}{8}$

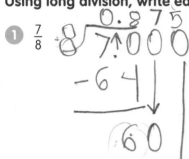

$$\begin{array}{r} 0.875 \\ 8\overline{)7.000} \\ -6\ 4 \\ \hline 6\ 0 \\ -5\ 6 \\ \hline 4\ 0 \\ -4\ 0 \\ \hline 0 \end{array}$$

2 $\frac{19}{4}$

3 $\frac{52}{40}$

4 $10\frac{13}{25}$

ENGAGE

a Write $\frac{9}{2}$ as a decimal. How do you write $\frac{2}{9}$ as a decimal?

b Now, try $\frac{9}{4}$ and $\frac{4}{9}$. What do you notice? Share your observations.

c Think of another two numbers that will result in the same observations in **b** when written in fractions. Share the numbers and fractions.

LEARN Write rational numbers as repeating decimals using long division

1 Since $\frac{1}{3}$ means 1 divided by 3, you can write $\frac{1}{3}$ as a decimal using long division.

```
    0.333      Divide 1 by 3.
3) 1.000      Add zeros after the decimal point.
   9
   ──
   10
    9
   ──
   10
    9
   ──
    1       The remainder will not terminate with 0.
```

So, $\frac{1}{3}$ = 0.333...

When you divide 1 by 3, the division process will not terminate with a remainder of 0. The digit 3 keeps repeating infinitely. A decimal, such as 0.333…, is called a repeating decimal.

A repeating decimal, such as 0.333…, has a group of one or more digits that repeat endlessly.

For the repeating decimal 0.333…, the digit 3 repeats itself. You can write 0.333… as $0.\overline{3}$, with a bar above the repeating digit 3. So, 0.333… = $0.\overline{3}$.

2 Using long division, write the rational number $\frac{13}{12}$ as a repeating decimal.

```
        1.0833
    12) 13.0000
        12
        1 00
          96
          40
          36
            40
            36
             4
```

Divide 13 by 12.

Add zeros after the decimal point.

Stop dividing when the digits continue to repeat themselves.

The remainder will not terminate with 0.

So, $\frac{13}{12} = 1.0833...$

$= 1.08\overline{3}$

Math Talk

If you see a repeating decimal such as 0.246246..., where 2, 4, and 6 repeat as a group of digits, how do you write the repeating decimal using bar notation?

Activity Classifying rational numbers in decimal form

Work in pairs.

① On a spreadsheet, label four columns with the following column heads.

| | Sheets | Charts | SmartArt Graphics | WordArt | |

	A	B	C	D
1	Rational Numbers in Decimal Form	Terminating, Repeating, or Neither	Number of Decimal Digits (Terminating Decimal)	Digits that Repeat (Repeating Decimal)
2				

Enter each rational number below in the first column, labeled "Rational Numbers in Decimal Form." Make sure that the cells in this column are formatted to display decimals up to 8 decimal places.

$\frac{5}{16}$, $\frac{141}{25}$, $-\frac{40}{111}$, $-\frac{15}{16}$, $\frac{14}{5}$, $\frac{1}{8}$, $-\frac{9}{44}$, $\frac{2}{11}$, $\frac{5}{4}$, and $-\frac{40}{9}$.

For example, if you enter $\frac{5}{16}$ into the spreadsheet, the entry will show the decimal form of this fraction.

Determine whether the decimal is terminating, repeating, or neither. Enter either "Terminating," "Repeating," or "Neither" in the second column.

If the decimal terminates, record the number of decimal digits in the third column. If the decimal repeats, record the repeating digits in the fourth column.

Example:

Sheets	Charts	SmartArt Graphics	WordArt

	A	B	C	D	

	Rational Numbers in Decimal Form	Terminating, Repeating, or Neither	Number of Decimal Digits (Terminating Decimal)	Digits that Repeat (Repeating Decimal)
1				
2	0.3125	Terminating	4	

(2) **Mathematical Habit 3** Construct viable arguments

Did you find any decimals that neither terminated nor repeated? What can you conclude about the decimal form of a rational number?

TRY Practice writing rational numbers as repeating decimals using long division

Using long division, write each rational number as a repeating decimal. Use bar notation to indicate the repeating digits.

1 $\dfrac{5}{9}$

2 $\dfrac{11}{6}$

Using a calculator, write each rational number as a repeating decimal. Use bar notation to indicate the repeating digits.

3 $\dfrac{23}{54}$

4 $\dfrac{78}{37}$

ENGAGE

a Compare $\frac{3}{8}$ and 0.35. Which is greater? What strategies did you use to compare?

b Compare $\frac{2}{3}$ and 0.4. Which is less? What strategies did you use to compare?

c Discuss when you should change fractions to decimals or decimals to fractions in order to compare them. Use examples to justify your answers.

LEARN Compare rational numbers

1 Compare the two rational numbers, $\frac{3}{4}$ and $\frac{4}{5}$, using the symbols > or <.

Write each rational number as a decimal first.

$$\frac{3}{4} = 0.75 \qquad \frac{4}{5} = 0.8$$

To compare the rational numbers, we compare their decimal forms, 0.75 and 0.8.

0.7**5**
0.8**0**

Compare the corresponding place value of two decimals from left to right. Stop at the first pair of digits which are different.

Since 7 tenths < 8 tenths, 0.75 < 0.8.

You may also use a number line to compare these decimals.

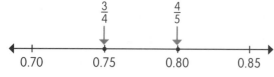

0.75 lies to the left of 0.80. So, 0.75 < 0.80.

$$\frac{3}{4} < \frac{4}{5}$$

2 Compare the positive rational numbers, $\frac{11}{8}$ and $\frac{15}{11}$, using the symbols > or <.

$\frac{11}{8} = 1.375$ Write each rational number as a decimal.

$\frac{15}{11} = 1.3636...$
$\quad = 1.\overline{36}$

Compare the decimals, 1.375 and $1.\overline{36}$.

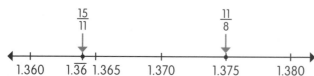

From the number line, 1.375 lies to the right of $1.\overline{36}$. So, $1.375 > 1.\overline{36}$.

$$\frac{11}{8} > \frac{15}{11}$$

3 Compare the negative rational numbers, $-\frac{2}{11}$ and $-\frac{3}{16}$, using the symbols > or <.

▶ **Method 1**
Compare using a number line.

$-\frac{2}{11} = -0.\overline{18}$ Write each rational number as a decimal.

$-\frac{3}{16} = -0.1875$

Use the absolute values of $-0.\overline{18}$ and -0.1875 to help you graph the decimals on a number line.

$|-0.\overline{18}| = 0.\overline{18}$
$|-0.1875| = 0.1875$

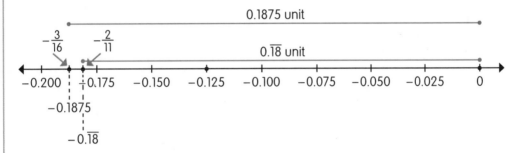

From the number line, -0.1875 lies farther to the left of 0 than $-0.\overline{18}$.
So, $-0.\overline{18} > -0.1875$

$\qquad -\frac{2}{11} > -\frac{3}{16}$

▶ **Method 2**
Compare using place value.

You can also write an inequality using the absolute value of the two numbers.

$|-0.\overline{18}| < |-0.1875|$

The two numbers are negative, so the number with the greater absolute value is farther to the left of 0. It is the lesser number.

$-0.\overline{18} > -0.1875$

$\qquad -\frac{2}{11} > -\frac{3}{16}$

TRY Practice comparing rational numbers

Compare each pair of rational numbers using the symbols > or <. Draw a number line to help you.

1 $\frac{7}{10}$ ◯ $\frac{13}{16}$

$\frac{7}{10} = $ _____ $\frac{13}{16} = $ _____   Write each rational number as a decimal.

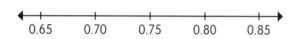

Use a number line to compare the decimals.

_____ ◯ _____   Compare the decimals.

So, $\frac{7}{10}$ ◯ $\frac{13}{16}$.

2 $\frac{24}{7}$ ◯ $\frac{10}{3}$

3 $-\frac{3}{5}$ ◯ $-\frac{4}{5}$

4 $-10\frac{3}{4}$ ◯ $-\frac{41}{5}$

5 -4.063 ◯ $-4\frac{1}{6}$

INDEPENDENT PRACTICE

Using long division, write each rational number as a terminating decimal.

1 $76\frac{1}{2}$

2 $-39\frac{2}{5}$

3 $-\frac{47}{10}$

4 $\frac{5}{16}$

5 $\frac{7}{20}$

6 $\frac{7}{8}$

Simplify each rational number. Then, use long division to write each rational number as a terminating decimal.

7 $\frac{99}{36}$

8 $\frac{12}{15}$

9 $\frac{9}{48}$

10 $-\frac{132}{8}$

11 $-\frac{48}{50}$

12 $-\frac{14}{128}$

Using long division, write each rational number as a repeating decimal with 3 decimal places. Identify the pattern of repeating digits using bar notation.

13 $\frac{5}{6}$

14 $-8\frac{2}{3}$

Write each rational number as a repeating decimal using bar notation. You may use a calculator.

15 $\dfrac{8}{55}$

16 $\dfrac{456}{123}$

17 $-\dfrac{987}{110}$

18 $\dfrac{11}{14}$

19 $-\dfrac{10}{13}$

20 $\dfrac{4{,}005}{101}$

 Refer to the list of rational numbers below for **21** **and** **22**. **You may use a calculator.**

$$-\dfrac{23}{32}, \ \dfrac{7}{15}, \ -\dfrac{368}{501}, \ -\dfrac{19}{26}, \ \dfrac{37}{44}$$

21 Write each rational number as a decimal with at most 6 decimal places.

22 Using your answers in **21**, list the numbers from least to greatest using the symbol <. Graph a number line between −1 and 1 with 0 in the middle. Then, place each rational number on the number line.

Answer the question.

23 **Mathematical Habit 2** Use mathematical reasoning

Maria tries to compare $-\dfrac{2}{3}$ and $-\dfrac{5}{8}$ using absolute values. She finds their decimal equivalents to be $-0.\overline{6}$ and -0.625, and she knows $|-0.\overline{6}| > |-0.625|$. Explain why Maria must reverse the inequality in her final answer, $-\dfrac{2}{3} < -\dfrac{5}{8}$.

Evaluate $-1 + (-3)$.

Method 1

Add using counters.

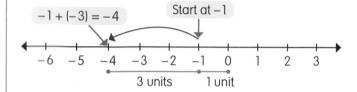

So, $(-1) + (-3) = -4$.

Method 2

Add using a number line.

$-1 + (-3) = -4$ Start at -1

$$\begin{array}{ccccccccccc} -6 & -5 & -4 & -3 & -2 & -1 & 0 & 1 & 2 & 3 \end{array}$$

3 units   1 unit

Start at -1. Then, add -3, a jump of **3 to the left** to reach -4.

Distance of sum from 0: $|-1| + |-3| = 1 + 3$
$$= 4$$

You move in a negative direction, so the sum is negative.

$-1 + (-3) = -4$

> When you add integers with the same sign on a horizontal number line:
> - move to the right, or in the positive direction, to add a positive integer.
> - move to the left, or in the negative direction, to add a negative integer.

How do you evaluate $(-1) + (-3)$ using a vertical number line?

3 Adding Integers

Learning Objectives:
- Add integers with the same sign.
- Add integers to their opposites.
- Add integers with different signs.

N
ze
ad

THINK

a   Will the sum of two integers be always greater than each of the integers? Wh
    think so?

b   Discuss what possible patterns you can observe when adding two integers. G
    to justify your observations.

ENGAGE

In a golf game, par is considered the number of strokes a player needs to get to the
Par is scored as 0 points. Playing one under par is considered a score of –1.

a   Alex was playing golf. On the first hole, he scored two over par. On the second h
    scored three under par.

    Use ⚪ ⚫ to show Alex's score on the first two holes.

b   Name two possible par results of each round to achieve a score of –2.

c   If Alex scored two under par at his first hole, what are the possible pars he shoulc
    the next two holes to achieve a total score of –3?

 Add integers with the same sign

1   You can use counters to represent integers.

    ⚪ represents +1 and ⚫ represents – 1.

    You can use counters to represent the positive integer 3.

    ⚪⚪⚪ ⟶ $1 + 1 + 1 = 3$

    You can also use counters to represent the negative integer – 2.

    ⚫⚫ ⟶ $(–1) + (–1) = –2$

▶ **Method 3**

Add using absolute values.

First, add the absolute values of the two negative integers.

$|-1| + |-3| = 1 + 3$ Add the absolute values.
$ = 4$ This is the distance of the sum from 0.

Then, decide whether the sum is positive or negative.

$-1 + (-3) = -4$ Use the common sign, a negative sign, for the sum.

> When you use absolute values to add integers with the same sign, first add their absolute values, and then use the common sign.
>
> The sum of positive integers is positive.
> The sum of negative integers is negative.

Activity Adding integers with the same sign

① **Mathematical Habit 5 Use tools strategically**
Use two different methods to illustrate each solution.
a $2 + 3$ b $(-2) + (-3)$ c $-4 + (-1)$

② **Mathematical Habit 2 Use mathematical reasoning**
Explain how to add two integers with the same sign. How are the absolute values of the addends related to the sum?

③ **Mathematical Habit 3 Construct viable arguments**
Is the sum of positive integers always positive? Is the sum of negative integers always negative? Explain your answer.

TRY Practice adding integers with the same sign

Evaluate each sum.

1 − 3 + (− 5).

▶ **Method 1**
Add using counters.

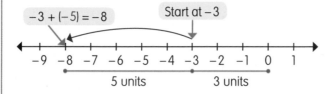

− 3 + (− 5) = _____

▶ **Method 2**
Add using a number line.

− 3 + (− 5) = − 8   Start at − 3

```
 ◄─┼──┼──┼──┼──┼──┼──┼──┼──┼──┼─►
   −9 −8 −7 −6 −5 −4 −3 −2 −1  0  1
       └──────5 units──────┘└3 units┘
```

Start at − 3. Then, add − 5, a jump of
5 to the left to reach _____.

− 3 + (− 5) = _____

▶ **Method 3**
Add using absolute values.

$|-3| + |-5|$ = _____ + _____   Add the absolute values.

= _____   Simplify.

− 3 + (− 5) = _____   Use the common sign, a negative sign, for the sum.

2 − 15 + (− 7)   **3** − 18 + (− 22)

ENGAGE

1. Choose an integer. Trade with your partner. Use to show how you would add the number your partner chose and its opposite.

2. A kettle of water at room temperature was boiled. After boiling, the water was left to cool down back to room temperature. Use a number line to find the total change in temperature.

   What can you say about the sum of a number and its opposite? Explain your thinking.

LEARN Add integers to their opposites

1. You have learned that each integer has an opposite. For example, the opposite of 1 is −1. 1 and −1 form a **zero pair**.

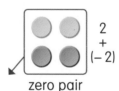

Remove one zero pair.

You write 1 + (−1) = 0.

2. Evaluate 2 + (−2).

   ▶ **Method 1**

   Add using counters.

   Remove two zero pairs.

   2 + (−2) = 0

   > **Math Note**
   > **Commutative Property of Addition:**
   > If *a* and *b* are integers, then
   > $a + b = b + a$. Hence, 2 + (−2) and
   > (−2) + 2 give the same answer.

   ▶ **Method 2**

   Add using a number line.

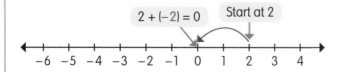

   Start at 2. Then, add −2, a jump of **2 to the left** to reach 0.

   2 + (−2) = 0

   2 and −2 are called **additive inverses** because 2 and its opposite −2 have a sum of zero.

    **Math Talk**
   Write a rule for the sum of a number and its additive inverse. How are the absolute values of a number and its additive inverse related?

③ There are real-world situations in which opposite quantities combine to make zero.

Examples of real-world situations involving opposite quantities include:

a A hydrogen atom has a charge of zero, because it contains one positively charged proton and one negatively charged electron.

b You put a 3-ounce stone on a scale and then remove it.
The overall change in weight on the scale is 0 ounces.

c You heat up an oven, and then turn it off so that it returns to room temperature.
The overall change in temperature is 0°F.

d You ride 50 feet up in an elevator and ride 50 feet back down.
Overall, your change in position is 0 feet.

Practice adding integers to their opposites

Evaluate each sum.

① $-5 + 5.$

> **Method 1**
> Add using counters

$-5 + 5 = $ _____

> **Method 2**
> Add using a number line.

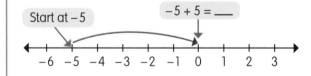

Start at -5. Then, add 5, a jump of

5 to the right to reach _____.

$-5 + 5 = $ _____

② $9 + (-9)$

③ $-21 + 21$

ENGAGE

The temperature recorded at 5 A.M. was −12°F. The temperature rose to 13°F at 4 P.M. What was the change in temperature? What was a possible temperature recorded at noon?

LEARN Add two integers with different signs

Activity Exploring addition of integers

Work in pairs.

⬤ represents +1 and ⬤ represents −1.

⬤ + ⬤ represent a zero pair.

① Use counters to add two integers with different signs.

   a Evaluate 3 + (−2).

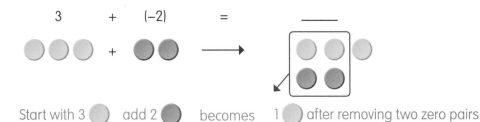

Start with 3 ⬤   add 2 ⬤   becomes   1 ⬤ after removing two zero pairs

   b Evaluate (−3) + 2.

> ⚠ **Caution**
> −3 + 2 ≠ −5

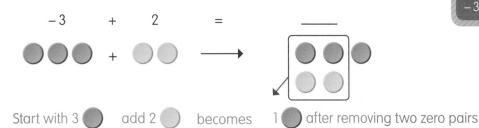

Start with 3 ⬤   add 2 ⬤   becomes   1 ⬤ after removing two zero pairs

② Use counters to evaluate each sum.

   a 7 + (−2) and (−7) + 2   **b** (−8) + 5 and 8 + (−5)

③ **Mathematical Habit 2 Use mathematical reasoning**

Explain how to add two integers with different signs. How are the absolute values of the addends related to the sum?

1 Suppose the temperature was − 8°F at 7 A.M. Five hours later, the temperature has risen 10°F. Find the new temperature.

Temperature at 7 A.M.

As the temperature rose, you can find the new temperature by finding − 8 + 10.

Evaluate − 8 + 10.

▶ **Method 1**
Add using counters.

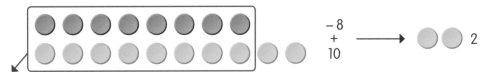

Remove eight zero pairs

$$-8 + 10 = 2$$

The new temperature is 2°F.

▶ **Method 2**

Add using a number line.

Start at –8   –8 + 10 = 2

$$-8 + 10 = 2$$

8 units

10 units

–10 –8 –6 –4 –2 0 2 4 6 8

Start at – 8. Then, add 10, a jump of **10 to the right** to reach 2.

Distance of sum from 0: $|10| - |-8| = 10 - 8$
$$= 2$$

$$-8 + \mathbf{10} = -8 + \mathbf{8} + \mathbf{2}$$
$$= \quad 0 \quad + 2$$
$$= \quad 2$$

The new temperature is 2°F.

▶ **Method 3**

Add using absolute values.

First, find the difference between the absolute values of the two integers.

$|10| - |-8| = 10 - 8$ Subtract the lesser absolute value from the greater one.
$\quad\quad\quad = 2$ Simplify.

Then, decide whether the sum is positive or negative.

$-8 + 10 = 2$ Use the sign of the addend with the greater absolute value, the positive sign of 10.

The new temperature is 2°F.

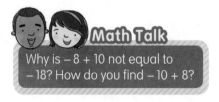

Math Talk

Why is $-8 + 10$ not equal to -18? How do you find $-10 + 8$?

When you use absolute values to add integers with different signs, first subtract the lesser absolute value from the greater one, and then use the sign of the integer with the greater absolute value.

TRY Practice adding two integers with different signs

Evaluate each sum.

1 −11 + 6.

▶ **Method 1**

Add using counters.

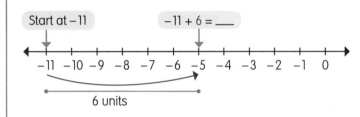
$$\begin{array}{l} -11 \\ + \\ 6 \end{array}$$

−11 + 6 = _____

▶ **Method 2**

Add using a number line.

Start at −11   −11 + 6 = ___

−11 −10 −9 −8 −7 −6 −5 −4 −3 −2 −1 0

6 units

Start at −11. Then, add 6, a jump of **6 to the right**

to reach _____.

−11 + 6 = _____

▶ **Method 3**

Add using absolute values.

$|-11| - |6| =$ _____ − _____   Subtract the lesser absolute value from the greater one.
         = _____   Simplify.

−11 + 6 = _____   Use the sign of the addend with the greater absolute value, the negative sign of −11.

2 −10 + 3

3 11 + (−25)

In a game, you start out with 15 points. At each turn, you pick a card. 3 points are awarded for a blue card picked and 5 points are deducted for a red card picked. Alan had a total of 14 points at the end of 5 turns. How many blue and red cards did he pick?

LEARN Add more than two integers with different signs

1 Evaluate $-9 + 2 + (-3)$.

▶ **Method 1**

Add using a number line.

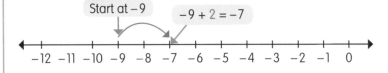

$-9 + 2 = -7$

Move to the right when adding a positive integer. Move to the left when adding a negative integer.

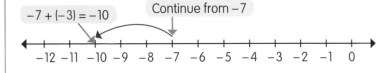

$-7 + (-3) = -10$

So, $-9 + 2 + (-3) = -7 + (-3)$
$= -10$

You can also add 2 and -3 first. Then, add -9 to the result.
$-9 + 2 + (-3) = -9 + (-1)$
$= -10$

Start at -9. Then, add 2, a jump of **2 to the right** to reach -7.

Next, add -3, a jump of **3 to the left** to reach -10.

Math Note

Associative Property of Addition: If a, b, and c are integers, then $(a + b) + c = a + (b + c)$.

▶ **Method 2**

Add using absolute values.

First, group integers with the same sign.

$-9 + 2 + (-3) = -9 + (-3) + 2$ Commutative property of addition

Next, add -9 and -3.

> Add their absolute values because the integers have the same sign.

$|-9| + |-3| = 9 + 3$ Add the absolute values.
$\qquad\qquad\quad = 12$ Simplify.
$\quad -9 + (-3) = -12$ Use the common sign, a negative sign, for the sum.

Then, continue by adding 2 to -12.

> Subtract their absolute values because the integers have different signs.

$|-12| - |2| = 12 - 2$ Subtract the lesser absolute value from the greater one.
$\qquad\qquad\quad = 10$ Simplify.

$\quad -12 + 2 = -10$ Use the sign of the addend with the greater absolute value, the negative sign of -12.

$-9 + 2 + (-3) = \mathbf{-9 + (-3)} + 2$
$\qquad\qquad\quad = \mathbf{-12} + 2$
$\qquad\qquad\quad = -10$

TRY Practice adding more than two integers with different signs

Evaluate each sum.

1 $10 + (-3) + 6$

2 $-7 + (-23) + 15$

ENGAGE

The temperature of a glass of water rose 4°F, fell 7°F, and then rose 2°F.

a   If the water was originally at 68°F, what was the final temperature?

b   If the final temperature of the water was 72°F, what was the original temperature?

Draw a number line to explain your thinking.

LEARN Add integers with different signs in a real-world situation

1 The water level in a large tank rises 5 feet, falls 9 feet, and then rises 3 feet.
   Overall, how far does the water level rise or fall?

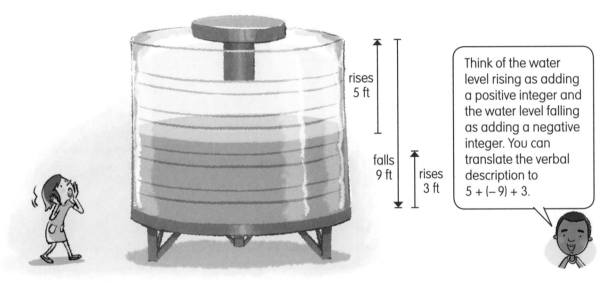

rises
5 ft

falls
9 ft   rises
         3 ft

Think of the water
level rising as adding
a positive integer and
the water level falling
as adding a negative
integer. You can
translate the verbal
description to
5 + (− 9) + 3.

Evaluate 5 + (− 9) +3.

▶ **Method 1**
Add using a number line.

5 + (−9) = −4   Start at 5

        −5 −4 −3 −2 −1   0   1   2   3   4   5   Start at 5. Then, add − 9, a jump of
                                                         9 to the left to reach − 4.

5 + (− 9) = − 4

Continue from − 4   − 4 + 3 = − 1

        −5 −4 −3 −2 −1   0   1   2   3   4   5   Next, add 3, a jump of 3 to
                                                         the right to reach − 1.

− 4 + 3 = − 1

5 + (− 9) + 3 = − 4 + 3 = − 1

Overall, the water level falls 1 foot.

▶ **Method 2**

Add using absolute values.

First, add 5 and (– 9).

$|-9| - |5| = 9 - 5$ Subtract the lesser absolute value from the greater one.
        $= 4$ Simplify.

    $5 + (-9) = -4$ Use the sign of the addend with the greater absolute value, the negative sign of – 9.

> You can evaluate 5 + (– 9) + 3 by adding from left to right. First, add 5 and (– 9). Then, add 3 to the result.

Then, add 3 to – 4.

$|-4| - |3| = 4 - 3$ Subtract the lesser absolute value from the greater one.
        $= 1$ Simplify.

    $(-4) + 3 = -1$ Use the sign of the addend with the greater absolute value, the negative sign of – 4.

$$5 + (-9) + 3 = -4 + 3$$
$$= -1$$

Overall, the water level falls 1 foot.

TRY Practice adding integers with different signs in a real-world situation

Solve.

1 A submarine is at 400 feet below sea level. If it ascends 150 feet and then descends 320 feet, how far is it above or below sea level?

> Think of the submarine ascending as adding a positive integer, and descending as adding a negative integer. You can translate the written description as – 400 + 150 + (– 320).

LET'S EXPLORE

The sum of three integers is 0. Each integer is nonzero. What could the integers be?

⬛ + ⬛ + ⬛ = 0

INDEPENDENT PRACTICE

Evaluate each sum using a number line.

1 − 3 + (− 9)

2 − 8 + (− 4)

3 7 + (− 7)

4 − 9 + 9

5 − 10 + 6

6 − 17 + 9

Evaluate each sum using the absolute values.

7 − 23 + (− 9)

8 − 11 + (− 34)

9 − 15 + (− 7)

10 12 + (− 18)

11 − 40 + 26

12 − 75 + 19

Evaluate each sum.

13 − 8 + 4 + 5

14 5 + (− 10) + (− 6)

15 − 6 + (− 8) + (− 12)

16 − 13 + (− 17) + 7

17 − 20 + 16 + (− 7)

18 − 11 + (− 8) + 14

Solve.

19 The temperature is − 4°F. What will the temperature be if the temperature rises 20°F?

20 Mr. Clark parked his car in a parking garage 33 feet below street level. He then got in an elevator and went up 88 feet to his office. How far above street level is his office?

? ft above street level

Street level

33 ft below street level

21 A hiker starts hiking in Death Valley at an elevation of 143 feet below sea level. He climbs up 400 feet in elevation. What is his new elevation relative to sea level?

22 Emma was playing a board game with her friends. On her first turn, she moved 6 spaces forward. On her second turn, she moved another 5 spaces forward. On her third turn, she moved 4 spaces backward. How many squares forward or backward from her starting point was she after her third turn?

23 **Mathematical Habit 2** Use mathematical reasoning
In a game, all scores with even numbers are recorded as positive numbers. Odd numbers are recorded as negative numbers. Explain how to find Diego's total score in a game if his individual scores during the game are 9, 12, 7, 18, and 19.

Subtracting Integers

Learning Objectives:
- Subtract integers by adding their opposites.
- Find the distance between two integers.

THINK

a   Will the difference between two integers be always positive? Why do you think so?

b   What are the possible patterns you can observe when subtracting two integers? Give examples to justify your observations.

ENGAGE

Brianna went to a school fair. She played a game that cost 4 tickets. She won 1 ticket. Did she end up losing or winning tickets? Use to explain your reasoning.

LEARN   Subtract integers by adding their opposites

Activity Exploring subtraction of integers

Work in pairs.

⬤ represents + 1 and ⬤ represents − 1.

⬤ + ⬤ represent a zero pair.

① Use counters to work out and complete the subtraction of a positive integer.

a Evaluate $5 - (+2)$ and compare with $5 + (-2)$.

b Evaluate $-5 - (+2)$ and compare with $-5 + (-2)$.

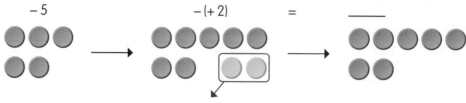

-5 $-(+2)$ $=$ _____

Start with 5 ⬤

add 2 zero pairs
so that you can
remove 2 ◯

becomes _____ ⬤

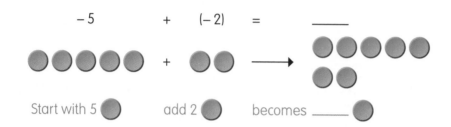

-5 $+$ (-2) $=$ _____

Start with 5 ⬤   add 2 ⬤   becomes _____ ⬤

② Use counters to evaluate each expression.

a $6 - 4$ and $6 + (-4)$

b $-6 - 4$ and $-6 + (-4)$

③ Use counters to work out and complete the subtraction of a negative integer.

a Evaluate $5 - (-2)$ and compare with $5 + 2$.

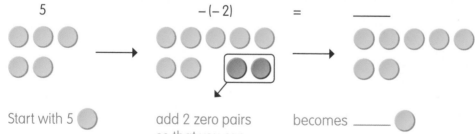

5 $-(-2)$ $=$ _____

Start with 5 ◯

add 2 zero pairs
so that you can
remove 2 ⬤

becomes _____ ◯

5 $+$ 2 $=$ _____

Start with 5 ◯   add 2 ◯   becomes _____ ◯

b Find $-5 - (-2)$ and compare with $-5 + 2$.

$$-5 - (-2) \quad = \quad \underline{}$$

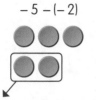
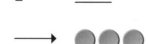

Start with 5  becomes _____ ⬤

and remove 2 ⬤

$$-5 \quad + \quad 2 \quad = \quad \underline{}$$

 +

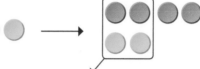

Start with 5 ⬤   add 2 ⬤   becomes _____ ⬤ after removing

two zero pairs

④ Use counters to evaluate each expression.

a $7 - (-3)$ and $7 + 3$ **b** $-7 - (-3)$ and $-7 + 3$

⑤ **Mathematical Habit 7** **Make use of structure**

Based on your results in ① to ④, explain how you can subtract integers.

1 Pedro scored 3 points in the first round of a game show and lost 5 points in the second round. Find Pedro's final score.

You can translate the written description as 3 − 5.
Instead of subtracting 5 from 3, we can add its opposite, which is − 5.

$$3 - 5 = 3 + \underbrace{(-5)}_{\text{opposite of 5}}$$

Evaluate 3 + (− 5).

▶ **Method 1**
Add using counters.

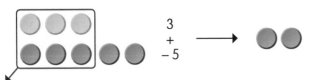

Remove three zero pairs.

$$3 - 5 = 3 + (-5)$$
$$= -2$$

Pedro's final score is − 2.

▶ **Method 2**
Add using a number line.

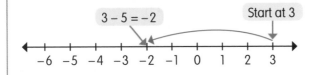

Start at 3. Then, add − 5, a jump of 5 to the left to reach − 2.

Pedro's final score is − 2.

2 You can use opposites to subtract negative integers.

For example, find 3 − (− 5).

The opposite of − 5 is 5. Instead of subtracting − 5 from 3, you can add its opposite, which is 5.

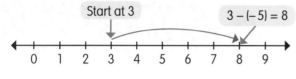

$$3 - (-5) = 3 \underbrace{+ 5}_{\text{opposite of } -5}$$
$$= 8$$

So, 3 − (− 5) can be rewritten as 3 + 5 to give an answer of 8.

Instead of subtracting an integer, you can add its additive inverse or opposite as follows:

- Subtracting a positive integer, b, is the same as adding its opposite, $-b$.
  So, $a - b = a + (-b)$.

- Subtracting a negative integer, $-b$, is the same as adding its opposite, b.
  So, $a - (-b) = a + b$.

When you subtract integers on a horizontal number line,
- move to the left to subtract a positive integer.
- move to the right to subtract a negative integer.

3 A diver went 24 feet below the surface of the ocean, and then 47 feet farther down. What is the diver's new position relative to the surface?

You can translate the written description as $-24 - 47$.

Ocean surface

24 ft

47 ft

Evaluate $-24 - 47$.

$-24 - 47 = -24 + (-47)$ Rewrite subtraction as adding the opposite.

Using absolute values,
$|-24| + |-47| = 24 + 47$ Add the absolute values, because the addends have the same sign.

$\qquad\qquad = 71$ Simplify.

$-24 - 47 = -24 + (-47)$
$\qquad\qquad = -71$ Use the common sign, a negative sign, for the sum.

The diver's new position is 71 feet below the surface of the ocean.

4 Evaluate $-15 - (-21)$.

$-15 - (-21) = -15 + 21$ Rewrite subtraction as adding the opposite.

Using absolute values,
$|21| - |-15| = 21 - 15$ Subtract the absolute values, because the addends have different signs.

$\qquad\qquad = 6$ Simplify.

$-15 - (-21) = -15 + 21$
$\qquad\qquad = 6$ Use a positive sign, because 21 has a greater absolute value.

5 Evaluate $-11 - (-5) - (-20)$.

5 is the additive inverse of -5.
20 is the additive inverse of -20.

$-11 - (-5) - (-20) = -11 + 5 + 20$ Rewrite subtraction as adding the opposite.
$\qquad\qquad\qquad\quad = -6 + 20$ Add from left to right.
$\qquad\qquad\qquad\quad = 14$ Simplify.

Evaluate each expression.

1. 21 – 30

   21 – 30 = 21 + _____   Rewrite subtraction as adding the opposite.

   Using absolute values,

   $|-30| - |21| = 30 - 21$ Subtract the absolute values because the
                                       addends have different signs.

   = _____   Simplify.

   21 – 30 = 21 + _____

   = _____   Use a negative sign, because – 30 has
                                       a greater absolute value.

2. 17 – (– 4)

   17 – (– 4) = 17 + _____   Rewrite subtraction as adding the opposite.

   = _____   Add.

Solve.

3. A fishing boat drags its net 35 feet below the ocean's surface. Then, it lowers the net by an
   additional 12 feet. Find the fishing net's new position relative to the ocean's surface.

   – 35 – _____ = – 35 + _____   Rewrite subtraction as adding the opposite.

   Using absolute values,

   _____ + _____ = _____   Add the absolute values because the addends have the
                                             same sign.

   – 35 – _____ = – 35 + _____   Use the common sign, a negative sign, for the sum.

   = _____   Simplify.

   The fishing net's new position is _____ feet below the ocean's surface.

4 A submarine was 1,200 feet below sea level. It then moved to 1,683 feet below sea level. How many feet did the submarine descend?

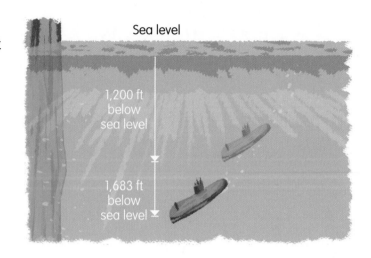

Sea level

1,200 ft
below
sea level

1,683 ft
below
sea level

Evaluate each expression.

5 $-25 - (-9)$

6 $-19 - (-7) - (-6)$

ENGAGE

1 The change in temperature recorded in November was between 2°F and 5°F. Draw a number line to find the change in temperature.
The change in temperature recorded in December was between −2°F and 5°F. Now, find the change in the temperature. What do you notice? Share your observations.

2 The lowest temperature recorded last month was below 0°F. This month, the lowest temperature recorded is above 0°F. If the difference between the two temperatures is 9°F, what could the temperatures be? List three possible sets of answers. Draw number lines to explain your thinking.

LEARN Find the distance between two integers

1. You can find the distance between two integers. First, plot the two integers on a number line. Then, count the units between them.

For example, find the distance between 3 and 7.

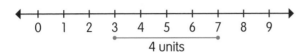

4 units

First, plot the integers 3 and 7 on the number line. Then, count the units from 3 to 7 or from 7 to 3.

Since you are finding the distance, and distance is always positive, it does not matter which integer you start counting from.

You can use absolute value to find the distance between two integers. It does not matter in which order you count, from 3 to 7, or from 7 to 3.

Distance between 3 and 7 can be represented as: $|7 - 3| = |3 - 7|$
$= 4$ units

For any two integers a and b, the distance between a and b is the absolute value of their difference, $|a - b|$. It does not matter which integer you decide to call a and which you decide to call b.

2 Find the distance between 2 and – 6.

▶ **Method 1**

Use a number line to plot the points and count the units.

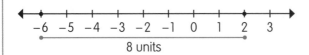

8 units

The distance between 2 and – 6 is 8 units.

▶ **Method 2**

Use absolute value to find the distance between integers with different signs.

Distance between 2 and – 6:

$|2 - (-6)| = |2 + 6|$ Rewrite subtraction as adding the opposite.

$= 8$ Add.

The distance between 2 and – 6 is 8 units.

You can also find the distance
between 2 and – 6 using $|-6 - 2|$.

TRY Practice finding the distance between two integers

Fill in each blank.

1 Find the distance between 3 and – 2.

▶ **Method 1**

Use a number line to plot the points and count the units.

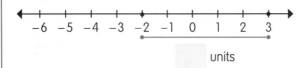

_____ units

The distance between 3 and – 2 is _____ units.

▶ **Method 2**

Use absolute value to find the distance between integers with different signs.

Distance between 3 and – 2:

$|3 - $_____$| = |3 + $_____$|$ Rewrite subtraction as adding the opposite.

$= $_____   Add.

The distance between 3 and – 2 is _____ units.

ENGAGE

1. The wind-chill temperature at 10 p.m. was – 8°F. One hour later, the wind-chill temperature had fallen to – 28°F. How do you find the change in temperature? Draw a number line to explain your reasoning.

2. The highest temperature recorded in California was 134°F. The lowest temperature was –43°F. How can you find the difference between the two temperatures? Draw a number line to explain your reasoning.

LEARN Find the distance between two integers in a real-world situation

1. The elevation of Death Valley in Eastern California is 86 meters below sea level. The elevation of the tallest mountain in California, Mount Whitney, is 4,421 meters above sea level. Find the difference in elevation between Death Valley and Mount Whitney.

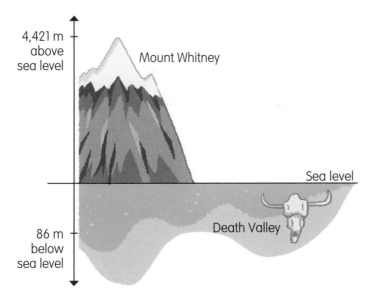

Elevation of Death Valley: – 86 m

Elevation of Mount Whitney: 4,421 m

Difference between the two elevations:

$$|4{,}421 - (-86)| = |4{,}421 + 86|$$ Rewrite subtraction as adding the opposite.
$$= 4{,}507$$ Add.

The difference in elevation is 4,507 meters.

TRY Practice finding the distance between two integers in a real-world situation

Solve.

1 A particular town has an elevation of 8 feet below sea level. Another town on top of a mountain has an elevation of 2,421 feet above sea level. What is the difference in elevation between the two towns?

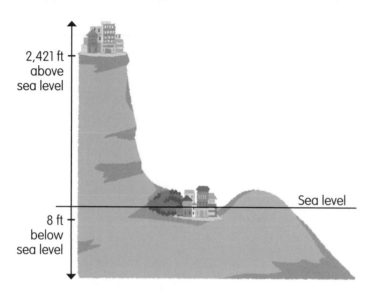

Elevation of town below sea level: _____ ft

Elevation of town on top of mountain: _____ ft

Difference between the two elevations:

| _____ − _____ | = | _____ + _____ | Rewrite subtraction as adding the opposite.

= _____ ft   Add.

The difference in elevation between the two towns is _____ feet.

Name: _____ Date: _____

INDEPENDENT PRACTICE

Evaluate each expression.

1 7 – 18

2 20 – 30

3 53 – 109

4 45 – (– 16)

5 –7 – (– 5)

6 – 94 – (– 68)

7 – 6 – 8 – 12

8 – 23 – 17 – 7

9 – 8 – (– 4) – 5

10 – 5 – (– 10) – 6

11 – 20 – (– 16) – (– 7)

12 – 11 – (– 8) – (– 14)

Evaluate the distance between each pair of integers.

13 4 and 20

14 16 and 52

15 – 15 and 36

16 – 7 and 41

17 – 28 and – 3

18 – 19 and – 8

Solve.

19 Ryan leaves to go skiing in Burlington, Vermont, when the temperature is − 4°C. The temperature drops 10°C when a cold front moves in. What is the new temperature?

20 The water level of the Dead Sea dropped from 390 meters below sea level in 1930 to 423 meters below sea level in 2010. By how much did the water level drop from 1930 to 2010?

21 **Mathematical Habit 6** Use precise mathematical language
Ms. Davis has only $420 in her bank account. Describe how to find the amount in her account after she writes a check for $590.

22 **Mathematical Habit 6** Use precise mathematical language
Kevin has trouble simplifying 15 − (− 36). Write an explanation to help him.

23 The lowest point in North America is in Death Valley, California, which is 86 meters below sea level at its lowest point. The highest point is Denali, a mountain in Alaska, with an elevation of 6,198 meters above sea level. What is the difference between their elevations?

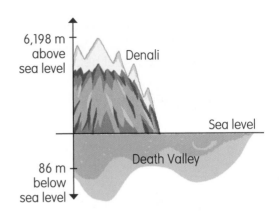

24 Ms. Scott has two freezers. Freezer A keeps frozen foods at a temperature of – 20°F, while Freezer B keeps frozen foods at a temperature of – 4°F. She transferred a package of frozen food from one freezer to the other.

a What is the temperature difference between the two freezers?

b If the temperature of the package rises after the transfer, from which freezer was the package taken?

25 You and a friend are playing a video game. Your score so far is 340 points and your friend's score is – 220 points. What is the difference between your scores?

26 Two record low monthly temperatures for Anchorage, Alaska, are – 34°F in January and 31°F in August. Find the difference between these two temperatures.

27 Town X is 120 feet above sea level,
Town Y is 25 feet below sea level,
and Town Z is 30 feet below sea level.
How high is

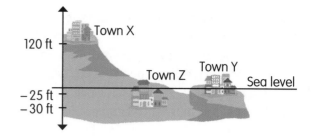

a Town X above Town Y?

b Town Y above Town Z?

c Town X above Town Z?

28 **Mathematical Habit 3** Construct viable arguments

a Find $|8 - 12|$ and $|8| - |12|$. Is $|8 - 12|$ equal to $|8| - |12|$?

b Find $|12 - 8|$ and $|12| - |8|$. Is $|12 - 8|$ equal to $|12| - |8|$?

c Jake thinks that to find the distance between two integers m and n, he can write $|m| - |n|$ or $|n| - |m|$. Use your answer in a and b to explain why you agree or disagree.

29 **Mathematical Habit 2** Use mathematical reasoning

Use the data in the following table. Which two gases have boiling points that are closest in value? Explain.

Gas	Temperature (°F)
Oxygen	−297
Hydrogen	−423
Nitrogen	−321

5 Multiplying and Dividing Integers

Learning Objective:
• Multiply and divide integers.

THINK

a Does the product or quotient of two integers with the same sign result in an answer with the same sign? Why do you think so?

b What are the possible patterns you can observe when multiplying or dividing two integers? Give examples to justify your observations.

ENGAGE

Show 2 × 4 using ◯◯. How do you show 2 × (– 4)? Create a real-world problem to model each situation. Share your real-world problems.

LEARN Multiply two or more integers

Activity Exploring multiplication rules using repeated addition

Work in pairs.

You can think of multiplying integers as repeated addition.

① Use counters and a number line to model and complete the multiplication of integers as repeated addition.

a Evaluate 3 · 2.

3 groups of 2   6

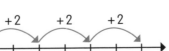

$3 \cdot 2 = 2 \cdot 3$
$\qquad = 2 + 2 + 2$

> Commutative property of multiplication:
> Two or more numbers can be multiplied in any order.

$\qquad = \_\_\_\_$

b Evaluate $3 \cdot (-2)$.

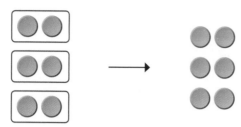

3 groups of (-2) -6

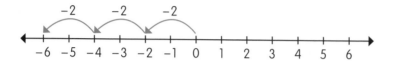

$$3 \cdot (-2) = (-2) \cdot 3$$
$$= -2 + (-2) + (-2)$$
$$= \underline{\hspace{2cm}}$$

The expression $3 \cdot (-2)$ can also be written as $3(-2)$.
The expression $(-2) \cdot 3$ can also be written as $-2(3)$.

(2) Use repeated addition to fill in the table.

Product	Equivalent Sum	Answer	Sign
3(2)	$2 + 2 + 2$	6	+
3(−2)	$-2 + (-2) + (-2)$		
2(5)	$5 + 5$		
2(−5)	$-5 + (-5)$		
4(3)			
4(−3)			

③ Use a number line to model and complete the multiplication as addition of the opposite.

a Evaluate $-3 \cdot 2$.

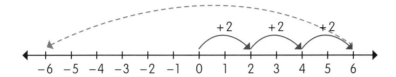

You can say that $-3 \cdot 2$ is the opposite of 3 groups of 2.

$-3 \cdot 2 = -(3)(2)$

$\quad = \underline{\hspace{1.5cm}}$

b Evaluate $-3 \cdot (-2)$.

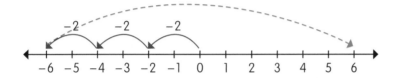

You can say that $-3 \cdot (-2)$ is the opposite of 3 groups of -2.

$-3 \cdot (-2) = -(3)(-2)$

$\quad = -(\underline{\hspace{1.5cm}})$

$\quad = \underline{\hspace{1.5cm}}$

④ Use addition of the opposite and your results from ② to fill in the table.

Product	Use Addition of Opposite	Use Results from ❷	Answer	Sign
$-3(-2)$	$-(3)(-2)$	$-(-6)$	6	+
$-2(-5)$	$-(2)(-5)$	$-(-10)$		
$-4(-3)$				

⑤ **Mathematical Habit 8** Look for patterns

Based on your observations in ① to ④,

a what do you observe about the sign of the product of two integers with the same sign?

b what do you observe about the sign of the product of integers with different signs?

1 Evaluate − 5(4).

− 5(4) = − 20   Product of two integers with different signs is negative.

2 Evaluate − 3 · (− 9).

− 3 · (− 9) = 27   Product of two integers with the same sign is positive.

3 Evaluate 2(− 3)(− 7).

▶ **Method 1**

2(− 3)(− 7) = − 6(− 7)   Product of two integers with different signs is negative.
= 42   Product of two integers with the same sign is positive.

▶ **Method 2**

2(− 3)(− 7) = 2 (21)   Product of two integers with the same sign is positive.
= 42   Product of two integers with the same sign is positive.

Math Note

Associative Property of Multiplication:
If a, b, and c are integers, then $(ab)c = a(bc)$.

 **Math Talk**

Will the product of three negative numbers be positive or negative? What can be said about the product of four negative numbers? Explain your answers.

TRY **Practice multiplying two or more integers**

Evaluate each product.

1 9(− 8)

2 − 6(9)

3 − 7 · (− 5)

4 $4 \cdot (-10)$　　　　　**5** $3(-4)(6)$　　　　　**6** $-5(9)(-2)$

ENGAGE

Water leaks out of a tank at 2 liters each day for 9 days. How do you find the total change in the amount of water in the tank during this time? Share your method.

LEARN Multiply two or more integers in a real-world situation

1 A helicopter's altitude changes at a rate of -17 feet per second. Find the change in the helicopter's altitude after 4 seconds.

Change in altitude = Rate · Time
$= -17 \cdot 4$　　　Substitute -17 for rate and 4 for time.
$= -68$ ft　　　Multiply. Product of two integers with different signs is negative.

The change in the helicopter's altitude is -68 feet.

Solve.

1 Samuel plays four rounds in a golf championship. The score for a round is recorded as positive (over par) or negative (under par). If Samuel scores 6 points under par for all four rounds, what is his total score for his game?

_____ · (− 6) = _____

His score is _____ points.

2 A shop owner sells 3 television sets at a loss. If the loss for each television set is $25, what is the shop owner's total loss?

ENGAGE

Divide 18 by 6. Now, divide − 18 by − 6. How does your knowledge of multiplying integers help you with dividing? Explain.

If the quotient of two numbers is 5, what possible numbers can they be?
If the quotient of two numbers is − 5, what possible numbers can they be?
List a few possible pairs of answers. How are they similar? How are they different? Explain.

LEARN Divide two integers

1 Division is the inverse (or reverse) of multiplication.

Multiplication	**Division**
$3(5) = \mathbf{15}$	$15 \div 5 = \mathbf{3}$
$3(- 5) = \mathbf{-15}$	$-15 \div (- 5) = \mathbf{3}$
$(- 3)5 = \mathbf{-15}$	$-15 \div 5 = \mathbf{-3}$
$(- 3)(- 5) = \mathbf{15}$	$15 \div (- 5) = \mathbf{-3}$

For the relationship between multiplication and division, you can conclude the following:

- When you divide two integers with the same sign, the quotient is positive.

  For example, $2 \div 3 = \frac{2}{3}$ and $-2 \div (-3) = \frac{2}{3}$.

- When you divide two integers with different signs, the quotient is negative.

  For example, $-2 \div 3 = -\frac{2}{3}$ and $2 \div (-3) = -\frac{2}{3}$.

Math Note

For negative fractions, the negative integer may be placed in either the numerator or the denominator:

$-\frac{m}{n} = \frac{-m}{n} = \frac{m}{-n}$, where m and n are integers with $n \neq 0$.

So,

$-2 \div 3 = \frac{-2}{3}$ and $2 \div (-3) = \frac{2}{-3}$

$\qquad = -\frac{2}{3}$ $\qquad\qquad = -\frac{2}{3}$

2 Evaluate $-25 \div (-5)$.

$-25 \div (-5) = 5$ Divide. Quotient of two integers with the same sign is positive.

3 Evaluate $-81 \div 3$.

$-81 \div 3 = -27$ Divide. Quotient of two integers with different signs is negative.

4 Evaluate $96 \div (-4)$.

$96 \div (-4) = -24$ Divide. Quotient of two integers with different signs is negative.

TRY Practice dividing two integers

Evaluate each quotient.

1 $-36 \div (-4)$

2 $-35 \div 5$

3 $45 \div (-3)$

ENGAGE

If an elevator in a skyscraper descends 1,500 feet in 60 seconds, how can you find the change in height per second? Discuss.

LEARN Divide two integers in a real-world situation

1 A submarine descends 720 feet in 6 minutes. Find the submarine's change in elevation per minute.

> A descent is in the negative direction. So, we translate the change in elevation as -720 feet.

Change in elevation per minute: $-\dfrac{720}{6} = -120$ ft/min

The submarine's change in elevation per minute is -120 feet per minute.

TRY Practice dividing two integers in a real-world situation

Solve.

1 Find the change in elevation per minute of a hiker who descended 320 feet in 40 minutes.

INDEPENDENT PRACTICE

Evaluate each product.

1 $5 \cdot (-7)$

2 $12 \cdot (-9)$

3 $-6 \cdot 8$

4 $-3 \cdot 15$

5 $-4 \cdot (-12)$

6 $-8 \cdot (-20)$

7 $-14 \cdot 0$

8 $0 \cdot (-50)$

9 $-3 \cdot 12 \cdot 7$

10 $8 \cdot (-4) \cdot 2$

11 $20 \cdot 5 \cdot (-5)$

12 $-4 \cdot 10 \cdot (-6)$

13 $-7 \cdot (-2) \cdot 10$

14 $9 \cdot (-6) \cdot (-4)$

15 $-2 \cdot (-8) \cdot (-7)$

16 $-5 \cdot (-12) \cdot (-3)$

17 $14 \cdot 0 \cdot (-15)$

18 $-30 \cdot (-2) \cdot 0$

19 $-6 \cdot (-7) \cdot 2 \cdot 5$

20 $-8 \cdot (-2) \cdot (-4) \cdot 12$

21 $-9 \cdot (-5) \cdot (-4) \cdot (-3)$

Evaluate each quotient.

22 $125 \div (-25)$

23 $300 \div (-15)$

24 $-100 \div 25$

25 $-32 \div 4$ **26** $-480 \div (-12)$ **27** $-144 \div (-24)$

28 $0 \div (-8)$ **29** $0 \div (-111)$

Solve.

30 While returning to the glider port, Susan descended at a rate of 380 feet per minute for 3 minutes. Calculate her change in altitude.

31 A scuba diver took 6 minutes to rise to the surface at a rate of 20 feet per minute. How far was he below sea level?

32 A scientist measures the change in height per second of a diving osprey as -198 feet per second. Find the change in the osprey's position after 2 seconds.

33 [**Mathematical Habit** **2**] **Use mathematical reasoning**
Nicole wrote $-25 \div (-100) = \frac{-25}{-100} = -\left(\frac{1}{4}\right)$ and $-2 \cdot (-2) = -4$. Discuss and correct her mistakes.

34 [**Mathematical Habit** **2**] **Use mathematical reasoning**
Ian has trouble solving $-12 \div 3 \cdot 2 \div (-4)$. Write an explanation to help him.

Order of Operations with Integers

Learning Objective:
• Use addition, subtraction, multiplication, and division with integers.

THINK

Ravi thinks he can evaluate $8 \div (3 - 1) \cdot 2 + 4$ and $-8 \div (3 - 1) \cdot 2 + 4$ the same way. Do you agree? Use a context for expression to justify your reasoning.

ENGAGE

Use the order of operations to evaluate $8 \div 2 - 3 + 4(-5)$. List the steps you would follow.

Create a mathematical expression involving the use of the order of operations. Trade your expression with a partner and solve it.

LEARN Apply the order of operations with integers

① The order of operations for integers is the same as the order of operations for whole numbers, fractions, and decimals.

 For expressions involving parentheses, evaluate expressions within parentheses first.

 Evaluate exponents.

 Working from left to right, perform multiplication and division.

 Working from left to right, perform addition and subtraction.

For expressions with parentheses, there may be more than one way of solving.
For example, evaluate $-13 + (-4) \cdot (2 - 10) + 8$.

▶ **Method 1**

Follow the order of operations.

$-13 + (-4) \cdot \underbrace{(2 - 10)} + 8$	Subtract within the parentheses.
$= -13 + \underbrace{(-4) \cdot (-8)} + 8$	Multiply.
$= -13 + \quad 32 \quad + 8$	Use the associative property of addition.
$= -13 + \quad\quad 40$	Add.
$= \quad\quad 27$	Add.

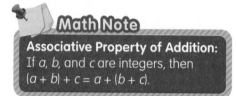

Math Note

Associative Property of Addition:
If a, b, and c are integers, then
$(a + b) + c = a + (b + c)$.

▶ **Method 2**

Use the distributive property first.

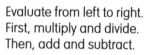

Caution

$(-4)(2 - 10) \neq (-4)(2) + (-4)(10)$

$-13 + (-4) \cdot (2 - 10) + 8$	
$= -13 + (-4) \cdot (2) - (-4) \cdot (10) + 8$	Use the distributive property.
$= -13 + (-8) - (-40) + 8$	Multiply.
$= -13 + (-8) + 40 + 8$	Rewrite subtraction as adding the opposite.
$= -13 + 40 + (-8) + 8$	Use the commutative property of addition.
$= 27$	Add.

2 Evaluate $-9 - 32 \div 4 - 21$.

$-9 - 32 \div 4 - 21$	
$= -9 - 8 - 21$	Divide.
$= -9 + (-8) + (-21)$	Rewrite subtraction as adding the opposite.
$= -9 + (-21) + (-8)$	Use the commutative property of addition.
$= -30 + (-8)$	Add.
$= -38$	Add.

Evaluate from left to right.
First, multiply and divide.
Then, add and subtract.

3 Evaluate $-5 + (8 - 12) \cdot (-4)$.

$-5 + \underbrace{(8 - 12)} \cdot (-4)$	
$= -5 + \underbrace{(-4) \cdot (-4)}$	Simplify within the parentheses.
$= -5 + \quad 16$	Multiply.
$= \quad 11$	Add.

Evaluate from left to right. First, evaluate
within the parentheses. Next, multiply
and divide. Then, add and subtract.

Evaluate each expression.

1 $14 + 8 - 9 \cdot 6$

$14 + 8 - 9 \cdot 6 = 14 + 8 - \underline{\hspace{1cm}}$ Multiply.

$= 14 + 8 + (\underline{\hspace{1cm}})$ Rewrite subtraction as adding the opposite.

$= 22 + (\underline{\hspace{1cm}})$ Simplify.

$= \underline{\hspace{1cm}}$ Add.

2 $(-25 - 5) \div 6 - 21$

$(-25 - 5) \div 6 - 21 = \underline{\hspace{1cm}} \div 6 - 21$ Subtract within parentheses.

$= \underline{\hspace{1cm}} - 21$ Divide.

$= \underline{\hspace{1cm}}$ Subtract.

3 $-14 - (3 + 3) \cdot 2$

4 $48 \div (-8 + 6) + 2 \cdot 28$

ENGAGE

A game show awards 30 points for each correct answer and deducts 50 points for each incorrect answer. A contestant answers 2 questions incorrectly and 3 questions correctly. How do you write an expression to find the contestant's final score? Discuss.

LEARN Apply the order of operations with integers in a real-world situation

1. Ana uses a piece of rectangular paper to make a paper box. The paper's dimensions are 12 inches by 9 inches. To make the paper box, Ana cuts 4 identical rectangles from the corners of the paper. These cut-off rectangles are shown in the diagram on the right. What is the area of the piece of paper that remains?

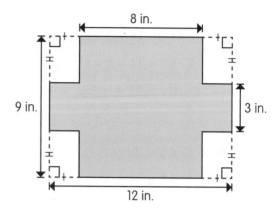

Length of 1 cut-off rectangle: $\left(\dfrac{9-3}{2}\right) = 3$ in.

Width of 1 cut-off rectangle: $\left(\dfrac{12-8}{2}\right) = 2$ in.

Area of remaining paper:

Area of original paper − Area of 4 cut-off rectangles
= 12 · 9 − 4(3 · 2)   Write an expression.
= 108 − 24   Multiply.
= 84 in²   Subtract.

The area of the remaining paper is 84 square inches.

TRY Practice applying the order of operations with integers in a real-world situation

Solve.

1. Luis drew a hexagon on a 3-inch piece of square paper.

   He cut 4 identical right triangles from the corners of the paper.

   The height of each triangle was $\dfrac{1}{2}$ the length of the paper.

   The base of each triangle was $\dfrac{1}{3}$ the length of the paper.

   What was the area of the piece of paper that remained after these triangles were cut off?

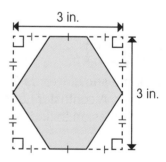

INDEPENDENT PRACTICE

Evaluate each expression.

1 $-3 \cdot 5 + 7$

2 $50 \div (-5) + (-4)$

3 $4 \cdot (-6) + (-3) \cdot 5$

4 $11 - 2 \cdot 8 - (-9)$

5 $-64 \div 4 \cdot 5 - 37$

6 $-28 - 350 \div 7 + 8$

7 $100 - (8 - 15) \cdot 9$

8 $70 \div (-4 - 3) + 60$

9 $(4 + 2) \cdot 3 - 8 \cdot (2 + 3)$

10 $-20 + 4 \cdot (2 + 7) - 35$

11 $15 \div (4 + 1) - 8 \cdot 3$

12 $24 \div 4 - (-13 + 3) \cdot 2$

13 $-12 + 50 \div (-2 - 3) + 72 \div (4 + 2)$

14 $180 \div (4 + 16) - 8 \cdot 3 + 7 \cdot (2 + 3)$

Solve.

15 Ella made a sketch of an octagonal window on a 27-inch square piece of paper. First, she cut 4 identical isosceles triangles from the corners of the paper. Then, she cut a square from the center of the octagon. Each leg of a cut-off triangle is $\frac{1}{3}$ the length of the paper. The side length of the cut-out square is also $\frac{1}{3}$ the length of the paper. What was the area of the sketch after she removed the triangles and the square?

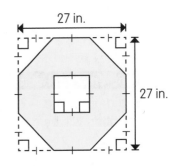

27 in.

27 in.

16 **Mathematical Habit 2** Use mathematical reasoning

Suppose that Lillian shows you some of her homework:

$$-2(6 - 8) = -2(6) - 2(8)$$
$$= -12 - 16$$
$$= -28$$

Lillian made a common error when she used the distributive property to evaluate the expression $-2(6 - 8)$. Evaluate the expression using the order of operations. Then, explain how Lillian can correctly use the distributive property to evaluate the expression.

17 Sarah took three turns in a video game. She scored -120 points during her first turn, 320 points during her second turn, and -80 points during her third turn. What was her average score for the three turns?

18 **Mathematical Habit 6** Use precise mathematical language

Benjamin wrote: $-20 + 4 \cdot 2 + 7 - 35 = -19$. Where can he place the parentheses so that the equation will be a true statement?

7 Operations with Fractions and Mixed Numbers

Learning Objectives:
• Add and subtract fractions and mixed numbers.
• Multiply and divide fractions and mixed numbers.

> **New Vocabulary**
> least common denominator
> complex fraction

THINK

Gracie thinks that when she adds the mixed number $-a\frac{b}{c}$ and the fraction $\frac{x}{y}$, the answer will be negative. She also thinks that their difference, product, and quotient will also be negative. Do you agree?

Explain your reasoning.

ENGAGE

Add $\frac{1}{5}$ and $\frac{2}{3}$. Now, add $\frac{1}{5}$ and $-\frac{2}{3}$. How does having a negative addend change the sum? Explain.

LEARN Add rational numbers

① A rational number is a number that can be written as $\frac{m}{n}$, where m and n are integers with $n \neq 0$. If $\frac{m}{n}$ is negative, either m or n can be negative but not both m and n.

You may rewrite rational numbers with a common denominator before you add them.

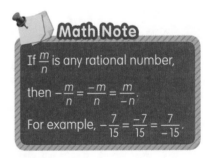

Math Note

If $\frac{m}{n}$ is any rational number,

then $-\frac{m}{n} = \frac{-m}{n} = \frac{m}{-n}$.

For example, $-\frac{7}{15} = \frac{-7}{15} = \frac{7}{-15}$.

The sum of two rational numbers with the same denominator:

Let $\frac{a}{b}$ and $\frac{c}{b}$ be any rational numbers.

$\frac{a}{b} + \frac{c}{b} = \frac{a+c}{b}$

The sum of two rational numbers with different denominators:

Let $\frac{a}{b}$ and $\frac{c}{d}$ be any rational numbers.

$\frac{a}{b} + \frac{c}{d} = \frac{ad+bc}{bd}$

To add two rational numbers such as $\frac{1}{5}$ and $\frac{-2}{3}$, you can apply the rules you know for adding integers.

First, find the least common denominator (LCD) of $\frac{1}{5}$ and $\frac{-2}{3}$, which is 15. Then, use the LCD to write equivalent fractions and evaluate.

$$\frac{1}{5} + \frac{-2}{3} = \frac{1 \cdot \mathbf{3}}{5 \cdot \mathbf{3}} + \frac{-2 \cdot \mathbf{5}}{3 \cdot \mathbf{5}}$$ Write equivalent fractions using the LCD.

$$= \frac{3}{15} + \frac{-10}{15}$$ Multiply.

$$= \frac{3 + (-10)}{15}$$ Simplify using a single denominator.

$$= \frac{-7}{15}$$ Add.

2   Evaluate $\frac{-2}{7} + \frac{3}{-5}$.

$$\frac{-2}{7} + \frac{3}{-5} = \frac{-2 \cdot (\mathbf{-5})}{7 \cdot (\mathbf{-5})} + \frac{3 \cdot \mathbf{7}}{-5 \cdot \mathbf{7}}$$ Write equivalent fractions using the LCD.

$$= \frac{10}{-35} + \frac{21}{-35}$$ Multiply.

$$= \frac{10 + 21}{-35}$$ Simplify using a single denominator.

$$= \frac{31}{-35}$$ Add.

$$= -\frac{31}{35}$$ Write an equivalent fraction.

3   Evaluate $1\frac{2}{3} + \left(-2\frac{1}{6}\right)$.

$$1\frac{2}{3} + \left(-2\frac{1}{6}\right) = 1\frac{2 \cdot 2}{3 \cdot 2} + \left(-2\frac{1}{6}\right)$$ Rewrite the fraction part of each mixed number using the LCD.

$$= 1\frac{4}{6} + \left(-2\frac{1}{6}\right)$$ Multiply.

$$= 1 + \frac{4}{6} + (-2) + \left(-\frac{1}{6}\right)$$ Rewrite the sum.

$$= 1 + (-2) + \frac{4}{6} + \left(-\frac{1}{6}\right)$$ Use the commutative property of addition.

$$= -1 + \left(\frac{3}{6}\right)$$ Add the integers and the fractions.

$$= \frac{-6}{6} + \frac{3}{6}$$ Write an equivalent fraction for the integer part using the same LCD.

$$= -\frac{3}{6}$$ Add the like fractions.

$$= -\frac{1}{2}$$ Write in simplest form.

> **Caution**
>
> $-2\frac{1}{6}$ is the sum of -2 and $-\frac{1}{6}$. Both the fraction part and the integer part of the mixed number are negative.
>
> $$-2\frac{1}{6} = -2 + \left(-\frac{1}{6}\right)$$
> $$= -2 - \frac{1}{6}$$
> $$-2\frac{1}{6} \ne -2 + \frac{1}{6}$$

④ Evaluate $\frac{2}{5} + \left(\frac{-4}{15}\right) + \frac{1}{10}$.

▶ **Method 1**

Add two rational numbers at a time, working from left to right.

$$\frac{2}{5} + \left(\frac{-4}{15}\right) + \frac{1}{10} = \frac{2 \cdot 3}{5 \cdot 3} + \left(\frac{-4}{15}\right) + \frac{1}{10}$$ Write equivalent fractions for the first two fractions using the LCD.

$$= \frac{6}{15} + \left(\frac{-4}{15}\right) + \frac{1}{10}$$ Multiply.

$$= \frac{6 + (-4)}{15} + \frac{1}{10}$$ Write the first two fractions using a single denominator.

$$= \frac{2}{15} + \frac{1}{10}$$ Add.

$$= \frac{2 \cdot 2}{15 \cdot 2} + \frac{1 \cdot 3}{10 \cdot 3}$$ Write equivalent fractions using the LCD of the fractions in the new sum.

$$= \frac{4}{30} + \frac{3}{30}$$ Multiply.

$$= \frac{7}{30}$$ Add the like fractions.

▶ **Method 2**

Use a common denominator for all three fractions.

Finding the LCD of $\frac{2}{5}$, $\frac{-4}{15}$, and $\frac{1}{10}$ is the same as finding the least common multiple (LCM) of 5, 15, and 10.

$\begin{array}{r|ccc} 5 & 5, & 10, & 15 \\ \hline & 1, & 2, & 3 \end{array}$ Divide by the common prime factor 5.
                 Stop dividing because 1, 2, and 3 have no common factor other than 1.

$5 \cdot 1 \cdot 2 \cdot 3 = 30$ Multiply the factors.

The LCM of 5, 10, and 15 is 30.

$$\frac{2}{5} + \left(\frac{-4}{15}\right) + \frac{1}{10} = \frac{2 \cdot 6}{5 \cdot 6} + \frac{-4 \cdot 2}{15 \cdot 2} + \frac{1 \cdot 3}{10 \cdot 3}$$ Write equivalent fractions using the LCD of all three fractions.

$$= \frac{12}{30} + \left(\frac{-8}{30}\right) + \frac{3}{30}$$ Multiply.

$$= \frac{12 + (-8) + 3}{30}$$ Rewrite using a single denominator.

$$= \frac{7}{30}$$ Add.

Evaluate each expression.

1 $\dfrac{-1}{9} + \dfrac{2}{-5}$

$\dfrac{-1}{9} + \dfrac{2}{-5} = \dfrac{(-1)()}{9(-5)} + \dfrac{2()}{(-5)(9)}$ Write equivalent fractions using the LCD.

$= \dfrac{(-1)() + 2()}{9(-5)}$ Rewrite using a single denominator.

$= \dfrac{ + }{-45}$ Multiply.

$= \underline{}$ Add.

2 $-1\dfrac{1}{6} + 3\dfrac{4}{9}$

$-1\dfrac{1}{6} + 3\dfrac{4}{9} = -1\dfrac{}{} + 3\dfrac{}{}$ Rewrite the fraction part of each mixed number using the LCD.

$= -1 + 3 + \dfrac{}{} + \dfrac{}{}$ Use the commutative property of addition to group the integers, and then the fractions.

$= \underline{} + \dfrac{}{}$ Add.

$= \underline{}$ Write as a mixed number.

3 $\dfrac{1}{6} + \left(\dfrac{-5}{9}\right) + \left(\dfrac{-1}{3}\right)$

▶ **Method 1**

Add two rational numbers at a time, working from left to right.

$\dfrac{1}{6} + \dfrac{-5}{9} + \dfrac{-1}{3} = \dfrac{}{} + \dfrac{}{} + \dfrac{-1}{3}$ Write equivalent fractions for first two fractions using the LCD.

$= \dfrac{}{} + \dfrac{-1}{3}$ Add the numerators of the first two fractions.

$= \dfrac{}{} + \dfrac{}{}$ Write equivalent fractions using the LCD.

$= \dfrac{ + }{}$ Write using a single denominator.

$= \underline{}$ Add.

▶ **Method 2**

Use a common denominator for all three fractions.

$$\frac{1}{6} + \frac{-5}{9} + \frac{-1}{3} = \frac{\quad}{\quad} + \frac{\quad}{\quad} + \frac{\quad}{\quad}$$ Write equivalent fractions using the LCD.

$$= \frac{\quad + \quad + \quad}{\quad}$$ Write using a single denominator.

$$= \underline{\quad}$$ Add.

ENGAGE

Subtract $\frac{a}{b}$ from $\frac{p}{q}$. Now, subtract $\frac{p}{q}$ from $\frac{a}{b}$. How does changing the order of the fractions affect the result? Explain.

LEARN Subtract rational numbers

1. As with fractions, you may need to rewrite rational numbers so that they have a common denominator before you subtract.

> **The difference between two rational numbers with the same denominator:**
>
> Let $\frac{a}{b}$ and $\frac{c}{b}$ be any rational numbers. $\frac{a}{b} - \frac{c}{b} = \frac{a - c}{b}$
>
> **The difference between two rational numbers with different denominators:**
>
> Let $\frac{a}{b}$ and $\frac{c}{d}$ be any rational numbers. $\frac{a}{b} - \frac{c}{d} = \frac{ad - bc}{bd}$

For example, subtract $\frac{1}{2}$ from $\frac{2}{5}$.

$$\frac{2}{5} - \frac{1}{2} = \frac{2 \cdot 2}{5 \cdot 2} - \frac{1 \cdot 5}{2 \cdot 5}$$ Write equivalent fractions using the LCD.

$$= \frac{4}{10} - \frac{5}{10}$$ Multiply.

$$= \frac{4 - 5}{10}$$ Rewrite using a single denominator.

$$= \frac{-1}{10}$$ Subtract.

$$= -\frac{1}{10}$$ Write an equivalent fraction.

> Remember that subtracting a number is the same as adding its opposite.
> For example, $4 - 5 = 4 + (-5)$
> $\qquad\qquad\quad = -1$

⚠️ **Caution**

The phrase "subtract a from b" does not mean $a - b$. It means $b - a$.

So, the phrase "subtract $\frac{1}{2}$ from $\frac{3}{5}$" means $\frac{3}{5} - \frac{1}{2}$.

2 Evaluate $\dfrac{1}{6} - \dfrac{3}{4}$.

$\dfrac{1}{6} - \dfrac{3}{4} = \dfrac{1 \cdot 2}{6 \cdot 2} - \dfrac{3 \cdot 3}{4 \cdot 3}$ Write equivalent fractions using the LCD.

$= \dfrac{2}{12} - \dfrac{9}{12}$ Multiply.

$= \dfrac{2 - 9}{12}$ Rewrite using a single denominator.

$= \dfrac{-7}{12}$ Subtract.

$= -\dfrac{7}{12}$ Rewrite an equivalent fraction.

3 Evaluate $2\dfrac{1}{4} - 4\dfrac{2}{3}$.

$2\dfrac{1}{4} - 4\dfrac{2}{3} = 2\dfrac{1 \cdot 3}{4 \cdot 3} - 4\dfrac{2 \cdot 4}{3 \cdot 4}$ Write equivalent fractions for the fraction part of each mixed number using the LCD.

$= 2\dfrac{3}{12} - 4\dfrac{8}{12}$ Multiply.

$= 2 + \dfrac{3}{12} - 4 - \dfrac{8}{12}$ Rewrite.

$= 2 - 4 + \left(\dfrac{3}{12} - \dfrac{8}{12} \right)$ Use the commutative property of addition.

$= -2 + \left(-\dfrac{5}{12} \right)$ Subtract the integers and the fractions.

$= -2\dfrac{5}{12}$ Simplify.

> You can rewrite $-4\dfrac{8}{12}$ as $-4 - \dfrac{8}{12}$ or $(-4) + \left(\dfrac{-8}{12} \right)$.

4 Evaluate $\dfrac{1}{3} - \dfrac{11}{12} - \dfrac{1}{2}$.

▶ **Method 1**

Subtract two rational numbers at a time, working from left to right.

$\dfrac{1}{3} - \dfrac{11}{12} - \dfrac{1}{2} = \dfrac{1 \cdot 4}{3 \cdot 4} - \dfrac{11}{12} - \dfrac{1}{2}$ Write equivalent fractions for the first two fractions using their LCD.

$= \dfrac{4}{12} - \dfrac{11}{12} - \dfrac{1}{2}$ Multiply.

$= \dfrac{4 - 11}{12} - \dfrac{1}{2}$ Rewrite the first two fractions using a single denominator.

$= \dfrac{-7}{12} - \dfrac{1}{2}$ Subtract.

$= \dfrac{-7}{12} - \dfrac{1 \cdot 6}{2 \cdot 6}$ Write equivalent fractions using the LCD.

$= \dfrac{-7}{12} - \dfrac{6}{12}$ Multiply.

$= \dfrac{-7 - 6}{12}$ Rewrite using a single denominator.

$= \dfrac{-13}{12}$ Subtract.

$= -1\dfrac{1}{12}$ Rewrite the improper fraction as a mixed number.

▶ **Method 2**

Use a common denominator for all three fractions.

$$\frac{1}{3} - \frac{11}{12} - \frac{1}{2} = \frac{1 \cdot 4}{3 \cdot 4} - \frac{11}{12} - \frac{1 \cdot 6}{2 \cdot 6}$$ Write equivalent fractions using the LCD for all three fractions.

$$= \frac{4}{12} - \frac{11}{12} - \frac{6}{12}$$ Multiply all products.

$$= \frac{4 - 11 - 6}{12}$$ Rewrite using a single denominator.

$$= \frac{-13}{12}$$ Subtract.

$$= -1\frac{1}{12}$$ Rewrite the improper fraction as a mixed number.

TRY Practice subtracting rational numbers

Evaluate each expression.

1 $\frac{1}{4} - \frac{3}{10}$

$$\frac{1}{4} - \frac{3}{10} = \frac{1 \cdot \boxed{}}{4 \cdot \boxed{}} - \frac{3 \cdot \boxed{}}{10 \cdot \boxed{}}$$ Write equivalent fractions using the LCD.

$$= \frac{\boxed{}}{20} - \frac{\boxed{}}{20}$$ Multiply.

$$= \frac{\boxed{} - \boxed{}}{20}$$ Rewrite using a single denominator.

$$= \frac{\boxed{}}{20}$$ Subtract.

$$= -\frac{\boxed{}}{20}$$ Rewrite an equivalent fraction.

2 $\frac{7}{8} - \frac{9}{10}$

3 $3\frac{1}{4} - 7\frac{5}{6}$

4 $\frac{3}{7} - \frac{27}{28} - \frac{3}{14}$

What is $\frac{1}{2}$ of $\frac{1}{3}$? What is $\frac{1}{2}$ of $-\frac{1}{3}$? Draw a sketch to show your thinking.

LEARN Multiply rational numbers

1. You have learned how to multiply positive fractions and how to multiply positive and negative integers. So, you can multiply both positive and negative rational numbers using the same rules for the signs of the products.

Multiply rational numbers with the same sign.

Examples:

$$\frac{1}{2} \cdot \frac{3}{4} = \frac{1 \cdot 3}{2 \cdot 4} = \frac{3}{8}, \text{ and } \left(-\frac{1}{2}\right) \cdot \left(-\frac{3}{4}\right) = \frac{1 \cdot 3}{2 \cdot 4} = \frac{3}{8}.$$

Multiply rational numbers with different signs.

Examples:

$$\frac{1}{2} \cdot \left(-\frac{3}{4}\right) = -\frac{1 \cdot 3}{2 \cdot 4} = -\frac{3}{8}, \text{ and } \left(-\frac{1}{2}\right) \cdot \frac{3}{4} = -\frac{1 \cdot 3}{2 \cdot 4} = -\frac{3}{8}.$$

Math Note

Multiplying Positive and Negative Rational Numbers:

Two signs are the same:
$(+) \cdot (+) = (+)$
$(-) \cdot (-) = (+)$
The product is positive.

Two signs are different:
$(+) \cdot (-) = (-)$
$(-) \cdot (+) = (-)$
The product is negative.

2. Evaluate $-\frac{3}{7} \cdot \frac{8}{15}$.

$$-\frac{3}{7} \cdot \frac{8}{15} = \frac{-3 \cdot 8}{7 \cdot 15}$$ Multiply the numerators, and multiply the denominators.

$$= \frac{^{-1}\cancel{-3} \cdot 8}{7 \cdot \cancel{15}_5}$$ Divide the numerator and denominator by their greatest common factor (GCF), 3.

$$= -\frac{8}{35}$$ Simplify.

3 Evaluate $-2\frac{3}{5} \cdot \left(-1\frac{1}{4}\right)$.

$$-2\frac{3}{5} \cdot \left(-1\frac{1}{4}\right) = -\frac{13}{5} \cdot \left(-\frac{5}{4}\right)$$ Write as improper fractions.

$$= \frac{13 \cdot \overset{1}{\cancel{5}}}{\underset{1}{\cancel{5}} \cdot 4}$$ Divide the numerator and denominator by their GCF, 5.

$$= \frac{13}{4}$$ Simplify.

$$= 3\frac{1}{4}$$ Write as a mixed number.

TRY Practice multiplying rational numbers

Evaluate each product.

1 $-\frac{4}{5} \cdot \frac{20}{21}$

$$-\frac{4}{5} \cdot \frac{20}{21} = \underline{\hspace{2cm}}$$ Multiply the numerators, and multiply the denominators.

$$= \underline{\hspace{2cm}}$$ Divide the numerator and denominator by their GCF, _____ .

$$= \underline{\hspace{2cm}}$$ Simplify.

2 $-3\frac{1}{4} \cdot \left(-2\frac{2}{3}\right)$

$$-3\frac{1}{4} \cdot \left(-2\frac{2}{3}\right) = -\frac{\boxed{}}{4} \cdot \left(-\frac{\boxed{}}{3}\right)$$ Write as improper fractions.

$$= \underline{\hspace{2cm}}$$ Divide the numerator and denominator by their GCF, _____ .

$$= \underline{\hspace{1cm}}$$ Simplify.

$$= \underline{\hspace{2cm}}$$ Write as a mixed number.

ENGAGE

Do the rules for multiplying negative fractions apply to dividing negative fractions? How do you know? Explain your reasoning by providing specific examples.

LEARN Divide rational numbers

1 You have learned that dividing by a fraction is the same as multiplying by the reciprocal of the fraction.

You can use this same method to divide rational numbers, but you need to apply what you know about dividing numbers with the same or different signs.

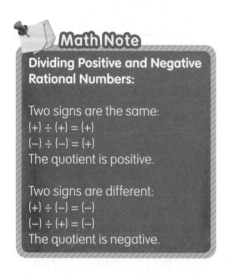

Math Note

Dividing Positive and Negative Rational Numbers:

Two signs are the same:
$(+) \div (+) = (+)$
$(-) \div (-) = (+)$
The quotient is positive.

Two signs are different:
$(+) \div (-) = (-)$
$(-) \div (+) = (-)$
The quotient is negative.

Two numbers are reciprocals if their product is 1.

3 and -3 are not reciprocals because their product is -9, not 1.

-5 and $-\frac{1}{5}$ are reciprocals because their product is 1.

So, $3 \div \frac{1}{5} = 3 \cdot 5$.

The quotient of two rational numbers may be written as a **complex fraction**. A complex fraction is a fraction in which the numerator, the denominator, or both the numerator and denominator contain a fraction.

An example of a complex fraction whose numerator and denominator contain a fraction is

$\left(\frac{1}{3}\right)$ ⟶ **Numerator**
$\overline{\left(\frac{5}{6}\right)}$ ⟶ **Denominator**

Other examples of complex fractions include $\dfrac{\left(\frac{2}{7}\right)}{8}$, $\dfrac{3}{\left(-\frac{5}{2}\right)}$, and $\dfrac{\left(-4\frac{1}{2}\right)}{\left(-1\frac{5}{16}\right)}$.

To simplify a complex fraction, rewrite the fraction using a division symbol '÷'.

$$\frac{\left(\frac{1}{3}\right)}{\left(\frac{5}{6}\right)} = \frac{1}{3} \div \frac{5}{6} \qquad \text{Rewrite as a division expression.}$$

$$= \frac{1}{3} \cdot \frac{6}{5} \qquad \text{Multiply } \frac{1}{3} \text{ by the reciprocal of } \frac{5}{6}.$$

$$= \frac{1 \cdot 6}{3 \cdot 5} \qquad \text{Multiply the numerators and denominators.}$$

$$= \frac{1 \cdot \overset{2}{\cancel{6}}}{\underset{1}{\cancel{3}} \cdot 5} \qquad \text{Divide the numerator and the denominator by the GCF, 3.}$$

$$= \frac{2}{5} \qquad \text{Simplify.}$$

2 Evaluate $-\frac{5}{6} \div \frac{1}{24}$.

$$-\frac{5}{6} \div \frac{1}{24} = -\frac{5}{6} \cdot \frac{24}{1} \qquad \text{Multiply } -\frac{5}{6} \text{ by the reciprocal of } \frac{1}{24}.$$

$$= \frac{-5 \cdot 24}{6 \cdot 1} \qquad \text{Multiply the numerators and denominators.}$$

$$= \frac{-5 \cdot \overset{4}{\cancel{24}}}{\underset{1}{\cancel{6}} \cdot 1} \qquad \text{Divide the numerator and denominator by the GCF, 6.}$$

$$= \frac{-20}{1} \qquad \text{Simplify.}$$

$$= -20 \qquad \text{Write as a negative integer.}$$

3 Evaluate $-5\frac{1}{3} \div \left(-2\frac{2}{5}\right)$.

$$-5\frac{1}{3} \div \left(-2\frac{2}{5}\right) = \frac{-16}{3} \div \frac{-12}{5} \qquad \text{Write as improper fractions.}$$

$$= \frac{-16}{3} \cdot \frac{5}{-12} \qquad \text{Multiply } \frac{-16}{3} \text{ by the reciprocal of } \frac{-12}{5}.$$

$$= \frac{\overset{4}{\cancel{16}} \cdot 5}{3 \cdot \underset{3}{\cancel{12}}} \qquad \begin{array}{l}\text{Multiply the numerators and denominators.}\\ \text{Divide the numerators and denominators by the GCF, 4.}\end{array}$$

$$= \frac{20}{9} \qquad \text{Simplify.}$$

$$= 2\frac{2}{9} \qquad \text{Write as a mixed number.}$$

4 Evaluate $\dfrac{\left(-\frac{1}{4}\right)}{\left(\frac{1}{2}\right)}$.

$$\dfrac{\left(-\frac{1}{4}\right)}{\left(\frac{1}{2}\right)} = -\frac{1}{4} \div \frac{1}{2} \qquad \text{Rewrite as a division expression.}$$

$$= -\frac{1}{4} \cdot \frac{2}{1} \qquad \text{Multiply } -\frac{1}{4} \text{ by the reciprocal of } \frac{1}{2}.$$

$$= -\frac{2}{4} \qquad \text{Multiply numerators and denominators.}$$

$$= -\frac{1}{2} \qquad \text{Write in simplest form.}$$

> $\dfrac{a}{b}$ means the same as $a \div b$. So,
> $\dfrac{\left(-\frac{1}{4}\right)}{\left(\frac{1}{2}\right)}$ is the same as $-\frac{1}{4} \div \frac{1}{2}$.

TRY Practice dividing rational numbers

Evaluate each quotient.

1 $\dfrac{3}{20} \div \left(-\dfrac{6}{35}\right)$

2 $-3\dfrac{1}{3} \div \left(-1\dfrac{1}{4}\right)$

3 $\dfrac{\left(\frac{1}{4}\right)}{\left(-\frac{3}{8}\right)}$

ENGAGE

A clock's battery is running low. Every 6 hours, the clock slows down by $\frac{1}{2}$ hour. How do you find out how much time the clock slows down by in 1 hour? Share your method.

LEARN Add, subtract, multiply, and divide rational numbers in a real-world situation

1. Mr. Turner has a partial roll of wire $18\frac{1}{4}$ feet long. He needs $25\frac{1}{2}$ feet of wire for a remodeling project. How much wire is he short of?

$18\frac{1}{4} - 25\frac{1}{2}$	Write an expression for this situation.
$= 18\frac{1}{4} - 25\frac{1 \cdot 2}{2 \cdot 2}$	Write equivalent fractions for the fraction parts using the LCD, 4.
$= 18\frac{1}{4} - 25\frac{2}{4}$	Multiply.
$= 18 + \frac{1}{4} - 25 - \frac{2}{4}$	Rewrite.
$= 18 - 25 + \left(\frac{1}{4} - \frac{2}{4}\right)$	Use the commutative property of addition to group the integers, and then the fractions.
$= -7 + \left(-\frac{1}{4}\right)$	Subtract the integers and then the fractions.
$= -7\frac{1}{4}$	Subtract.

He is short of $7\frac{1}{4}$ feet of wire.

TRY Practice adding, subtracting, multiplying, and dividing rational numbers in a real-world situation

Solve.

1. Philadelphia suffered a severe snowstorm in 1996 that left $30\frac{7}{10}$ inches of snow on the ground. Another severe snowstorm occurred in 2010, when $28\frac{1}{2}$ inches of snow fell.

a Write a subtraction expression for the difference in depth of these two record snowfalls.

b Rewrite the expression as an addition expression.

c Find the difference between the two record snowfalls.

2. A pancake recipe requires $1\frac{2}{3}$ cups of flour to make 20 pancakes and you have 9 cups of flour.

a How many pancakes can you make with 1 cup of flour?

b How many pancakes can you make with 9 cups of flour?

INDEPENDENT PRACTICE

Evaluate each expression. Give your answer in simplest form.

1 $\frac{1}{2} + \left(-\frac{5}{6}\right)$

2 $\frac{-6}{7} + \frac{3}{14}$

3 $-\frac{1}{7} + \frac{-3}{5}$

4 $2\frac{1}{2} + \left(-3\frac{4}{5}\right)$

5 $\frac{-1}{7} + \frac{-5}{6} + \frac{-1}{3}$

6 $\frac{3}{5} - \frac{2}{3}$

7 $\frac{-1}{7} - \frac{3}{14}$

8 $5\frac{2}{5} - 8\frac{3}{7}$

9 $\frac{1}{3} - \left(-\frac{2}{5}\right) - \frac{3}{4}$

Evaluate each product. Give your answer in simplest form.

10 $-\frac{7}{25} \cdot \frac{5}{14}$

11 $\frac{5}{8} \cdot \left(-\frac{4}{15}\right)$

12 $\frac{7}{30} \cdot \left(-\frac{6}{7}\right)$

13 $-\frac{8}{27} \cdot \left(-\frac{9}{40}\right)$

14 $-\frac{11}{16} \cdot \left(-\frac{4}{33}\right)$

15 $\frac{5}{8} \cdot \left(-2\frac{4}{5}\right)$

16 $-\frac{3}{22} \cdot 1\frac{5}{6}$

17 $3\frac{1}{8} \cdot \left(-\frac{3}{10}\right)$

18 $-4\frac{1}{2} \cdot \left(-1\frac{8}{9}\right)$

Evaluate each quotient. Give your answer in simplest form.

19 $-10 \div \left(-\dfrac{5}{6}\right)$

20 $\dfrac{9}{25} \div (-18)$

21 $-\dfrac{3}{8} \div \left(-\dfrac{1}{8}\right)$

22 $-\dfrac{1}{4} \div \dfrac{3}{8}$

23 $\dfrac{5}{12} \div \left(-\dfrac{1}{6}\right)$

24 $-1\dfrac{1}{4} \div \dfrac{3}{4}$

25 $\dfrac{8}{15} \div \left(-2\dfrac{2}{3}\right)$

26 $3\dfrac{3}{4} \div \left(-\dfrac{1}{4}\right)$

27 $2\dfrac{1}{2} \div \left(-1\dfrac{2}{3}\right)$

28 $-2\dfrac{2}{7} \div \left(-1\dfrac{3}{7}\right)$

29 $\dfrac{-7}{\left(-\dfrac{7}{3}\right)}$

30 $\dfrac{\left(-\dfrac{2}{3}\right)}{4}$

31 $\dfrac{\left(-\dfrac{3}{4}\right)}{\left(-\dfrac{5}{8}\right)}$

32 $\dfrac{\left(-\dfrac{1}{5}\right)}{\left(1\dfrac{2}{15}\right)}$

Solve.

33 Daniel biked $15\dfrac{9}{10}$ miles on Saturday and $6\dfrac{7}{10}$ miles on Sunday. How much farther did Daniel bike on Saturday than on Sunday?

34 A recipe calls for $\frac{3}{4}$ cup of flour, but David has only $\frac{1}{3}$ cup of flour. How much more flour does he need?

35 A weather report showed that the rainfall in Janesville was $2\frac{2}{3}$ inches during the first half of January. At the end of January, the total rainfall was $3\frac{1}{4}$ inches. How much did it rain in the second half of January?

36 The sum of two rational numbers is $5\frac{1}{2}$. If one of the numbers is $6\frac{3}{14}$, find the other number.

37 **Mathematical Habit 3** **Construct viable arguments**

Melanie adds $\frac{1}{a} + \left(-\frac{1}{b}\right)$ and says the answer is $\frac{1}{a-b}$. Give an example to show that Melanie is wrong.

38 **Mathematical Habit 6** Use precise mathematical language

Juan multiplies two mixed numbers, $-4\frac{3}{5}$ and $1\frac{2}{7}$, as follows:

$$-4\frac{3}{5} \cdot 1\frac{2}{7} = -4 \cdot 1 \cdot \frac{3}{5} \cdot \frac{2}{7}$$

$$= -4 \cdot \frac{3 \cdot 2}{5 \cdot 7}$$

$$= -4\frac{6}{35}$$

Describe Juan's mistakes. What is the correct answer?

39 Package A weighs $5\frac{1}{2}$ pounds and Package B weighs $1\frac{1}{4}$ pounds. Find the average weight of the two packages.

40 A scientist measured the weight of some damp soil. After exposing the soil to the air for $4\frac{1}{2}$ weeks, the scientist found that the weight had decreased by $5\frac{5}{8}$ ounces. Find the soil's average weight loss per week.

41 A plank measures $4\frac{3}{4}$ feet. Rachel cuts off $\frac{2}{5}$ of the plank. How long is the plank now?

8 Operations with Decimals

Learning Objectives:
• Add and subtract decimals.
• Multiply and divide numbers in decimal or percent form.

THINK

Sofia evaluated the expression as shown.

$$-3.2\,(-2.5 + 0.3) \div 0.4 = -3.2 \cdot (-2.2) \div 0.4$$
$$= -5.4 \div 0.4$$
$$= -13.5$$

Do you agree with Sofia's solution? Explain your reasoning.

ENGAGE

A company made a profit of $1.65 million in January but a loss of $2.8 million in February. How do you find how much the company lost in total within these two months? Share your method.

LEARN Add and subtract decimals

1 The table shows the monthly profits and losses in dollars of a company for the first three months of one year.

January	February	March
− $2.14 million	− $1.5 million	$2.17 million

From the table, the negative decimals mean that the company lost money doing business in January and February. It made a profit in March.

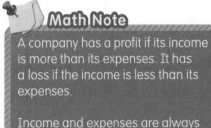

Math Note

A company has a profit if its income is more than its expenses. It has a loss if the income is less than its expenses.

Income and expenses are always positive, but business losses can be represented by negative numbers.

You can find the company's combined loss for January and February, as well as the net profit or loss the company made at the end of the three months.

To find the combined loss for January and February, evaluate the sum of -2.14 and -1.5. In this case, you are adding two negative decimals, -2.14 and -1.5.

Using absolute values,

$|-2.14| + |-1.5| = 2.14 + 1.5$ Add the absolute values.
             $= 3.64$ Simplify.

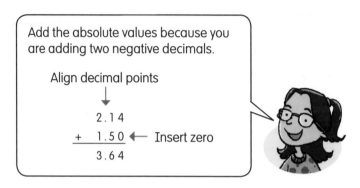

Add the absolute values because you are adding two negative decimals.

Align decimal points

$$\begin{array}{r} 2.14 \\ +\ 1.50 \\ \hline 3.64 \end{array}$$ ← Insert zero

$-2.14 + (-1.5) = -3.64$ Use the common sign, a negative sign.

The combined loss for January and February was $3.64 million.

To find the net profit or loss of the company at the end of the three months, evaluate the sum of -2.14, -1.5, and 2.17. Since $-2.14 + (-1.5) = -3.64$, you only need to find $-3.64 + 2.17$. In this case, you are adding two decimals with different signs.

Using absolute values,

$|-3.64| - |2.17| = 3.64 - 2.17$ Subtract the lesser absolute value from the greater one.
             $= 1.47$ Simplify.

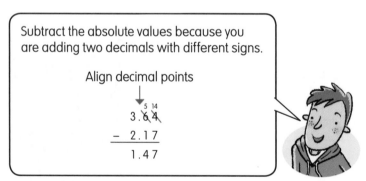

Subtract the absolute values because you are adding two decimals with different signs.

Align decimal points

$$\begin{array}{r} \overset{5\ \ 14}{3.6\cancel{4}} \\ -\ 2.17 \\ \hline 1.47 \end{array}$$

$-3.64 + 2.17 = -1.47$ Use a negative sign because -3.64 has a greater absolute value.

Since -1.47 is negative, you know that the company had a net loss at the end of the three months. The company had a net loss of $1.47 million.

2 Evaluate − 4.52 + 3.26.

Using absolute values,

|− 4.52| − |3.26| = 4.52 − 3.26   Subtract the lesser absolute value from the greater one.
               = 1.26   Simplify.

− 4.52 + 3.26 = − 1.26   Use a negative sign because − 4.52 has a greater absolute value.

3 Evaluate − 7.4 − 5.18.

− 7.4 − 5.18 = − 7.4 + (− 5.18)   Rewrite subtraction as adding the opposite.

Using absolute values,

|− 7.4| + | − 5.18| = 7.4 + 5.18   Add the absolute values.
              = 12.58   Simplify.

− 7.4 − 5.18 = − 12.58   Use the common sign, a negative sign.

TRY Practice adding and subtracting decimals

Evaluate each expression.

1 2.35 + (− 6.13)

Using absolute values,

_____ − _____ = _____ − _____   Subtract the lesser absolute value from the greater absolute value.

              = _____   Simplify.

2.35 + (− 6.13) = _____   Use a _____ sign because

_____ has a greater absolute value.

2 − 8.6 − 3.27

3 3.38 + (− 5.6)

ENGAGE

a How can you multiply 3.2 by 0.5 in different ways?

b What happens to the product when one of the numbers is negative? What happens when both the numbers are negative? Explain your reasoning.

c How can you multiply 0.75 by a fraction? How can you multiply 0.75 by an integer? How can you multiply 0.75 by another decimal? How does each multiplication differ?

LEARN Multiply numbers in decimal or percent form

1 The rules for multiplying integers also apply to multiplying numbers in decimal form. For example, evaluate the product of − 2.05 and 1.2.

First, multiply the two decimals without their signs. Then, apply what you know about multiplying numbers with the same or different signs.

$$
\begin{array}{r}
{}^{1} \\
2.0\,5 \leftarrow \text{ 2 decimal places} \\
\times \quad 1.2 \leftarrow \underline{+\,1\,\text{decimal place}} \\
\hline
4\,1\,0 \\
2\,0\,5 \\
\hline
2.4\,6\,0 \leftarrow \text{ 3 decimal places}
\end{array}
$$

The product of − 2.05 and 1.2 has a negative sign because the two decimals have different signs.

So, the product of − 2.05 and 1.2 is − 2.46.

− 2.05 · 1.2 = − 2.46

② Evaluate $6.72 \cdot (-0.4)$.

$$
\begin{array}{r}
\overset{2}{6}.7\,2 \\
\times\qquad 0.4 \\
\hline
2\,6\,8\,8 \\
0\,0\,0 \\
\hline
2.6\,8\,8
\end{array}
$$

6.72 ← 2 decimal places
0.4 ← +1 decimal place

2.688 ← 3 decimal places

Multiply the numbers without their signs.

Add.

$6.72 \cdot (-0.4) = -2.688$

Product of two decimals with different signs is negative.

③ Evaluate $-51 \cdot (-8.5)$.

$$
\begin{array}{r}
5\,1 \\
\times\qquad 8.5 \\
\hline
2\,5\,5 \\
4\,0\,8 \\
\hline
4\,3\,3.5
\end{array}
$$

51 ← 0 decimal place
8.5 ← +1 decimal place

433.5 ← 1 decimal place

Multiply the numbers without their signs.

Add.

$-51 \cdot (-8.5) = 433.5$

Product of two decimals with the same sign is positive.

④ Evaluate 6% of 530.

$$
\begin{array}{r}
\overset{1}{5}\,3\,0 \\
\times\qquad 0.0\,6 \\
\hline
3\,1\,8\,0 \\
0\,0\,0 \\
0\,0\,0 \\
\hline
0\,3\,1.8\,0
\end{array}
$$

530 ← 0 decimal place
0.06 ← +2 decimal places

031.80 ← 2 decimal places

Multiply the numbers without their signs.

Add.

$6\% \cdot 530 = 31.8$

Product of two numbers with the same sign is positive.

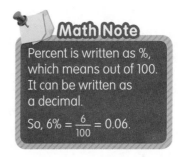

Math Note

Percent is written as %, which means out of 100. It can be written as a decimal.

So, $6\% = \frac{6}{100} = 0.06$.

Evaluate each product.

1 − 7.2 ⋅ 4.6

2 − 37 ⋅ (− 9. 2)

3 8% of $230

ENGAGE

You have learned to multiply and divide fractions using positive and negative integers. Use your knowledge of fractions to divide 0.28 by − 0.4. Explain your strategy.

a How can you divide 0.28 by −0.4 in different ways?

b What happens to the quotient when one of the numbers is negative? What happens when both the numbers are negative? Explain your reasoning.

c How can you divide 0.56 by a fraction? How can you divide 0.56 by an integer? How can you divide 0.56 by another decimal? How does each division differ?

LEARN Divide numbers in decimal form

1 The rules for dividing integers also apply to dividing numbers in decimal form.

For example, evaluate − 24.18 ÷ 2.6.

First, divide the two decimals without their signs. Then, use what you know about dividing numbers with the same or different signs.

$$2.6 \overline{)24.18} \longrightarrow \begin{array}{r} 9.3 \\ 26\overline{)241.8} \\ \underline{234} \\ 7\,8 \\ \underline{7\,8} \\ 0 \end{array}$$

Place the decimal point in the quotient above the decimal point in the dividend.

Make the divisor a whole number by multiplying both the divisor and the dividend by 10.

− 24.18 ÷ 2.6 = − 9.3

Use a negative sign because the two decimals have different signs.

2 Evaluate $13.14 \div (-1.8)$.

$$1.8 \overset{\curvearrowright}{\smash{)}}\, 13.\overset{\curvearrowright}{14} \quad \longrightarrow \quad \begin{array}{r} 7.3 \\ 18 \overline{)\, 131.4} \\ 126 \\ \hline 5\ 4 \\ 5\ 4 \\ \hline 0 \end{array}$$

Make the divisor a whole number by multiplying both the divisor and the dividend by 10.

Place the decimal point in the quotient above the decimal point in the dividend.

$13.14 \div (-1.8) = -7.3$

TRY Practice dividing numbers in decimal form

State whether each quotient is positive or negative. Then, evaluate the quotient.

1 $-21.7 \div 0.7$

2 $-31.92 \div (-4.2)$

Tiana buys 4 boxes of paper clips. She pays with a $10 bill and receives $6.08 in change. How do you write an expression to find the price of 1 box of paper clips? Explain your reasoning.

LEARN Apply the order of operations to decimals in a real-world situation

1 A diver went 30.65 feet below the surface of the ocean, and then 46.5 feet further down. He then rose 52.45 feet. Find the diver's new depth.

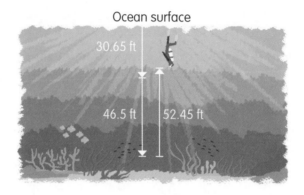

Ocean surface

30.65 ft

46.5 ft   52.45 ft

$-30.65 - 46.5 + 52.45$ Write an expression.
$= -30.65 + (-46.5) + 52.45$ Rewrite subtraction as adding the opposite.

Use absolute values to add the first two numbers.

$|-30.65| + |-46.5| = 30.65 + 46.5$ Add the absolute values of the first two numbers.
$= 77.15$ Simplify.

$-30.65 - 46.5 = -77.15$ Use the common sign, a negative sign.

Use absolute values to add the sum of the first two numbers to the third.

$|-77.15| - |52.45| = 77.15 - 52.45$ Subtract the lesser absolute value.
$= 24.7$ Simplify.

$-77.15 + 52.45 = -24.7$ Use a negative sign because -77.15 has a greater absolute value.

$-30.65 - 46.5 + 52.45 = -24.7$

The diver's new depth is 24.7 feet below the surface of the ocean.

2 A hot air balloon ascended at 0.7 meter per second for 8 seconds. It then descended at 0.5 meter per second for 6 seconds. Find the overall change in altitude.

$0.7 \cdot 8 - 0.5 \cdot 6 = 5.6 - 3.0$ Multiply.
$ = 2.6$ Subtract.

The overall change in altitude is 2.6 meters.

3 An electronic game system costs $399 plus a 4% sales tax. What is the total cost of the game system?

▶ **Method 1**
$\$399 + 0.04 \cdot \$399 = \$399 + \$15.96$ Multiply.
$ = \$414.96$ Add.

The total cost of the game system is $414.96.

The total cost is more than $399 because the customer must pay a 4% sales tax.

▶ **Method 2**
$\$399 \cdot 1.04 = \$414.96$ Multiply.

The total cost of the game system is $414.96.

TRY Practice applying the order of operations to decimals in a real-world situation

Solve.

1 A town's temperature drops by 1.6°F per hour for 1.2 hours. It then drops by 0.8°F per hour for 2.5 hours. Find the total change in temperature.

You can use a negative number to represent the hourly drop in temperature.

Total change in temperature:

$-1.6 \cdot$ _____ $+ (-0.8) \cdot$ _____ $=$ _____ $+ ($_____$)$

$=$ _____

The total change in temperature is _____ °F.

2 A baker usually uses 0.5 cup of sugar to bake a raisin cake. To bake a healthier raisin cake, he reduces the amount of sugar by 20% the usual amount. What amount of sugar does the baker use for baking the healthier raisin cake?

$0.5 - ($_____ $\cdot$ _____$) = 0.5 -$ _____   Multiply.

$=$ _____   Subtract.

The amount of sugar the baker uses is _____ cup.

3 Stratosphere Tower in Las Vegas, Nevada, is the tallest freestanding observation tower in the United States. Its height is 350.2 meters. The Eiffel Tower in Paris, France, is the country's tallest building. Its height is 324 meters. Find the difference in the structures' heights.

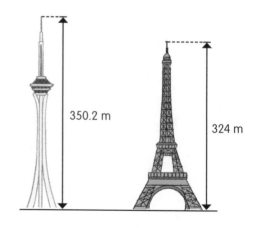

350.2 m

324 m

INDEPENDENT PRACTICE

Evaluate each sum or difference.

1 $-6.25 + 3.9$

2 $-2.074 + 1.8$

3 $-11.52 - 6.3$

4 $-29.4 - (-7.21)$

5 $-8.106 - 0.98$

Evaluate each product.

6 $0.3 \cdot (-4.8)$

7 $-1.6 \cdot 2.9$

8 $-3.25 \cdot (-1.7)$

9 $2.03 \cdot (-5.4)$

10 $-0.08 \cdot 3.2$

Evaluate each quotient.

11 $-29.52 \div 3.6$

12 $107.64 \div (-2.3)$

13 $-40.56 \div (-5.2)$

14 $9.758 \div 0.41$

Evaluate each expression.

15 $-0.59 - 1.2 - 3.4$

16 $-2.38 + 15.6 - 140.05$

17 $38.92 - 6.7 - (-12.04)$

18 $712.14 - 356.8 - (-9.03)$ **19** $11.3 - 5.1 + 3.1 \cdot 0.2 - 1.1$ **20** $(29.3 + 4) \div 3 + 0.5 \cdot 2$

Solve.

21 In Arizona, a minimum temperature of $-40.0°C$ was recorded at Hawley Lake in 1971. A maximum recorded temperature of $53.3°C$ was recorded at Lake Havasu City in 1994. Find the difference between these maximum and minimum temperatures.

22 A shop owner buys 5 handbags to sell in his shop. The owner pays $39.75 for each handbag. Later, the owner has to sell the handbags at a loss. If he charges $27.79 for each handbag, what is his total loss for the 5 handbags?

23 A state sales tax is 4.25%. Amy spends $208 at a department store, but only half of the merchandise she purchases is taxed. What is her total bill?

24 Kylie bought some T-shirts and a pair of shorts for $66.30. The pair of shorts costs $15.90, and each T-shirt costs $5.60. How many T-shirts did Kylie buy?

25 Ms. Parker wants to buy 10 books. Six of them cost $12.50 each, and the rest cost $26.35 each. If she only has $150, how much more does Ms. Parker need to buy all 10 books?

26 The recommended calcium intake for men and women is about 1.2 grams per day. A glass of milk contains about 0.27 gram of calcium. If a man drinks 3 glasses of milk, how much additional calcium does he need from other food sources?

27 **Mathematical Habit 6** Use precise mathematical language
Maya evaluated an expression as follows:

$$48 \div 2 \cdot (0.9 + 0.3) = 48 \div 2 \cdot 1.2$$
$$= 48 \div 2.4$$
$$= 20$$

She made a common mistake when applying the order of operations. Explain her mistake and help her solve the problem correctly.

28 One day in February, the temperature at 9 A.M. was − 6.8°F. At 3 P.M. on the same day, the temperature was 1.72°F.
a Find the change in temperature.

b Find the average hourly rate of change in temperature.

© 2020 Marshall Cavendish Education Pte Ltd

29 A submarine was cruising at 1,328.4 feet below sea level. It then rose at a rate of 14.76 feet per minute for 15 minutes.

    a Find the submarine's depth after it rose for 15 minutes.

    b If the submarine continued to rise at this same rate, find the time it took to reach the surface from the depth you found in **a**.

30 José is climbing a mountain. Using a rope, José climbs down from the top of a steep cliff for 4 minutes at a rate of 12.2 feet per minute. He then climbs back up for 10 minutes at a rate of 3.6 feet per minute. How far from the top of the cliff is he after 14 minutes?

31 Ms. Nelson owns 120 shares in a shipping company. On Monday, the value of each share dropped by $0.38. On Tuesday, the value of each share rose by $0.16. Find the total change in the value of Ms. Nelson's 120 shares.

32 A company suffered a loss of $5.4 million in its first year. It lost another $3.1 million in the second year. It made a profit of $4.9 million in the third year.

    a Find the average profit or loss for the first three years.

    b After its fourth year of business, the company's combined profit for all four years was $0. Find the company's profit or loss during the fourth year.

Mathematical Habit 3 **Construct viable arguments**

Katherine evaluated the following expression incorrectly.
Explain the mistake to Katherine and show her the correct solution.

Katherine's solution:
$-9 + 15 ÷ (-3) + 24 ÷ (3 + 5)$
$= 6 ÷ (-3) + 24 ÷ 3 + 5$
$= (-2) + 8 + 5$
$= 11$

Explanation:

Correct solution:

How do you check your answer?

Problem Solving with Heuristics

1 **Mathematical Habit 7** Make use of structure

The **4** key on your calculator is not working. Show how you can use the calculator to find 321 · 64.

2 **Mathematical Habit 2** Use mathematical reasoning

Isabella finds a way to use mental math to find the average of these numbers:

15, 19, 18, 12, 20

She guesses that the mean is about 17, and uses mental math to find out how far above or below this value each data item is:

− 2, 2, 1, − 5, 3

She uses mental math to add these amounts:

− 2 + 2 + 1 + (− 5) + 3 = − 1

Isabella then divides − 1 by 5 to get an average of − 0.2. She says this means that the average of the numbers is 0.2 less than 17, the number she estimated. Check that Isabella's method gives the correct average. Then, use the same method to find the average of these four numbers:

32, 35, 38, 36

CHAPTER WRAP-UP

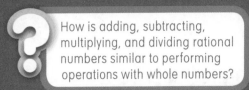

How is adding, subtracting, multiplying, and dividing rational numbers similar to performing operations with whole numbers?

Rational Numbers

Fractions

Integers

include

Terminating or repeating decimals

are represented by

$\frac{m}{n}$ where m and n are integers with $n \neq 0$

can be expressed as

Absolute values

measure the distance of numbers from 0 on

can be mapped to

Real number line

operations are

Products of two numbers

Quotients of two numbers

Addition

Subtraction

with the same signs are

with different signs are

can be represented on

can be simplified using

Positive

Negative

Number line

Absolute values

move to the left when

move to the right when

Adding a negative number

Subtracting a positive number

Adding a positive number

Subtracting a negative number

KEY CONCEPTS

- Rational numbers are found in every segment on the number line.

- Rational numbers can be expressed in the form $\frac{m}{n}$ where m and n are integers with $n \neq 0$.

- The decimal form of a rational number is either terminating or repeating.

- You can use a number line or absolute values to add or subtract integers, rational numbers, and decimal numbers. The sum of positive numbers is positive. The sum of negative numbers is negative.

- Subtracting a number is the same as adding its opposite, or additive inverse.
  Example:
  $3 - (-2) = 3 + 2$

- To evaluate the sum or difference of rational numbers with the same denominators, add or subtract their numerators.
  Examples:
  $\frac{1}{5} + \frac{2}{5} = \frac{1+2}{5} = \frac{3}{5}$ and $\frac{2}{3} - \frac{1}{3} = \frac{2-1}{3} = \frac{1}{3}$

- To evaluate the sum or difference of rational numbers with different denominators, rewrite the rational numbers using a common denominator, and then add or subtract.
  Example:
  $\frac{1}{2} - \frac{2}{3} = \frac{3}{6} - \frac{4}{6} = \frac{3-4}{6} = -\frac{1}{6}$

- The product or quotient of two numbers with the same sign is positive. The product or quotient of two numbers with different signs is negative.
  Examples:
  $-3(-2) = 6$ and $3(-2) = -6$

Name: _____ Date: _____

Write each number in $\frac{m}{n}$ form where m and n are integers with $n \neq 0$.
Simplify your answers.

1 20.75

2 −0.48

3 $4\frac{6}{13}$

4 $-\frac{39}{56}$

5 1.34

6 60%

For each pair of numbers, find the absolute value of each number. Then, determine which number is farther from 0 on the number line.

7 −16 and −18

8 $-\frac{15}{4}$ and $\frac{18}{7}$

9 2.36 and −2.7

10 $\frac{31}{3}$ and $\frac{40}{6}$

Use long division to write each rational number as a decimal. Use the bar notation if the rational number is a repeating decimal.

11 $\frac{7}{56}$

12 $9\frac{13}{20}$

13 $\frac{100}{11}$

14 $-\dfrac{5}{12}$

15 $-2\dfrac{9}{55}$

16 47%

Evaluate each sum or difference.

17 $-6 + 14$

18 $-25 + (-9)$

19 $52 + (-52)$

20 $46 + (-17) + 38$

21 $35 - 140$

22 $-61 - 28$

23 $-8 - (-50)$

24 $\dfrac{1}{4} - \dfrac{7}{8}$

25 $-6\dfrac{1}{7} + 3\dfrac{5}{14}$

Evaluate each product or quotient.

26 $-5 \cdot 11$

27 $-30 \cdot (-4)$

28 $144 \div (-6)$

29 $-48 \div (-3)$

30 $-126 \div 9$

31 $\dfrac{-5}{8} \cdot \dfrac{8}{15}$

32 $-\dfrac{3}{4} \cdot \left(-1\dfrac{2}{3}\right)$

33 $5\dfrac{1}{4} \div \left(-\dfrac{7}{12}\right)$

34 $\dfrac{\left(-\dfrac{2}{3}\right)}{\left(-\dfrac{8}{15}\right)}$

Evaluate each expression.

35 $12.3 - 8.1 + 2\dfrac{1}{10} \cdot 0.4 - 1.6$

36 $(25.7 + 4) \div 3 + 0.8 \cdot 2$

37 $10 - 32.86 \div 5.3 + 7\left(\dfrac{81}{100}\right)$

38 $3.25(0.9 - 0.74) + 6.3$

39 $\dfrac{\dfrac{1}{3} - \dfrac{1}{4}}{\dfrac{1}{8} + \dfrac{1}{2}}$

40 $8.5 - \dfrac{\left(-\dfrac{1}{6}\right)}{\left(-\dfrac{5}{18}\right)}$

Solve.

41 Gavin dug a hole that was $16\frac{1}{2}$ inches deep. He left a pile of dirt next to the hole that was $8\frac{3}{4}$ inches high. Show how you could use subtraction to find the distance from the top of the pile of dirt to the bottom of the hole.

42 A hiker descended 320 feet in 40 minutes. Find the hiker's average change in elevation per minute.

43 A hot air balloon descends 305 feet per minute for 4 minutes and then ascends at a rate of 215 feet per minute for another 2 minutes. Find the total change in the balloon's altitude.

44 Suppose you deposit $12.50 into your savings account each week for 4 weeks and then withdraw $4.80 each week for the next two weeks. Find the total change in the amount of money in your account.

45 A game show awards 30 points for each correct answer and deducts 50 points for each incorrect answer. A contestant answers 2 questions incorrectly and 3 questions correctly. What is his final score?

46 The price of a stock falls $1.50 each day for 7 days.
   a Find the total change in the price of the stock.

   b If the value of the stock was $36 before the price of the stock started falling for 7 days, find the price of the stock after those 7 days.

47 Matthew uses 24 boards that are each $5\frac{3}{4}$ feet long to build a tree house. The wood costs $1.65 per foot. Find the total cost of the wood.

Answer each question.

48 Which expressions are equivalent to $-3\frac{2}{5} - \left(-\frac{3}{4}\right)$? Choose all that apply.

(A) $-3\frac{2}{5} + \left(\frac{3}{4}\right)$

(B) $3\frac{2}{5} + \left(\frac{3}{4}\right)$

(C) $-3\frac{2}{5} + \left(+\frac{3}{4}\right)$

(D) $3\frac{2}{5} + \left(-\frac{3}{4}\right)$

(E) $-3\frac{2}{5} - \left(\frac{3}{4}\right)$

49 Which expressions have products that are negative? Choose all that apply.

(A) $\left(\frac{3}{4}\right)(-2)\left(-\frac{1}{5}\right)$

(B) $(-5)(-0.3)\left(-\frac{1}{2}\right)$

(C) $\left(2\frac{3}{5}\right)(2)\left(\frac{4}{5}\right)$

(D) $(6)(-2)(-5)(3)$

(E) $(-0.4)(-2.5)(-1.2)(0.6)$

(F) $\left(-1\frac{2}{3}\right)(-10)\left(\frac{1}{5}\right)(-0.2)$

50 At midnight, the temperature was $-3.8°F$. It rose $5.7°F$ by noon, and dropped $4.8°F$ by the following midnight. Find the final temperature. Write your answer and your work or explanation in the space below.

51 At the start of the year, the value of an investment was $14,589. At the end of six months, the value of the investment has decreased to $11,445.54. What was the mean decrease per month, in dollars? Write your answer and your work or explanation in the space below.

© 2020 Marshall Cavendish Education Pte Ltd

Name: _____ Date: _____

Drive Through the Death Valley

1 While taking a road trip along CA 190, Sean observed on the mileage sign that the Death Valley Junction was 83 miles away, after Panamint Valley Road. He continued to travel on CA 190, and observed that the Death Valley Junction was 17 miles away while he was near the eastern boundary of Death Valley National Park. How much distance did Sean cover between the two mileage signs? Show your work.

2 The lowest point along Death Valley is Badwater Basin, which is 282 feet below sea level, and the highest point is the Telescope Peak, which is 11,049 feet above sea level. What is the difference in altitude between Badwater Basin and Telescope Peak? Show your work. Use a number line to help you.

3. On the way back home, Sean decided to stop at a gas station. Each gallon of gas cost $3.19. He purchased 12 gallons of gas and paid with a $50 bill. How much change did Sean receive?

Rubric

Point(s)	Level	My Performance
7–8	4	• Most of my answers are correct. • I showed complete understanding of the concepts. • I used effective and efficient strategies to solve the problems. • I explained my answers and mathematical thinking clearly and completely.
5–6	3	• Some of my answers are correct. • I showed adequate understanding of the concepts. • I used effective strategies to solve the problems. • I explained my answers and mathematical thinking clearly.
3–4	2	• A few of my answers are correct. • I showed some understanding of the concepts. • I used some effective strategies to solve the problems. • I explained some of my answers and mathematical thinking clearly.
0–2	1	• A few of my answers are correct. • I showed little understanding of the concepts. • I used limited effective strategies to solve the problems. • I did not explain my answers and mathematical thinking clearly.

Teacher's Comments

STEAM

Extreme Temperatures

Weather describes day-by-day outdoor conditions. Climate, however, describes decades of weather patterns. Over recent decades, the planet has experienced increasingly higher average temperatures.

No part of the globe can escape the effects of increased average temperatures, or global warming. Around the world, global warming leads to more extreme weather.

Task

Work in pairs or small groups to create an extreme weather infographic for your state.

1. The National Oceanic and Atmospheric Administration (NOAA), provides online access to U.S. climate and weather information through the National Centers for Environmental Information (NCEI). Use the site to search for data.

2. Collect and display data from the year you were born to the current year.

3. Use number lines and equations to show yearly ranges in temperature and precipitation.

4. Gather and illustrate economic data associated with extreme weather in your state, such as agricultural losses, transportation challenges, and property damages.

5. Use art materials or digital tools to create an infographic or a visual display of your research. Share your work.

Chapter 2

Algebraic Expressions

How much does it cost?

When is the last time you went on a school field trip? Where did you go? Perhaps you visited a local museum, an aquarium, or a national monument such as the Statue of Liberty National Monument. Or perhaps you visited one of the locations on the National Register of Historic Places. Those include places as small as a one-room schoolhouse in Iowa and as large as the Grand Canyon in Arizona.

Most field trips come with expenses. After all, you probably traveled by bus, paid for an entrance ticket, and took time for lunch. Before leaving, your teacher planned ahead, using algebraic expressions to calculate the costs for a given number of students.

In this chapter, you will learn how to write algebraic expressions and to use algebraic reasoning to solve real-world problems, such as how much does it cost to go on a field trip.

How do you simplify, expand, or factor algebraic expressions?

Name: _____   Date: _____

Recognizing parts of an algebraic expression

A variable can be used to represent an unknown value or quantity. An algebraic expression is a mathematical phrase that includes variables, numbers, and operation symbols.

Operation symbol

Constant term ↘   ↓   ↙ Coefficient

$7 + 2x$ ← Variable

Numerical term   Algebraic term

▶ Quick Check

Consider the algebraic expression $3x + 4$. Then, answer each question.

1 How many terms are there?

2 What is the coefficient of the algebraic term?

3 What is the constant term?

4 What is the operation symbol?

Evaluating algebraic expressions

Evaluate an algebraic expression by replacing all its variables with their assigned values.

Given that $a = 5$ in the expression $2a - 3$, find the value of the expression.

$2a - 3 = (2 \cdot 5) - 3$
$= 10 - 3$
$= 7$

▶ Quick Check

5 Fill in the table.

x	$x + 9$	$7x$	$5x - 2$
0	$0 + 9 = 9$		
2			
-1			
7			

Simplifying algebraic expressions

Simplify expressions by adding or subtracting the coefficients of like terms (terms that have the same variables with the same corresponding exponents). Algebraic terms cannot be added to or subtracted from constant terms.

Can be Simplified	Cannot be Simplified
• $4a + 3 + 6 = 4a + 9$ • $6x - 2x + 5 = 4x + 5$	• $4x + 3y + 7$ has no like terms. • $2a - b + 3$ has no like terms.

▶ **Quick Check**

State whether each expression can be simplified. Explain your reasoning.

⑥ $2k - 3 + k$

⑦ $7x + 3 - 3y$

⑧ $6u + 5w - 1$

⑨ $4g - 3g - g$

Simplify each expression.

⑩ $4t + 1 + 6$

⑪ $5p - 5p$

⑫ $4y + 5y + 3$

⑬ $4m - 3m - 3$

Expanding algebraic expressions

Expand algebraic expressions by applying the distributive property to remove the parentheses.

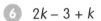
$3(p + 2) = 3(p) + 3(2)$
$\qquad\quad = 3p + 6$

$6(w - 4) = 6(w) - 6(4)$
$\qquad\quad = 6w - 24$

▶ **Quick Check**

Expand each expression.

⑭ $4(h + 2)$

⑮ $5(4 + 5c)$

⑯ $3(4x - 11)$

⑰ $7(3 - 5p)$

Factoring algebraic expressions

Factoring is the inverse of expansion. Factor an algebraic expression by writing it as a product of its factors. Use the distributive property to factor expressions whose terms have a common factor.

$$2x + 10 = 2(x) + 2(5) \quad \text{The common factor of } 2x \text{ and } 10 \text{ is } 2.$$
$$= 2(x + 5)$$

▶ **Quick Check**

Factor each expression.

⑱ $6m + 3$

⑲ $4v + 14$

⑳ $10p - 2$

㉑ $6 - 18c$

Recognizing equivalent expressions

Equivalent expressions are expressions that are equal for any values of the variables. Use an equal sign to relate equivalent expressions.

$4(x + 3)$ and $4x + 12$ are equivalent expressions because they are equal for all values of x. So, you can write $4x + 12 = 4(x + 3)$.

▶ **Quick Check**

Choose an equivalent expression.

㉒ $6y - 3$ is equivalent to

   a $3(3y - 1)$ b $3(2y - 1)$ c $3(2y - 3)$ d $6(3y - 1)$

Writing algebraic expressions to represent unknown quantities

Mason is 2 years older than his brother Evan.

- When Evan is 12 years old, Mason will be $(12 + 2) = 14$ years old.
- When Evan is x years old, Mason will be $(x + 2)$ years old.

▶ **Quick Check**

x is an unknown number. Write an expression for each of the following.

㉓ 7 more than the number

㉔ Product of 8 and the number

㉕ 5 less than twice the number

㉖ 3 more than half the number

Adding Algebraic Terms

Learning Objective:
- Simplify algebraic expressions with integral, decimal, and fractional coefficients by adding like terms.

THINK

The perimeter of a triangle is $2x$ centimeters long. What are the possible lengths of each of its three sides?

ENGAGE

Use ▮ to represent $+x$ and ▮ to represent $-x$. How do you find $3x + 3x$? How about $3x + (-3x)$?

How is this similar to what you know about $3 + (-3)$? Explain.

Now, show three different expressions to represent $2x$ using algebra tiles. Include the use of negative terms. Draw a sketch of your methods to record your thinking.

LEARN Simplify algebraic expressions with integral coefficients by adding like terms

1 You have learned how to simplify an algebraic expression like $2x + 4x$, where x is a variable, by adding the like terms.

▮ represents $+x$.

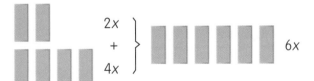

So, $2x + 4x = 6x$.

Math Note

In the algebraic term, $2x$, the number that is multiplied by the variable x is called the coefficient.

2 You can also add algebraic expressions involving negative terms.

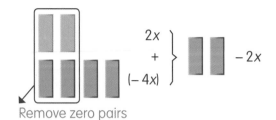 represents $+x$ and 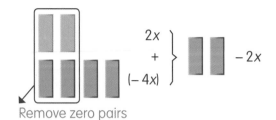 represents $-x$.

a Simplify $2x + (-4x)$.

Remove zero pairs

So, $2x + (-4x) = -2x$.

Math Note
x and $-x$ form a zero pair.

b Simplify $-2x + 4x$.

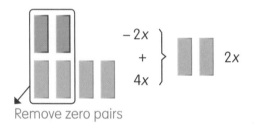

Remove zero pairs

So, $-2x + 4x = 2x$.

Caution
$-2x + 4x \neq -6x$

c Simplify $-2x + (-4x)$.

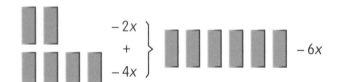

So, $-2x + (-4x) = -6x$.

Simplify each expression.

1 $4x + (-2x)$

2 $7x + (-9x)$

3 $-4y + 6y$

4 $-10y + 3y$

5 $-5m + (-2m)$

6 $-3m + (-3m)$

ENGAGE

Show how you use a bar model to represent $0.7p + 0.4p$. Will the sum be greater than p? How do you know? Explain your reasoning.

LEARN Simplify algebraic expressions with decimal or fractional coefficients by adding like terms

1 Simplify the expression $0.9p + 0.7p$.

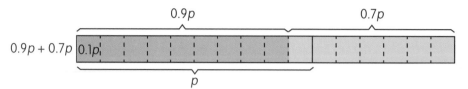

Represent the term $0.9p$ with nine $0.1p$ sections and the term $0.7p$ with seven $0.1p$ sections.

From the bar model,
$0.9p + 0.7p = 1.6p$.

The sum is the total number of colored sections in the model.

2 Simplify $m + \frac{2}{3}m$.

▶ **Method 1**
Draw a bar model.

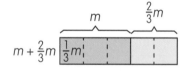

Represent the term m using a bar divided into three $\frac{1}{3}m$ sections.

From the bar model, $m + \frac{2}{3}m = \frac{5}{3}m$.

▶ **Method 2**
Use a common denominator for both coefficients.

$m + \frac{2}{3}m = \frac{3}{3}m + \frac{2}{3}m$ Rewrite m as a fraction with denominator 3.

$\qquad = \frac{5}{3}m$ Simplify.

Math Note

In algebraic expressions, fractional coefficients that are greater than 1 are left as improper fractions.

③ Simplify $1.2x + (-0.5x)$.

$1.2x + (-0.5x) = 0.7x$

$1.2 + (-0.5) = 0.7$

④ Simplify $\frac{1}{4}y + \left(-\frac{1}{6}y\right)$.

To add $\frac{1}{4}y$ and $-\frac{1}{6}y$, rewrite the coefficients so that they have the same denominator.

The least common denominator (LCD) of $\frac{1}{4}$ and $\frac{1}{6}$ is 12.

Find the equivalent fractions of $\frac{1}{4}y$ and $-\frac{1}{6}y$ with denominator 12.

$\frac{1}{4}y + \left(-\frac{1}{6}y\right) = \frac{3}{12}y + \left(-\frac{2}{12}\right)y$

$\qquad\qquad\qquad = \frac{1}{12}y$

$\frac{1}{4} + \left(-\frac{1}{6}\right) = \frac{3}{12} + \left(-\frac{2}{12}\right)$

$\qquad\qquad = \frac{3 + (-2)}{12}$

$\qquad\qquad = \frac{1}{12}$

Math Note

The procedure for simplifying algebraic expressions with decimal or fractional coefficients is similar to that of simplifying decimals or fractions.

TRY **Practice simplifying algebraic expressions with decimal and fractional coefficients by adding like terms**

Simplify each expression.

① $0.8p + 0.5p$

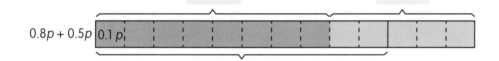

$0.8p + 0.5p$ | 0.1 p|

$0.8p + 0.5p = $ _____

2 $\frac{1}{2}p + \frac{2}{5}p$

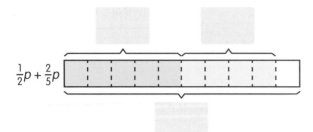

The LCD of $\frac{1}{2}$ and $\frac{2}{5}$ is _____.

So, p is divided into _____ p sections.

$\frac{1}{2}p + \frac{2}{5}p =$ _____

3 $-0.2y + 0.7y$

4 $1.3g + (-0.9g)$

5 $-m + \frac{5}{6}m$

6 $\frac{1}{4}x + \left(-\frac{2}{3}x\right)$

**Math Talk**

In **2** and **6**, you can multiply the two denominators to get the LCD. Does this always work? Explain.

INDEPENDENT PRACTICE

Simplify each expression.

1 $15p + (-3p)$

2 $-8r + 2r$

3 $16q + (-20q)$

4 $-7x + (-9x)$

Simplify each expression with decimal coefficients.

5 $0.2x + 0.8x$

6 $x + 0.6x$

7 $0.7b + 0.9b$

8 $0.5k + 1.6k$

9 $2.6p + (-0.3p)$

10 $-0.9r + 1.3r$

Simplify each expression with fractional coefficients.

11 $\frac{3}{7}p + \frac{2}{7}p$

12 $\frac{5}{8}m + \frac{7}{8}m$

13 $\frac{2}{3}b + \left(-\frac{1}{3}b\right)$

14 $-\frac{1}{9}h + \frac{5}{9}h$

Simplify each expression with fractional coefficients by rewriting the fractions.

15 $\frac{1}{6}a + \frac{1}{3}a$

16 $\frac{2}{5}p + \frac{7}{10}p$

17 $\frac{1}{4}b + \frac{1}{3}b$

18 $\frac{3}{5}x + \frac{3}{4}x$

19 $\frac{1}{2}k + \left(-\frac{1}{6}k\right)$

20 $-\frac{2}{3}m + \frac{3}{4}m$

Solve.

21 The figures show Rectangle A and Rectangle B. Write and simplify an algebraic expression for each of the following.

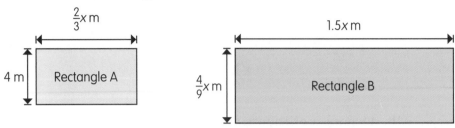

a The perimeter of Rectangle A.

b The perimeter of Rectangle B.

c The sum of the perimeters of the two rectangles.

22 The length and width of two rectangular gardens are shown. Find the sum of the areas of the two gardens in simplest form.

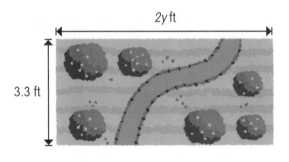

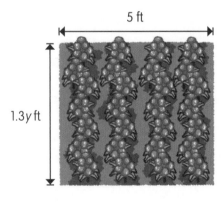

23 | Mathematical Habit 3 | Construct viable arguments

Jacob and Evan simplified the same algebraic expression. Their work is shown.

Jacob's work
$\frac{1}{5}x + 0.3x = \frac{1}{2}x$

Evan's work
$\frac{1}{5}x + 0.3x = 0.5x$

Describe a method each boy might have used to get his answer. Which method do you prefer? Why?

24 | Mathematical Habit 2 | Use mathematical reasoning

Which of the following expressions has a greater value if y is a positive number? Explain your reasoning.

$$1.4y + \frac{2}{5}y \quad \text{or} \quad \frac{1}{3}y + \frac{3}{4}y$$

25 Each day, a restaurant serves x meals that consist of $\frac{1}{4}$ of a chicken each. It also makes soup using $\frac{1}{2}$ of a chicken each day. The chef expresses the number of chickens she uses each day as $\frac{1}{4}x + \frac{1}{2}$. How many chickens does she use in three days?

26 **Mathematical Habit 2** Use mathematical reasoning

Maria simplified the algebraic expression $\frac{2}{3}x + \frac{1}{4}x$ as shown below.

$$\frac{2}{3}x + \frac{1}{4}x = \frac{3}{7}x$$

Describe and correct the error Maria made.

 # Subtracting Algebraic Terms

Learning Objective:
• Simplify algebraic expressions with integral, decimal, and fractional coefficients by subtracting like terms.

THINK

The perimeter of a triangle is $5\frac{1}{2}x$ centimeters. The length of one of its sides is $0.7x$ centimeters. Find the possible lengths of each of the other two sides.

ENGAGE

Use to represent $+x$ and ▮ to represent $-x$. How do you find $2x - x$? How about $2x - (-x)$?

How is this similar to what you know about $2 - (-1)$? Explain.

Create as many subtraction equations as you can with the numbers 2, 1, -2, and -1. Repeat with $2x$, x, $-2x$, and $-x$. What do you notice? Share your observations.

LEARN Simplify algebraic expressions with integral coefficients by subtracting like terms

1. You can simplify an algebraic expression like $5x - 3x$, where x is a variable, by subtracting the like terms.

▮ represents $+x$.

$5x - 3x$ ▮▮▮▧▧▧ $\longrightarrow$ $2x$ ▮▮

So, $5x - 3x = 2x$.

2 You can also subtract algebraic expressions involving negative terms.

▮ represents $+x$ and ▯ represents $-x$.

a Simplify $5x - (-3x)$.

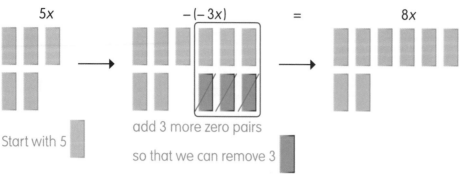

So, $5x - (-3x) = 8x$.

b Simplify $-5x - 3x$.

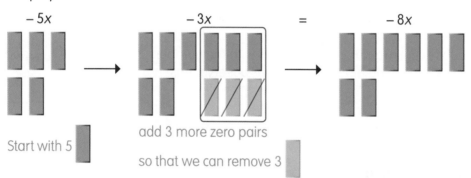

So, $-5x - 3x = -8x$.

c Simplify $-5x - (-3x)$.

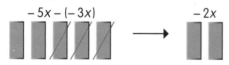

So, $-5x - (-3x) = -2x$.

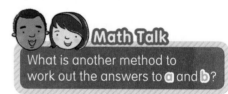

Math Talk

What is another method to work out the answers to **a** and **b**?

TRY **Practice simplifying algebraic expressions with integral coefficients by subtracting like terms**

Simplify each expression.

1 $3y - (-4y)$

2 $-6t - 6t$

3 $-5p - (-2p)$

4 $-3a - (-6a)$

ENGAGE

Draw a part-whole bar model to show how you can subtract $0.7y$ from $1.2y$. Share your method.

LEARN Simplify algebraic expressions with decimal or fractional coefficients by subtracting like terms

1 Simplify the expression $1.8y - 0.9y$.

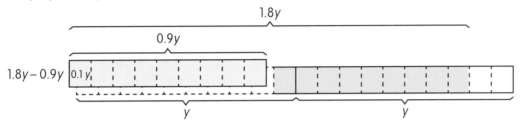

From the bar model, $1.8y - 0.9y = 0.9y$.

The difference is represented by the shaded parts that remain.

2 Simplify the expression $\frac{2}{3}b - \frac{1}{4}b$.

▶ **Method 1**

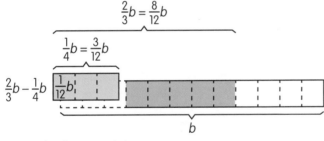

The LCD of $\frac{2}{3}$ and $\frac{1}{4}$ is 12. So, divide b into twelve $\frac{1}{12}b$ sections.

From the bar model,

$\frac{2}{3}b - \frac{1}{4}b = \frac{5}{12}b.$

▶ **Method 2**

$\frac{2}{3}b - \frac{1}{4}b = \frac{8}{12}b - \frac{3}{12}b$ The LCD of $\frac{2}{3}$ and $\frac{1}{4}$ is 12. Rewrite the coefficients as fractions with denominator 12.

$= \frac{5}{12}b$ Subtract.

③ Simplify the expression $4.6m - (-1.2m)$.

$$4.6m - (-1.2m) = 4.6m + 1.2m$$
$$= 5.8m$$

$4.6 - (-1.2) = 4.6 + 1.2$
$= 5.8$

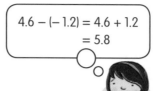

Math Note

Subtracting a negative number, $-b$, is the same as adding its opposite, b.

④ Simplify the expression $\frac{3}{4}n - \left(-\frac{5}{8}n\right)$.

$$\frac{3}{4}n - \left(-\frac{5}{8}n\right) = \frac{3}{4}n + \frac{5}{8}n$$
$$= \frac{6}{8}n + \frac{5}{8}n$$
$$= \frac{11}{8}n$$

$\frac{3}{4} - \left(-\frac{5}{8}\right) = \frac{3}{4} + \frac{5}{8}$
$= \frac{6}{8} + \frac{5}{8}$
$= \frac{11}{8}$

TRY Practice simplifying algebraic expressions with decimal or fractional coefficients by subtracting like terms

Simplify each expression.

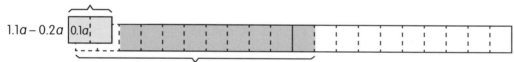

$1.1a - 0.2a = $ _____

② $-\frac{5}{6}a - \frac{1}{3}a$

③ $-0.7g - (-0.4)g$

④ $\frac{3}{4}p - \left(-\frac{1}{6}p\right)$

INDEPENDENT PRACTICE

Simplify each expression.

1 $12y - 8y$

2 $7p - (-6p)$

3 $-11x - 3x$

4 $-9k - (-12k)$

Simplify each expression with decimal coefficients.

5 $1.7p - 0.4p$

6 $2.3a - (-0.4a)$

7 $-0.2b - 1.4b$

8 $-4.2x - (-2.5x)$

Simplify each expression with fractional coefficients.

9 $\frac{7}{8}x - \frac{5}{8}x$

10 $\frac{9}{5}y - \frac{1}{5}y$

11 $-\frac{1}{3}m - \frac{2}{3}m$

12 $-\frac{3}{11}n - \left(-\frac{6}{11}n\right)$

Simplify each expression with fractional coefficients by rewriting the fractions.

13 $\frac{1}{4}a - \frac{1}{8}a$

14 $\frac{5}{6}m - \frac{2}{3}m$

15 $\frac{1}{2}h - \left(-\frac{3}{4}h\right)$

16 $\frac{4}{5}p - \frac{1}{3}p$

17 $\frac{3}{4}r - \frac{2}{3}r$

18 $-\frac{2}{3}y - \frac{2}{5}y$

19 $-\frac{3}{5}x - \left(-\frac{1}{4}x\right)$

20 $-\frac{1}{3}f - \left(-\frac{5}{7}f\right)$

Solve.

21 | Mathematical Habit 2 | Use mathematical reasoning

Luke simplified the algebraic expression $\frac{3}{2}x - \frac{1}{3}x$ as shown below.

$$\frac{3}{2}x - \frac{1}{3}x = \frac{18}{12}x - \frac{4}{12}x$$
$$= \frac{14}{12}x$$

Is Luke's simplification correct? Why or why not?

22 Rectangle A, shown below, is larger than Rectangle B. Write and simplify an algebraic expression that represents the difference in the areas of the two rectangles.

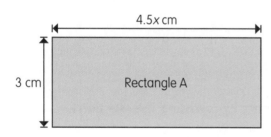

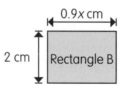

Simplifying Algebraic Expressions

Learning Objectives:
- Simplify algebraic expressions with more than two terms.
- Simplify algebraic expressions by using the commutative property of addition.
- Simplify algebraic expressions with two variables.

THINK

Explain how you would simplify the expression $\frac{2}{3}x - \frac{1}{3}y + (-0.2x) + 0.6y$.

ENGAGE

Use ▌ to represent $+x$, ▌ to represent $-x$, and ▨ to represent $+1$. Simplify the expression $2x + 3x + 4x$. What steps did you take? How does your method change when simplifying $2x - 3x + 4$? Explain your reasoning.

LEARN Simplify algebraic expressions with more than two terms and involving negative coefficients

1. Algebraic expressions may contain more than two terms. Not all the terms may be like terms. To simplify such expressions, first identify the like terms. Then, add or subtract the like terms.

$3x - 5x + 2$ can be simplified as shown.

$3x - 5x + 2 = 3x + (-5x) + 2$

Instead of subtracting $5x$ from $3x$, you can add its opposite, which is $-5x$.

▌ represents $+x$, ▌ represents $-x$, and ▨ represents $+1$.

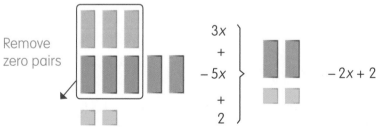

Remove zero pairs

$$\left.\begin{array}{c} 3x \\ + \\ -5x \\ + \\ 2 \end{array}\right\}$$

$-2x + 2$

So, $3x - 5x + 2 = -2x + 2$.

$-2x$ and 2 are not like terms, so $-2x + 2$ cannot be simplified further.

2 Simplify $-3x + 2x - 3 + 1$.

■ represents $+x$, ▌ represents $-x$, ▢ represents $+1$, and ■ represents -1.

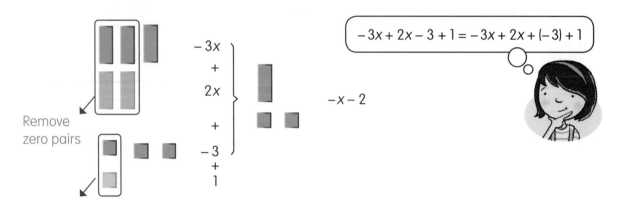

$$-3x + 2x - 3 + 1 = -3x + 2x + (-3) + 1$$

$-x - 2$

Remove zero pairs

$\left.\begin{array}{c} -3x \\ + \\ 2x \\ + \\ -3 \\ + \\ 1 \end{array}\right\}$

So, $-3x + 2x - 3 + 1 = -x - 2$.

TRY Practice simplifying algebraic expressions with more than two terms and involving negative coefficients

Simplify each expression.

1 $5 + (-2) + 4y$

2 $6x - 2x + 6 - 2$

3 $5 - 2 - 6x + x$

4 $-2k - 5k - 3 - 4$

ENGAGE

a Draw a bar model to show how you simplify $0.3 + 0.2 + 2$.

b Now, show how you simplify $0.3x + 0.2x + 2$. What should the value of x be for the expressions in **a** and **b** to be equivalent? Explain.

LEARN **Simplify algebraic expressions with more than two terms and involving decimal and fractional coefficients**

1. A bar model can help simplify expressions such as $0.2x + 0.5x + 2$.

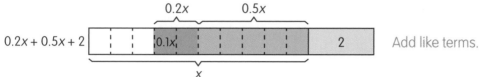

$0.2x + 0.5x + 2$

Add like terms.

The like terms are $0.2x$ and $0.5x$.

From the bar model,

$0.2x + 0.5x + 2 = 0.7x + 2$.

$0.7x$ and 2 are not like terms, so $0.7x + 2$ cannot be simplified further.

2. You can simplify algebraic expressions such as $\frac{1}{2}x - \frac{1}{4}x + 5 + 2$ by writing like terms with a common denominator.

$\frac{1}{2}x - \frac{1}{4}x + 5 + 2$

$\frac{1}{4}x$

$\frac{1}{2}x = \frac{2}{4}x$

x

Rewrite $\frac{1}{2}x$ as $\frac{2}{4}x$.

Then, subtract like terms.

From the bar model,

$\frac{1}{2}x - \frac{1}{4}x + 5 + 2 = \frac{1}{4}x + 7$.

3. Simplify the expression $\frac{2}{5}x + \frac{3}{10}x - 1 - 2$.

$\frac{2}{5}x + \frac{3}{10}x - 1 - 2 = \frac{4}{10}x + \frac{3}{10}x - 1 - 2$

Rewrite the coefficients as fractions with denominator 10. Two like terms are $\frac{4}{10}x$ and $\frac{3}{10}x$. Two other like terms are -1 and -2.

$= \frac{7}{10}x - 3$

Simplify.

Remember that
$-1 - 2 = -1 + (-2)$
$= -3$

④ Simplify the expression $5m - 7 - (-3m) + 2$.

$$\begin{aligned} 5m - 7 - (-3m) + 2 &= 5m - 7 + 3m + 2 \\ &= 5m + 3m - 7 + 2 \\ &= 8m - 5 \end{aligned}$$

Rewrite subtraction as adding the opposite.
Use commutative property to group like terms.
Simplify.

⑤ Simplify the expression $\frac{3}{8}b + \frac{2}{3} + \left(-\frac{1}{8}b\right) - \frac{1}{3}$.

$$\begin{aligned} \frac{3}{8}b + \frac{2}{3} + \left(-\frac{1}{8}b\right) - \frac{1}{3} &= \frac{3}{8}b + \frac{2}{3} - \frac{1}{8}b - \frac{1}{3} \\ &= \frac{3}{8}b - \frac{1}{8}b + \frac{2}{3} - \frac{1}{3} \\ &= \frac{2}{8}b + \frac{1}{3} \\ &= \frac{1}{4}b + \frac{1}{3} \end{aligned}$$

Rewrite addition of a negative coefficient as subtraction.

Group like terms.

Simplify.

Write fractions in simplest form.

TRY **Practice simplifying algebraic expressions with more than two terms and involving decimal and fractional coefficients**

Simplify each expression.

① $1.8m - 0.9m + 2$

$1.8m - 0.9m + 2$

$= \underline{\qquad} + \underline{\qquad}$

② $\frac{1}{3}d + \frac{7}{12}d - 5 - 1$

$\frac{1}{3}d + \frac{7}{12}d - 5 - 1 = \underline{\qquad} d + \frac{7}{12}d - 5 - 1$

$= \underline{\qquad} d - \underline{\qquad}$

③ $3.4a + 5 + (-0.2a) - 3$

④ $\frac{1}{2}k - 8 - \left(-\frac{2}{5}k\right) + 2$

ENGAGE

Use ▌ to represent $+x$ and ▌ to represent $+y$. Represent the stories given using algebra tiles.

Then, write an expression for the total number of pieces of fruit in each story.

a Logan has two bags of x apples. He buys one more bag of x apples.

b Molly has one bag of x apples. She buys one bag of y pears, and then another two bags of x apples.

How are the expressions different? Explain.

LEARN Simplify algebraic expressions with two variables

1 You have learned how to simplify expressions with one variable. Some expressions like $x + y + 2x$ contain two variables, each representing a different unknown quantity.

To simplify $x + y + 2x$, you can add the like terms as shown below.

▌ represents $+x$ and ▌ represents $+y$.

$$
\begin{array}{ll}
x & x \\
+ & + \\
y & 2x \\
+ & + \\
2x & y
\end{array}
$$

$x + y + 2x = x + 2x + y$ Group like terms.
         $= 3x + y$ Simplify.

2 Simplify algebraic expressions such as $4x + 3y - x - 2y$ by first grouping the like terms. Then, add or subtract the like terms.

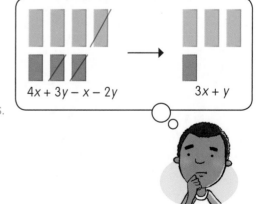

x $2y$

$4x + 3y - x - 2y$ | | | | | y | y

         $4x$ $3y$

$4x + 3y - x - 2y = (4x - x) + (3y - 2y)$ Group like terms.
              $= 3x + y$ Simplify.

$4x + 3y - x - 2y$ $3x + y$

3 Simplify the expression $5y + 3x + 2y + 2x$.

$5y + 3x + 2y + 2x = (5y + 2y) + (3x + 2x)$ Group like terms.
$\qquad\qquad\qquad = 7y + 5x$ Add like terms.

Caution
$7y + 5x \neq 12xy$

4 Simplify the expression $6c + 5d - c - 8d$.

$6c + 5d - c - 8d = (6c - c) + (5d - 8d)$ Group like terms.
$\qquad\qquad\qquad = 5c - 3d$ Simplify.

**Math Talk**

When adding or subtracting algebraic expressions,
how do you identify the like terms?

TRY Practice simplifying algebraic expressions with two variables

Simplify each expression.

1 $6a + 9b + a + b$

$6a + 9b + a + b$

$= \underbrace{\rule{1cm}{0.4pt} + \rule{1cm}{0.4pt}} + \underbrace{9b + b}$

$= \rule{1.5cm}{0.4pt} + \rule{1cm}{0.4pt}$

2 $3x + 2y - 2x - 3y$

$3x + 2y - 2x - 3y$

$= \underbrace{\rule{1cm}{0.4pt} - \rule{1cm}{0.4pt}} + \underbrace{\rule{1cm}{0.4pt} - \rule{1cm}{0.4pt}}$

$= \rule{1.5cm}{0.4pt} - \rule{1cm}{0.4pt}$

3 $2.5x + 1.8z + 1.6x - 0.9z$

4 $\frac{2}{3}a - \frac{1}{6}a + \frac{3}{5}b - \frac{3}{10}b$

INDEPENDENT PRACTICE

Simplify each expression with one variable.

1 $0.3x + 0.6x + 3$

2 $\frac{2}{7}x + \frac{3}{7}x + 4$

3 $0.8x - 0.2x - 5$

4 $\frac{7}{8}x - \frac{1}{8}x - 5$

Simplify each expression with three algebraic terms.

5 $0.3p + 0.2p + 0.4p$

6 $0.2p + 0.8p - 0.6p$

7 $\frac{1}{3}y + \frac{1}{6}y + \frac{5}{12}y$

8 $\frac{1}{2}a + \frac{2}{3}a - \frac{1}{6}a$

Simplify each expression with one variable.

9 $7x + 6 + 4x$

10 $8y + 4 - 6y$

11 $1.8x - 0.6 - 0.7x$

12 $\frac{4}{7}x + \frac{1}{5} + \frac{2}{7}x$

Simplify each expression with two variables.

13 $2x + 4x + 7y$

14 $4x - (-x) - 3y$

15 $9x - 7x + 3y$

16 $7p - (-2p) + 3q - (-q)$

17 $2.3a + 3.5b - 1.8a - 2.7b$

18 $3.4h + 2.1k - 1.2h - (-0.4k)$

19 $\frac{3}{5}a + \frac{1}{6}b + \frac{2}{5}a + \frac{1}{6}b$

20 $\frac{4}{5}x - \frac{2}{3}y - \left(-\frac{1}{10}x\right) + \frac{1}{6}y$

Find the perimeter of each triangle or rectangle.

21

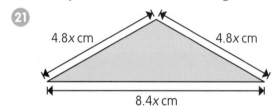

4.8x cm   4.8x cm

8.4x cm

22

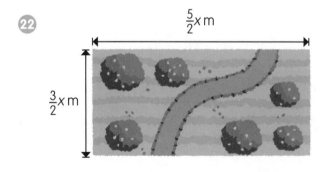

$\frac{5}{2}x$ m

$\frac{3}{2}x$ m

Expanding Algebraic Expressions

Learning Objective:
• Expand algebraic expressions with fractional, decimal, and negative factors.

THINK

Megan wants to insert two pairs of parentheses into the expression on the right side of the equation, so that it is equivalent to the expression on the left side.

$-5(x - y) + 6(2 - 0.5x) = 5y - 6x - 14 - 2 + 2x$

Identify where the pairs of parentheses should be inserted. Explain your answer.
(Hint: Take note of the change in signs after inserting the parentheses.)

ENGAGE

a   Use ▮ to represent $+x$ and ▢ to represent $+1$. Show how you expand $2(2x + 6)$.

b   Now, show how you expand $\frac{1}{2}(2x + 6)$. Share your method.

LEARN Expand algebraic expressions with fractional and decimal factors

1 You have learned how to expand algebraic expressions involving integers, such as $3(2x + 4)$ and $2(5x - 1)$. Use the distributive property to expand such expressions.

▮ represents $+x$ and ▢ represents $+1$.

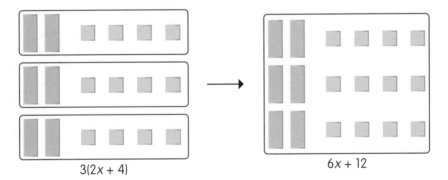

$3(2x + 4)$ $6x + 12$

$3(2x + 4) = 3(2x) + 3(4)$ $2(5x - 1) = 2(5x) - 2(1)$ Use the distributive property.
$\qquad\quad = 6x + 12$ $\qquad\quad = 10x - 2$ Multiply.

You will obtain an expression equivalent to the original expression after expanding. $3(2x + 4)$ and $6x + 12$ are equivalent expressions because the value of both expressions remains the same for all values of x. In the same way, $2(5x - 1)$ and $10x - 2$ are also equivalent expressions.

② Expand algebraic expressions like $\frac{1}{2}(2x + 4)$ using either bar models or the distributive property. This will produce an equivalent expression, just as expanding an expression with a whole number factor did.

▶ **Method 1**
Rearrange the bar model into two equal groups.

$2x + 4$ | x | x | 2 | 2 ⟶ $2x + 4$ | x | 2 | x | 2

$\frac{1}{2}(2x + 4)$

From the bar model,

$\frac{1}{2}(2x + 4) = x + 2$.

Rearrange the bar model into two equal groups to find one half of $(2x + 4)$.

▶ **Method 2**
Use the distributive property to expand $\frac{1}{2}(2x + 4)$.

$\frac{1}{2}(2x + 4) = \frac{1}{2}(2x) + \frac{1}{2}(4)$ Use the distributive property.

$\qquad = x + 2$ Multiply.

$\frac{1}{2}(2x + 4)$ and $x + 2$ are equivalent expressions.

③ Expand the expression $\frac{1}{3}(3x + 15)$.

▶ **Method 1**
Draw a bar model.

$3x + 15$ | x | 5 | x | 5 | x | 5

$\frac{1}{3}(3x + 15)$

Arrange the bar model for $3x + 15$ into three equal groups to find one third of $(3x + 15)$.

From the bar model, $\frac{1}{3}(3x + 15) = x + 5$.

▶ **Method 2**
Use the distributive property.

$\frac{1}{3}(3x + 15) = \frac{1}{3}(3x) + \frac{1}{3}(15)$ Use the distributive property.

$\qquad = x + 5$ Multiply.

4 You can also use the distributive property to expand expressions involving decimals.

$$0.7(0.2t - 3) = 0.7[0.2t + (-3)]$$ Rewrite subtraction as adding the opposite.
$$= 0.7(0.2t) + 0.7(-3)$$ Use the distributive property.
$$= 0.14t + (-2.1)$$ Multiply.
$$= 0.14t - 2.1$$ Rewrite the expression.

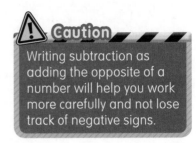

Caution

Writing subtraction as adding the opposite of a number will help you work more carefully and not lose track of negative signs.

TRY **Practice expanding algebraic expressions with fractional and decimal factors**

Expand each expression.

1 $\frac{1}{4}(8x + 12)$

> **Method 1**
> Draw a bar model.

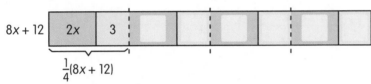

8x + 12   2x   3

$\frac{1}{4}(8x + 12)$

From the bar model, $\frac{1}{4}(8x + 12) = $ _____.

> **Method 2**
> Use the distributive property.

$$\frac{1}{4}(8x + 12) = \frac{1}{4}(\underline{\quad\quad}) + \frac{1}{4}(\underline{\quad\quad})$$

$$= (\underline{\quad\quad\quad})$$

2 $\frac{1}{3}(9x + 6)$

3 $\frac{1}{5}(25x + 15)$

Expand each expression. Write + or – in each ◯.

④ $0.3(2x + 5)$

$0.3(2x + 5) = 0.3(\underline{\hspace{1cm}}) + 0.3(\underline{\hspace{1cm}})$

$= \underline{\hspace{1cm}} + \underline{\hspace{1cm}}$

⑤ $0.5(1.4y - 2.1)$

$0.5(1.4y - 2.1) = 0.5 (\underline{\hspace{1cm}}) \bigcirc 0.5(-\underline{\hspace{1cm}})$

$= \underline{\hspace{1cm}} \bigcirc (-\underline{\hspace{1cm}})$

$= \underline{\hspace{1cm}} \bigcirc \underline{\hspace{1cm}}$

Expand each expression.

⑥ $0.4(3y + 2)$

⑦ $0.2(4x - 3.1)$

ENGAGE

How can you use an area model to expand $2(x + 1)$. Now, explain how you would expand $-2(x + 1)$ in different ways.

LEARN Expand algebraic expressions with negative factors

1. When expanding algebraic expressions with negative factors, such as $-3(x+2)$ and $-5(y-2)$, use the distributive property and apply the rules for multiplying integers.

$$-3(x+2) = -3(x) + (-3)(2) \quad \text{Use the distributive property.}$$
$$= -3x + (-6) \quad \text{Multiply.}$$
$$= -3x - 6 \quad \text{Rewrite the expression.}$$

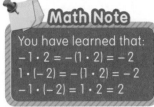

Math Note

You have learned that:
$-1 \cdot 2 = -(1 \cdot 2) = -2$
$1 \cdot (-2) = -(1 \cdot 2) = -2$
$-1 \cdot (-2) = 1 \cdot 2 = 2$

$$-5(y-2) = -5[y + (-2)] \quad \text{Rewrite subtraction as adding the opposite.}$$
$$= -5(y) + (-5)(-2) \quad \text{Use the distributive property.}$$
$$= -5y + 10 \quad \text{Multiply.}$$

2. Expand the expression $-3\left(-\dfrac{2}{3}a + \dfrac{1}{5}\right)$.

$$-3\left(-\frac{2}{3}a + \frac{1}{5}\right) = -3\left(-\frac{2}{3}a\right) + (-3)\left(\frac{1}{5}\right) \quad \text{Use the distributive property.}$$
$$= 2a - \frac{3}{5} \quad \text{Multiply.}$$

3. Expand the expression $-(-0.4k - 2.5)$.

$$-(-0.4k - 2.5) = -1[-0.4k + (-2.5)] \quad \text{Rewrite the expression.}$$
$$= -1(-0.4k) + (-1)(-2.5) \quad \text{Use the distributive property.}$$
$$= 0.4k + 2.5 \quad \text{Multiply.}$$

4. Expand the expression $-\dfrac{1}{3}(p + 2q)$.

$$-\frac{1}{3}(p + 2q) = -\frac{1}{3}(p) + \left(-\frac{1}{3}\right)(2q) \quad \text{Use the distributive property.}$$
$$= -\frac{1}{3}p - \frac{2}{3}q \quad \text{Multiply.}$$

TRY Practice expanding algebraic expressions with negative factors

Expand each expression.

1. $-4(3d - 2)$

2. $-7(5k + e)$

3. $-4(0.6x - 4)$

4. $-\frac{1}{4}\left(-3y + \frac{1}{2}\right)$

ENGAGE

Show how you use bar models to simplify each expression.

a $2p + 5p$

b $2(p + 5p)$

c $2(p + 5q)$

d $2(p + 5q) - q$

What changes each time? Are there any rules you can develop based on what you noticed? Discuss.

LEARN Expand and simplify algebraic expressions

1. When you simplify an algebraic expression, you may need to expand it first before adding or subtracting the like terms.

   To simplify an expression like $4(p + 5q) - 3q$, you need to expand $4(p + 5q)$ first.

   $$
   \begin{aligned}
   4(p + 5q) - 3q &= 4(p) + 4(5q) - 3q &&\text{Use the distributive property.}\\
   &= 4p + 20q - 3q &&\text{Multiply.}\\
   &= 4p + 17q &&\text{Simplify.}
   \end{aligned}
   $$

2. Expand and simplify the expression $-2(0.5y - 3) + y$.

   $$
   \begin{aligned}
   -2(0.5y - 3) + y &= -2[0.5y + (-3)] + y &&\text{Rewrite the expression.}\\
   &= (-2)(0.5y) + (-2)(-3) + y &&\text{Use the distributive property.}\\
   &= -y + 6 + y &&\text{Multiply.}\\
   &= -y + y + 6 &&\text{Group like terms.}\\
   &= 6 &&\text{Simplify.}
   \end{aligned}
   $$

3. Expand and simplify the expression $4(2n + 5) - (m - 1)$.

   $$
   \begin{aligned}
   4(2n + 5) - (m - 1) &= 4(2n + 5) + (-1)[m + (-1)] &&\text{Rewrite the expression.}\\
   &= 4(2n) + 4(5) + (-1)(m) + (-1)(-1) &&\text{Use the distributive property.}\\
   &= 8n + 20 + (-m) + 1 &&\text{Multiply.}\\
   &= 8n + (-m) + 20 + 1 &&\text{Group like terms.}\\
   &= 8n - m + 21 &&\text{Remove parentheses and simplify.}
   \end{aligned}
   $$

Caution

$8n - m \neq 7nm$

Expand and simplify each expression.

1. $2(2a + 3b) + 5b$

$$2(2a + 3b) + 5b = 2(2a) + 2(\underline{}) + \underline{}$$
$$= \underline{} + \underline{} + \underline{}$$
$$= \underline{} + \underline{}$$

2. $-3\left(\dfrac{1}{2}k - 4\right) - 2k$

3. $5(2h - 3) - (2k - 1)$

4. $3(2w + 3) - 2(0.5w - 1)$

5. $4p - 2(0.1p - 4)$

INDEPENDENT PRACTICE

Expand each expression.

1 $\frac{1}{4}(4x + 8)$

2 $\frac{1}{3}(6b + 9)$

3 $\frac{1}{2}(p + 2)$

4 $\frac{1}{5}(4a + 3)$

5 $\frac{1}{2}(4k - 6)$

6 $\frac{1}{3}(16a - 8)$

7 $\frac{1}{3}(5b - 1)$

8 $\frac{2}{5}(k - 10)$

9 $3(4x + 0.2)$

10 $4(0.1y + 5)$

11 $0.2(3x + 4)$

12 $0.6(3h + 5)$

13 $0.2(m - 3)$

14 $0.3(p - 3)$

15 $0.4(1.5d + 0.5)$

16 $1.2(0.3x - 1.4)$

Expand each expression with a negative factor.

17 $-2(x + 1)$

18 $-3(2x + 5)$

19 $-3(4a + 9b)$

20 $-7(2k - h)$

21 $-4\left(p + \dfrac{1}{2}\right)$

22 $-\dfrac{1}{2}\left(6x - \dfrac{1}{3}\right)$

23 $-2(5k + 1.7)$

24 $-3(0.2m + 5)$

25 $-5(q - 0.3)$

26 $-0.6(0.4y - 1)$

Expand and simplify each expression.

27 $3(2y + 1) + 4$

28 $3(2a + 5) - 8$

29 $2(x + 2) + 3x$

30 $6(b + 3) - 2b$

31 $5\left(\dfrac{1}{6}a + 1\right) + 3$

32 $4\left(\dfrac{1}{8}a - 3\right) - \dfrac{1}{2}a$

Expand and simplify each expression.

33 $0.2(x + 1) + 0.7x$

34 $0.5(y + 2) - 0.3y$

35 $-2(4m + 1) - m$

36 $10 - 3(2n - 1)$

37 $-0.8(r + 3) + 2.2r$

38 $-(1.2x + 7) + 1.5x$

Expand and simplify each expression with two variables.

39 $4x + 6(3y + x)$

40 $7a + 5(3a - b)$

41 $8g + 5(v - g)$

42 $4q + 6(p - 2q)$

43 $2(a + 2b) + (a + 3b)$

44 $3(m - 2n) + 6(n - 2m)$

45 $4(d + e) - 3(d - 2e)$

46 $3(3q - p) - (q - 6p)$

47 $-4(x + 3y) + 3(2x - 5y)$

48 $-7(y + 2t) - 3(y - t)$

Write an expression for the missing dimension of each shaded figure and a multiplication expression for its area. Then, expand and simplify the multiplication expression.

49

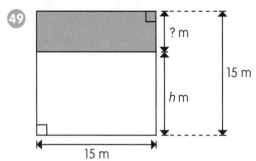

50

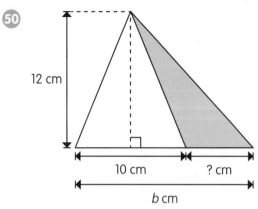

Write an expression for the area of the figure. Expand and simplify.

51

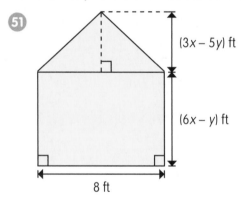

5 Factoring Algebraic Expressions

Learning Objectives:
• Factor algebraic expressions with two variables.
• Factor algebraic expressions with negative terms.

THINK

Cole wants to insert two terms to the expression on the right side of the equation, so that it is equivalent to the expression on the left side.

$-3 - 12x - 21y = -3(4x - y)$

Identify the terms and where they should be inserted. Explain how you arrived at your answer in two different ways.

ENGAGE

a   Use to represent $+x$, ▮ to represent $+y$, and ▢ to represent $+1$. How can you represent

$3x + 6$ using the algebra tiles? What are the factors of $3x + 6$?

b   Now, show $3x + 6y$. How do you factor $3x + 6y$ using algebra tiles? Draw a sketch of your method to record your thinking.

LEARN Factor algebraic expressions with two variables

1   You have learned how to factor an algebraic expression, such as $2x + 2$. You can factor the expression by using counters and tiles, or the greatest common factor (GCF).

▶ **Method 1**
Factoring $2x - 4$ results in an equivalent expression $2(x - 2)$.

▮ represents $+x$ and ▮ represents -1.

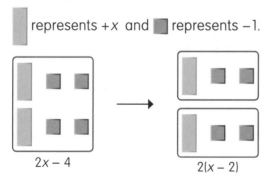

$2x - 4$

$2(x - 2)$

So, $2x - 4 = 2(x - 2)$.

You can check whether you have factored correctly by expanding $2(x - 2)$.

▶ **Method 2**
$$2x - 4 = 2x + (-4)$$
$$= 2(x) + 2(-2)$$
$$= 2(x - 2)$$

Rewrite the expression.
The GCF of $2x$ and -4 is 2.
Use the distributive property to factor 2 from each term.

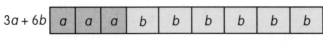

2 You can also factor expressions with two variables, like $3a + 6b$, using models or the GCF.

▶ **Method 1**

$3a + 6b$ | a | a | a | b | b | b | b | b | b |

Draw a group of three a sections and six b sections.

| a | b | b |

$3(a + 2b)$ | a | b | b |

| a | b | b |

Rearrange into three identical groups. Each group has one a section and two b sections to represent $(a + 2b)$.

From the bar model, $3a + 6b = 3(a + 6b)$.

▶ **Method 2**

$3a + 6b = 3(a) + 3(2b)$ The GCF of $3a$ and $6b$ is 3.
$\qquad\quad = 3(a + 2b)$ Factor 3 from each term.

Check

Expand the expression $3(a + 2b)$ to check the factoring.

$3(a + 2b) = 3(a) + 3(2b)$
$\qquad\qquad = 3a + 6b$

$3a + 6b$ is factored correctly.

3 Factor the expression $3x - 9y$.

▶ **Method 1**
Draw a bar model.

$3x - 9y$ | x | x | x | −y | −y | −y | −y | −y | −y | −y | −y | −y |

Draw a group of three x sections and nine $-y$ sections.

| x | −y | −y | −y |

$3(x - 3y)$ | x | −y | −y | −y |

| x | −y | −y | −y |

Rearrange into three identical groups. Each group has one x section and three $-y$ sections to represent $(x - 3y)$.

From the bar model, $3x - 9y = 3(x - 3y)$.

▶ **Method 2**

Use the distributive property.

$3x - 9y = 3x + (-9y)$ Rewrite the expression.
$\quad\quad\quad = 3(x) + 3(-3y)$ The GCF of $3x$ and $-9y$ is 3.
$\quad\quad\quad = 3(x - 3y)$ Factor 3 from each term.

The factors of 3 are 3 and 1.
3 is also a factor of -9
because $3(-3) = -9$.
So, the GCF of 3 and -9 is 3.

Check

Expand the expression $3(x - 3y)$ to check the factoring.

$3(x - 3y) = 3(x) + 3(-3y)$
$\quad\quad\quad\quad = 3x - 9y$

$3x - 9y$ is factored correctly.

TRY **Practice factoring algebraic expressions with two variables**

Factor each expression.

① $2j - 10k$

$2j - 10k = \underline{\quad\quad} + (\underline{\quad\quad})$ Rewrite the expression.

$\quad\quad\quad = \underline{\quad\quad} (\underline{\quad\quad}) + \underline{\quad\quad} (\underline{\quad\quad})$ The GCF of $2j$ and $-10k$ is 2.

$\quad\quad\quad = \underline{\quad\quad\quad\quad}$ Factor 2 from each term.

② $6a - 18b$

③ $8p - 12q$

ENGAGE

Decide if each expression given is completely factored. Explain why or why not.

a $3x + 2$

b $2x - 3y$

c $-4x + 8y$

d $-10x - 5$

If -6 is is a factor of an algebraic expression involving the terms $2x$ and $3y$, what are the possible algebraic expressions? Explain your thinking.

LEARN Factor algebraic expressions with negative terms

1 An expression such as $-2x - 3$ is not factored completely because you can factor out -1 from the expression.

$$-2x - 3 = -2x + (-3) \quad \text{Rewrite the expression.}$$
$$= (-1)(2x) + (-1)(3) \quad \text{The GCF of } -2x \text{ and } -3 \text{ is } (-1).$$
$$= -1(2x + 3) \quad \text{Factor } (-1) \text{ from each term.}$$
$$= -(2x + 3) \quad \text{Simplify.}$$

Check

Expand the expression $-(2x + 3)$ to check the factoring.

$$-(2x + 3) = (-1)(2x + 3)$$
$$= (-1)(2x) + (-1)(3)$$
$$= -2x - 3$$

$-2x - 3$ is factored correctly.

> The expression $-(2x + 3)$ is factored completely because the terms inside the parentheses have no common factors.

2 Factor the expression $-4a - 8$.

$$-4a - 8 = -4a + (-8) \quad \text{Rewrite the expression.}$$
$$= (-4)(a) + (-4)(2) \quad \text{The GCF of } -4a \text{ and } -8 \text{ is } (-4).$$
$$= -4(a + 2) \quad \text{Factor } (-4) \text{ from each term and simplify.}$$

Check

Expand the expression $-4(a + 2)$ to check the factoring.

$$-4(a + 2) = (-4)(a) + (-4)(2)$$
$$= -4a - 8$$

$-4a - 8$ is factored correctly.

TRY Practice factoring algebraic expressions with negative terms

Factor each expression.

1 $-5x - 3$

2 $-3f - 6$

3 $-8p - 10q$

INDEPENDENT PRACTICE

Factor each expression with two terms.

1 $2x + 8$

2 $5a + 5$

3 $3x - 12$

4 $4x - 16$

5 $2x + 8y$

6 $7a + 7b$

7 $5p + 15q$

8 $14w + 49m$

9 $4j - 16k$

10 $8t - 32u$

11 $2a - 10p$

12 $9h - 45f$

Factor each expression with negative terms.

13 $-p - 2$

14 $-x - 5$

15 $-2d - 7$

16 $-4y - 11$

17 $-3a - 6$

18 $-4x - 20$

19 $-5k - 25$

20 $-7u - 49$

21 $-1 - 4n$

22 $-3 - 6a$

23 $-12x - 16y$

24 $-25m - 10n$

Factor each expression with three terms.

25 $4x + 4y + 8$

26 $2a + 6b + 4$

27 $5p + 10q + 10$

28 $12d + 6e + 18$

29 $3s - 9t - 15$

30 $4a - 6b - 12$

31 $12a - 9b - 6$

32 $24g - 12h - 36$

Solve.

33 A rectangle has an area of $(12m - 30n)$ square units. Its width is 6 units. Factor the expression for the area to find an expression for the length of the rectangle.

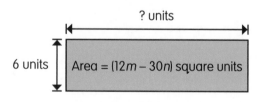

6 Writing Algebraic Expressions

Learning Objectives:
• Translate verbal descriptions into algebraic expressions with one or more variables.
• Translate verbal descriptions into algebraic expressions involving the distributive property.

THINK

Ava has x magnets. Leah has 25% fewer magnets than Ava. Katie has $\frac{1}{2}y$ magnets more than Leah. The three of them then share their magnets equally. How many magnets does each of them have after sharing the magnets? Simplify the expression, if necessary. Show two different methods the three girls can use to share the magnets among themselves, so that each of them has the same number of magnets.

ENGAGE

A wooden plank is x feet long. Draw a bar model and write an expression to represent the total length of two such planks.

Now, use the bar model to represent the length of $\frac{1}{3}$ of the total length of the two planks.

How do you write an expression to show it? Explain your reasoning.

LEARN Translate verbal descriptions into algebraic expressions with one variable

1. You have learned to translate verbal descriptions into algebraic expressions. You can translate verbal descriptions with variable terms that have decimal, fractional, and negative coefficients as in the following problem.

   Mia used two-thirds of a piece of ribbon that is y inches long, to tie her hair. Write an algebraic expression for the length of the piece of ribbon she used.

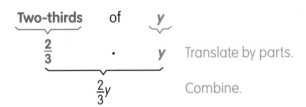

Math Note
$\frac{2}{3}y$ can also be expressed as $\frac{2y}{3}$.

The length of the piece of ribbon she used is $\frac{2}{3}y$ inches.

2 You can translate verbal descriptions into algebraic expressions using more than one operation. Simplify algebraic expressions when you can.

Seven sticks of clay are shared equally among 28 students. Each stick of clay weighs c grams. Write an algebraic expression for the weight of the clay that each student receives.

Product of 7 and c　　divided by　**28**

$$7 \cdot c \qquad \div \qquad 28 \qquad \text{Translate by parts.}$$

$$\frac{7c}{28} \qquad \text{Combine and simplify.}$$

$$= \frac{c}{4}$$

You can translate verbal descriptions into algebraic expressions by parts before you combine them into an expression.

Each student receives $\frac{c}{4}$ grams of clay.

3 Charles usually makes 7 quarts of fruit punch using r quarts of orange juice. This time, he uses 30% less orange juice. Write an expression for the number of quarts of fruit punch Charles makes this time.

7　　adds to　　**−0.3**　　times　　**r**

$$-0.3 \qquad \cdot \qquad r \qquad \text{Translate by parts.}$$

$$7 \qquad + \qquad -0.3r \qquad \text{Combine.}$$

$$7 + (-0.3r) = 7 - 0.3r$$

Charles makes $(7 - 0.3r)$ quarts of fruit punch this time.

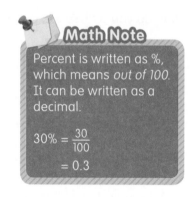

Math Note

Percent is written as %, which means *out of 100*. It can be written as a decimal.

$$30\% = \frac{30}{100}$$
$$= 0.3$$

4. Seven watermelons each weigh w pounds. A basket can hold 11 pounds less than two-fifths of the total weight of the watermelons. What weight can the basket hold?

Since w represents the weight of one watermelon, $7 \cdot w$ represents the weight of seven watermelons.

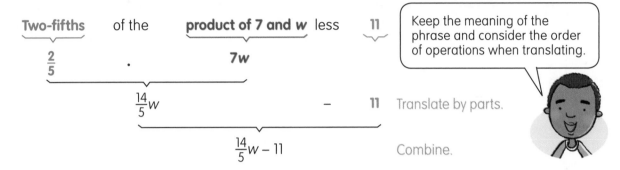

Two-fifths	of the	product of 7 and w	less	11
$\frac{2}{5}$	$\cdot$	$7w$		

$\frac{14}{5}w$ $\quad\quad\quad\quad - \quad\quad$ 11   Translate by parts.

Keep the meaning of the phrase and consider the order of operations when translating.

$\frac{14}{5}w - 11$ Combine.

The basket can hold $\left(\frac{14}{5}w - 11\right)$ pounds.

TRY Practice translating verbal descriptions into algebraic expressions with one variable

Solve.

1. The usual price of a ring was w dollars. Claire bought the ring at a price that was 25% cheaper than the usual price. Write an algebraic expression for the amount she paid for the ring.

w	reduced by	25%

_____ % of w

=

w $\quad - \quad$ _____ w Translate by parts.

_____ − _____   Combine.

= _____   Simplify.

She paid _____ dollars for the ring.

2 6n lumps of clay are shared among 14 students. Write an algebraic expression for the number of lumps of clay that each student will get.

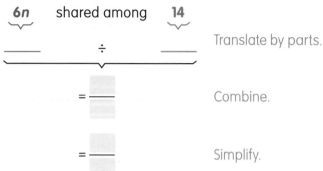

Each student gets _____ lumps of clay.

3 Tyler has w stickers and Megan has $\frac{1}{2}w$ stickers. Tyler gives one-tenth of his stickers and Megan gives two-fifth of her stickers to their cousin Joseph. Write an expression for the number of stickers Joseph receives.

_____ + _____ = _____

Joseph receives _____ stickers.

4 After baking some bread, Zoe has $\frac{2}{3}b$ pounds of butter left. Then, she uses $\frac{3}{4}$ pound for some white sauce. Write an algebraic expression for the amount of butter left in the end.

_____ − _____   Subtract $\frac{3}{4}$ from $\frac{2}{3}b$.

There are _____ pounds of butter left in the end.

Ms. Miller has a backyard that is in the shape of a rectangle as shown.

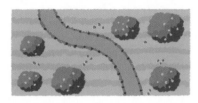

She wants to fence her backyard using wire. Write an algebraic expression with one variable to find the perimeter of her backyard.

Ms. Miller decides to fence off a small rectangular section from a corner of her rectangular backyard as shown.

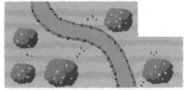

Will she need more or less wire? Explain your reasoning.

LEARN Translate real-world problems into algebraic expressions with one variable

1. You can use diagrams, models, or tables to represent the information in a real-world problem. These help you to solve problems involving algebraic expressions.

   Mr. Kim has a farm that is in the shape of a rectangle. Its width is x yards. Its length is 6 yards more than one-third of the width. Write an algebraic expression for the perimeter of Mr. Kim's farm.

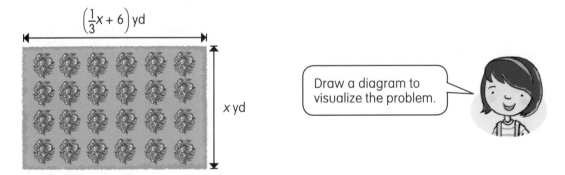

Draw a diagram to visualize the problem.

Perimeter of Mr. Kim's farm:

$$x + \left(\frac{1}{3}x + 6\right) + x + \left(\frac{1}{3}x + 6\right) = \frac{8}{3}x + 12 \quad \text{Add the like terms.}$$

The perimeter of Mr. Kim's farm is $\left(\frac{8}{3}x + 12\right)$ yards.

Solve.

1. Mr. Martin's backyard is in the shape of an isosceles triangle with a base of length $2y$ feet and sides of length $\left(\frac{2}{5}y + 3\right)$ feet each. Write an algebraic expression for the perimeter of Mr. Martin's backyard.

    _____ ft   _____ ft

    _____ ft

    Perimeter of Mr. Martin's backyard:

    _____ + _____ + _____ = _____   Add the like terms.

    The perimeter of Mr. Martin's backyard is _____ feet.

ENGAGE

Rafael has 6 apps on his phone. Emily has x more apps on her phone than Rafael. Draw a bar model and write an expression to show how many apps Emily has.

If Rafael has $2y$ apps on his phone, how many apps does Emily have? Explain your answer.

LEARN Translate verbal descriptions into algebraic expressions with more than one variable

1. Some situations may require you to use more than one variable.

    Adam has m coins. Rachel has $\frac{1}{2}r$ coins. Assuming Adam has more coins than Rachel, how many more does Adam have?

    m minus $\frac{1}{2}r$

    m $-$ $\frac{1}{2}r$ Translate by parts. Combine.

    Adam has $\left(m - \frac{1}{2}r\right)$ coins more than Rachel.

2 Eric made t dollars and his sister Lily made u dollars while working at a restaurant during their summer break. They gave 12% of their earnings to a local charity. Find the total amount they gave to the charity.

12%	of the	**sum of t and u**	
0.12	$\cdot$	$t + u$	Translate by parts.

0.12 $(t + u)$ Combine.

Eric and Lily gave [0.12$(t + u)$] dollars to the charity.

TRY **Practice translating verbal descriptions into algebraic expressions with more than one variable**

Solve.

1 There are $\frac{2}{3}x$ red balloons and y blue balloons. How many more blue balloons are there?

2 The price of a bag is p dollars and the price of a pair of shoes is $5q$ dollars. Ms. Scott bought both items and paid a sales tax of 20%. Write an algebraic expression for the amount of sales tax she paid.

A bowl cost x dollars and a cup cost $\frac{1}{2}x$ dollars. Mr. Perez bought 3 bowls and 6 cups. Draw a bar model to find the total cost of the items.

Then, Mr. Perez bought 5 plates and each plate cost y dollars. How do you find the total amount of money he spent? Show your method.

LEARN Translate real-world problems into algebraic expressions with more than one variable

1. Grapes, papayas, and strawberries are sold in a supermarket at the following prices:

| x dollars Per lb | y dollars Per lb | $\frac{3}{5}x$ dollars Per lb |

Julia bought 4.5 pounds of grapes, 2.65 pounds of papayas, and 6 pounds of strawberries. What is the total cost of the fruit she bought?

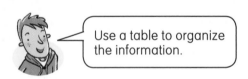

Use a table to organize the information.

Fruit	Price Per Pound	Total Weight	Cost
Grapes	x dollars	4.5 pounds	$4.5x$ dollars
Papayas	y dollars	2.65 pounds	$2.65y$ dollars
Strawberries	$\frac{3}{5}x$ dollars	6 pounds	$3.6x$ dollars

Total cost of fruit:

$4.5x + 2.65y + 3.6x = 4.5x + 3.6x + 2.65y$ Group the like terms.

$\qquad\qquad\qquad\quad = 8.1x + 2.65y$ Add the like terms.

The total cost of the fruit that she bought is $(8.1x + 2.65y)$ dollars.

Fill in the table. Then, solve.

1. The price of a buffet lunch is $14.80 per adult and $12 per child. For a group of m adults and n children, how much does the lunch cost before tax and tips?

Diners	Price Per Person	Number of Diners	Cost
Adult	$14.80		
Child		n	

Total cost of lunch before tax and tips:

_____ + _____

The total cost of lunch before tax and tips is _____ dollars.

Solve.

2. Lucas had m quarters in his pocket. He also had one dime and n nickels. What was the total value of his coins?

ENGAGE

Owen had k markers. He lost 6 markers. Draw a bar model and write an algebraic expression to show the number of markers he has left.

Owen then divided the markers he had left equally among 3 friends. How do you write an algebraic expression for the number of markers each friend received? Share your method.

1   Anya had n baseball cards that she wanted to give away. She gave 12 baseball cards to her brother and divided the rest of them equally among 4 friends. How many baseball cards did each friend receive?

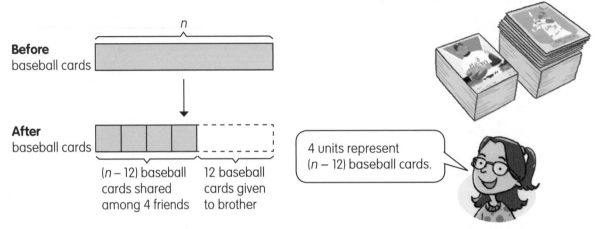

Before
baseball cards

After
baseball cards

$(n - 12)$ baseball cards shared among 4 friends   12 baseball cards given to brother

4 units represent $(n - 12)$ baseball cards.

From the bar model, the number of baseball cards each friend received was:

$\frac{1}{4}(n - 12) = \frac{1}{4}n - 3$ Use the distributive property.

Each friend received $\left(\frac{1}{4}n - 3\right)$ baseball cards.

Activity Using algebraic expressions in real-world situations

Work in groups.

Translate verbal descriptions into algebraic expressions.

Kayla used her cell phone for four days. Her average calling time was 130 minutes each day. Suppose that Kayla used the phone for m minutes on the fifth day. Write an algebraic expression for the average number of minutes she spent on the phone over five days.

1   Complete.

Total number of minutes spent over five days:

Total number of minutes spent over four days + Number of minutes spent on the fifth day

= _____ + m

Average minutes over five days:

$\dfrac{\text{Total number of minutes spent over five days}}{\text{Five days}}$ = _____

Math Note

Average number of minutes spent over four days

= $\dfrac{\text{Total number of minutes spent over four days}}{\text{Four days}}$

(2) Use a spreadsheet to solve real-world problems involving algebraic expressions.

a Label your spreadsheet and enter the values in column A as shown.

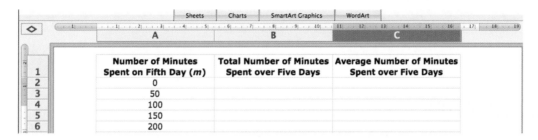

Enter the formula = 130*4+A2 in cell B2 to find the total number of minutes Kayla spent on her cell phone over five days. What is the value in cell B2 after you have entered the formula?

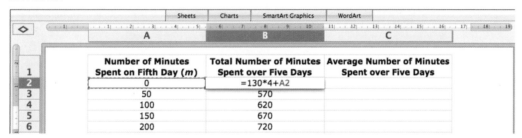

b Complete cell C2 with a formula to find the average number of minutes Kayla spent on her cell phone over five days.

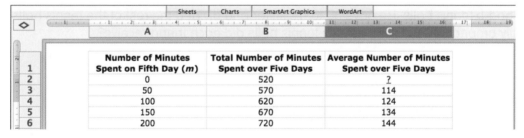

③ Karina would like to spend an average of 150 minutes a day on her cell phone over five days. Determine the number of minutes she can spend on the fifth day by repeating with different values in column A.

④ **Mathematical Habit 4** Use mathematical models

Based on your activity, what is the relationship between the algebraic expressions of ① and the formula used in the spreadsheet cell of ②? Explain how you can use technology to solve real-world problems.

TRY Practice translating real-world problems into algebraic expressions involving the distributive property

Solve.

❶ Alan had *b* tennis balls. He gave 30 to his sister and divided the rest of the tennis balls equally among 5 friends. How many tennis balls did each friend receive?

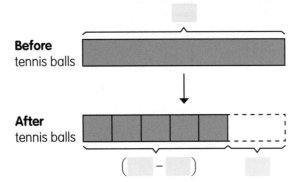

From the bar model, the number of tennis balls each friend received was:

_____ (_____ − _____) = _____   Use the distributive property.

Each friend received _____ tennis balls.

INDEPENDENT PRACTICE

Translate each verbal description into an algebraic expression. Simplify the expression when you can.

1. Sum of one-sixth of *x* and 2.8

2. One-half *u* subtracted from 3 times *u*

3. 4.5 times *q* divided by 9

4. 60% of one-half *x*

5. 120% of 5*x*

6. 7 times *z* reduced by a third of the product

7. 24% of *w* plus 50% of *y*

⑧ Three-fourths of v subtracted from 6 times two-ninths y

⑨ One-fourth of the sum of $2p$ and 11

⑩ Sum of $2x$, $\left(\frac{2}{3}x + 5\right)$, and $(11 - x)$

Solve. You may use a diagram, model, or table.

⑪ The length of $\frac{2}{3}$ of a rope is $(4u - 5)$ inches. Express the total length of the rope in terms of u.

⑫ If 50 lb = 22.68 kg, what is $\frac{15}{8}y$ pounds in kilograms?

⑬ The minute hand of a clock makes one complete round every 60 minutes. How many rounds does the minute hand make in $650x$ minutes?

⑭ Fifteen cards are added to n cards. 6 people then share the cards equally. Express the number of cards for each person in terms of n.

15 Yesterday, the pump price for gasoline was g dollars per gallon. The price increases by 10 cents per gallon today. If a driver pumps 12.4 gallons of gasoline today, how much does he have to pay?

16 Each algebraic expression contains an error. Fill in the table.

Verbal Description	Expression with Error	Description of Error	Correct Expression
35% of s plus 65% of t	$s + t$		
$\frac{1}{6}x$ subtracted from $\frac{1}{6}y$	$\frac{1}{6}x - \frac{1}{6}y$		
One more than half of n	$\frac{1}{2}n + n$		
$\frac{2}{3}x$ divided by $\frac{1}{5}$	$\frac{2}{15}x$		

17 The ratio of red counters to blue counters is 9 : 11. There are y blue counters. Express the number of red counters in terms of y.

18 When 18 boys joined a group of y students, the ratio of boys to girls in the group became 4 : 5. Write an algebraic expression for the number of girls in terms of y.

19 Andrew is x years old. Blake is 7 years younger than Andrew. In 5 years' time, Blake will be twice the age of Carla. How old is Carla now in terms of x?

20 A holiday touring group has an equal number of adults and children. When n oranges are given to the group, each adult gets two oranges while each child gets one orange, leaving 5 oranges in the box. Write an algebraic expression for the number of oranges given to the adults.

21 The list price of a camera was w dollars. Dylan bought the camera for $35 less than the list price. If the sales tax was 8%, how much did Dylan pay for the camera including the sales tax?

SALE
$35 off

22 At a museum, there were m visitors to an exhibition on the first day and 1,200 fewer visitors on the second day. On the third day, the number of visitors was 30% greater than the number of visitors on the second day. What was the average number of visitors at the exhibition over the three days?

23 A man drove x miles per hour for 3 hours and $(2x - 60)$ miles per hour for the next 4.75 hours.

a Express the total distance he traveled in terms of x.

b If $x = 64$, what is the total distance he traveled?

7 Real-World Problems: Algebraic Reasoning

Learning Objective:
• Solve real-world problems using algebraic reasoning.

THINK

A piece of string is $(w + 5)$ feet long. Ms. Reyes kept 60% of the piece of the string and used the rest to tie two boxes.

a If one of the pieces of string used to tie the box was at least $\frac{1}{3}$ as long as the other piece, find a possible length of the other piece of string.

b If one of the pieces of string was not more than $\frac{1}{3}$ of the length of the other piece, find a possible length of the other piece of string.

ENGAGE

Zachary bought 3 cartons of x eggs. He used 6 to make a cake. He then used the remaining eggs equally to make 2 pies. Draw a bar model to show how many eggs were used in each pie. Now, write an expression to explain your reasoning.

LEARN   Solve real-world problems using algebraic reasoning

1 After Seth gives Elena 6 pears, Elena has $(x + 6)$ pears. If she gives one-third of her pears to Dae, how many pears, in terms of x, does Dae have?

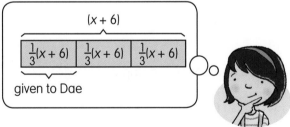

Number of pears that Dae has:

$\frac{1}{3}(x + 6)$ Translate verbal descriptions into algebraic expression.

$= \frac{1}{3} \cdot x + \frac{1}{3} \cdot 6$ Use the distributive property.

$= \frac{1}{3}x + 2$ Simplify.

Dae has $\left(\frac{1}{3}x + 2\right)$ pears.

Simplifying is a logical step after expanding.

2 There are *n* apples in a box. 5 apples are green and the rest are red. Jade and Kyle share the red apples in the ratio 2 : 3. How many red apples does Kyle get?

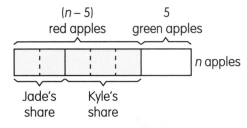

STEP 1 Understand the problem.

> How many apples are there in total?
> How many of the apples are red?
> How do Jade and Kyle share the red apples?
> What fraction of the red apples does Kyle get?
> What do I need to find?

STEP 2 Think of a plan.
I can draw a bar model or use algebraic reasoning.

STEP 3 Carry out the plan.

▶ **Method 1**
Draw a bar model.

$(n - 5)$ red apples   5 green apples

n apples

Jade's share   Kyle's share

From the bar model, the number of red apples Kyle gets is:

$\frac{3}{5}(n - 5) = \frac{3}{5}(n) - \frac{3}{5}(5)$ Use the distributive property.

$\qquad\qquad = \frac{3}{5}n - 3$

Kyle gets $\left(\frac{3}{5}n - 3\right)$ red apples.

▶ **Method 2**
Use algebraic reasoning.

Only red apples are shared. So, subtract 5 green apples from n apples.

Jade's apples : Kyle's apples
                2 : 3

So, Kyle gets 3 out of every 5 red apples.

Number of red apples: $n - 5$

Number of red apples Kyle gets:

$\frac{3}{5}(n - 5) = \frac{3}{5}(n) - \frac{3}{5}(5)$ Use the distributive property.

$\qquad = \frac{3}{5}n - 3$

Kyle gets $\left(\frac{3}{5}n - 3\right)$ red apples.

 Check the answer.
I can work backwards to check my answer.

Jade's apples : Kyle's apples
                2 : 3
$\frac{2}{5}(n - 5) : \frac{3}{5}(n - 5)$

Total number of red apples $= \frac{2}{5}(n - 5) + \frac{3}{5}(n - 5)$
$\qquad\qquad\qquad\qquad = n - 5$

Total number of apples = Number of red apples + Number of green apples
$\qquad\qquad\qquad\qquad = n - 5 + 5$
$\qquad\qquad\qquad\qquad = n$
My answer is correct.

TRY Practice solving real-world problems using algebraic reasoning

Solve.

① The area of a triangle is $(u + 10)$ square centimeters. The ratio of the area of the unshaded region to the area of the shaded region is 1 : 3. Using algebraic reasoning, express the area of the shaded region in terms of u.

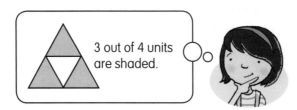

3 out of 4 units are shaded.

Area of shaded region:

$$\underline{}\Big(\underline{}\Big) = \underline{}$$ Use the distributive property. Simplify.

The area of the shaded region of the triangle is _____ square centimeters.

② There are 25 nickels and quarters. w coins are nickels and the rest are quarters.

? quarters w nickels

25 coins

a Write an algebraic expression for the number of coins that are quarters.

Number of quarters: _____ – _____

There are _____ quarters.

b Find the total value of the quarters.

Total value of quarters:

_____ • _____ = _____

The total value of the quarters is _____ dollars.

Luke thinks of three consecutive even numbers. Using x to represent one of the even numbers, write an expression for each of the other two even numbers. How do you find the sum of the three even numbers? Share and explain your method.

LEARN Solve real-world problems involving algebraic expressions

1 One number is n and a second number is $\left(\frac{2n}{3} + 2\right)$. A third number is $\frac{n}{6}$ less than the second number. Express the sum of the three numbers in terms of n.

First Number Second Number Third Number

Sum of three numbers: $n + \left(\frac{2n}{3} + 2\right) + \left(\frac{2n}{3} + 2 - \frac{n}{6}\right)$ Write the addition expression.

$$= n + \frac{2}{3}n + 2 + \frac{2}{3}n + 2 - \frac{1}{6}n$$ Rewrite the expression.

$$= n + \frac{2}{3}n + \frac{2}{3}n - \frac{1}{6}n + 2 + 2$$ Group like terms.

$$= \frac{6}{6}n + \frac{4}{6}n + \frac{4}{6}n - \frac{1}{6}n + 2 + 2$$ LCM of 3 and 6 is 6.

$$= \frac{13}{6}n + 4$$ Simplify.

The sum of the three numbers is $\left(\frac{13}{6}n + 4\right)$.

TRY Practice solving real-world problems involving algebraic expressions

Solve. Write + or − in each $\bigcirc$.

1 Hana has x comic books, Mario has $\left(\frac{2x}{5} + 1\right)$ comic books, and John has $\frac{x}{10}$ fewer comic books than Mario. Express the total number of comic books that Hana, Mario, and John have in terms of x.

Hana's Books Mario's Books John's Books

Total number of comic books: $x + \left(\frac{2x}{5} + 1\right) + \left(\underline{\quad}\bigcirc\underline{\quad}\right)$ Write the addition expression.

$$= x + \frac{2}{5}x + 1 + \underline{\quad}\bigcirc\underline{\quad}$$ Rewrite the expressions.

$$= x + \frac{2}{5}x + \underline{\qquad\qquad}$$ Group like terms.

$$= \underline{\qquad\qquad\qquad}$$ LCD of $\frac{2}{5}$ and $\frac{1}{10}$ is _____.

$$= \underline{\qquad}$$ Simplify.

The total number of comic books is _____.

Ms. Evans bought a total of 60 pens and pencils. There was an equal number of pens and pencils. She gave *x* percent of the pens and *y* percent of the pencils to her students. Use algebraic reasoning to write an algebraic expression for the number of pens and pencils that she gave her students. Share your reasoning.

LEARN Solve percent problems involving algebraic expressions using algebraic reasoning

1. There is an equal number of boys and girls in a group of 80 children. Within the group, *p* percent of the boys and *q* percent of the girls wear glasses. Write an algebraic expression for the number of children who wear glasses. Factor any terms with a common factor.

$80 \div 2 = 40$

There are 40 boys and 40 girls.

Number of boys who wear glasses $= 0.01p \cdot 40$
$\qquad\qquad\qquad\qquad\qquad\quad = 0.4p$

Number of girls who wear glasses $= 0.01q \cdot 40$
$\qquad\qquad\qquad\qquad\qquad\quad = 0.4q$

Number of children who wear glasses $= 0.4p + 0.4q$
$\qquad\qquad\qquad\qquad\qquad\qquad\quad = 0.4(p + q)$

> p percent $= \dfrac{p}{100}$ $\qquad$ q percent $= \dfrac{q}{100}$
> $\qquad\qquad = 0.01p$ $\qquad\qquad\qquad = 0.01q$

The number of children who wear glasses is $0.4(p+ q)$.

TRY Practice solving percent problems involving algebraic expressions using algebraic reasoning

Solve.

1. A store stocks *x* pairs of sneakers and *y* pairs of sandals. During a promotion, a pair of sneakers is priced at $50 and a pair of sandals at $36. The shop manages to sell half of the sneakers and 80% of the sandals. Write an expression for the total dollar amount the store makes.

INDEPENDENT PRACTICE

Solve.

1. In a factory, 40% of *k* liters of acid are added to 60% of *w* liters of water. Write an algebraic expression for the total volume of the solution.

2. Write an algebraic expression for the perimeter of the quadrilateral shown.

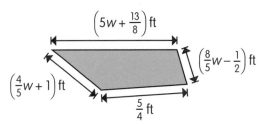

3. If the average daily sales amount in a store for the past 5 days was $(2.3q + 1.4)$ dollars, write an algebraic expression for the total sales amount for the past 5 days.

4 The weight of 2 similar science fiction books and 1 autobiography is $\frac{5}{6}w$ pounds. What is the total weight of 4 of these science fiction books and 2 of these autobiographies?

5 On her way to work, Ms. Lee waited 20 minutes at a subway station. The train ride took her $(x + 30)$ minutes to reach Grand Central Station. Then, she walked for another $\frac{1}{3}x$ minutes before reaching her office. How much time, in minutes, did Ms. Lee take to travel to her office?

6 A piece of ribbon measuring $(v + 4)$ feet in length was cut into two smaller pieces in the ratio 3 : 7. What was the length of the longer piece?

7 When one-fifth of the boys left, there were still b boys and g girls who stayed to see a musical performance. What was the total number of boys and girls at the beginning of the performance?

8 Mr. Gomez is paid at an hourly-rate of $15 and an overtime hourly-rate of 1.5 times his usual hourly-rate for his work. If Mr. Gomez puts in w regular hours and y overtime hours in a week, what is his total wage for the week?

9 Jaden is p years old now. In 10 years' time, he will be 3 times as old as Cody. Express Cody's age 10 years from now in terms of p.

10 Ms. Walker bought a computer for 15% off from the list price of p dollars. If the sales tax was 8%, how much did she pay for the computer including sales tax?

11 A farmer collected some eggs from his farm and found *b* eggs broken. He packed the remaining eggs in *c* egg cartons. Each egg carton can hold a dozen eggs and no eggs were leftover. Write an algebraic expression for the number of eggs he collected initially in terms of *b* and *c*.

12 A teacher from Anderson Middle School printed *k* nametags in preparation for a science fair. Half of the nametags were given out to students and 100 nametags were given out to parents. Three-fifths of the remaining nametags were given out to teachers and contest judges. How many nametags were not given out?

13 At the beginning of a journey, the fuel tank of a car was $\frac{3}{4}$ full. When the car reached its destination, it had consumed 60% of the gasoline in the tank. The full capacity of the fuel tank was *w* gallons.

a Write an algebraic expression for the amount of gasoline left in the fuel tank.

b If *w* = 15.5, how much gasoline was left in the tank at the end of the journey?

Mathematical Habit 3 **Construct viable arguments**

Briella expanded and simplified the expression $6(x + 3) - 2(x + 1) + 5$ as follows:

$$6(x + 3) - 2(x + 1) + 5 = 6x + 3 - 2x + 1 + 5$$
$$= 6x - 2x + 3 + 1 + 5$$
$$= 4x + 9$$

Explain to Briella her mistakes and show the correct solution.

Explanation:

Correct solution:

Problem Solving with Heuristics

1 **Mathematical Habit 2** Use mathematical reasoning

A planner was drawing up a floorplan of a children's playground for a neighborhood.

The playground was in the shape of a rectangle with length $(x + 5)$ meters and width

$(x - 3)$ meters. It was then decided that the length needed to be reduced to $\frac{4}{5}$ of the original

length, and the width needed to be increased to 1.2 times the original width.

a Find an expression for the perimeter of the new playground. Was there any change to the perimeter?

b If the shape of the playground were a square instead, do you think the decrease in length by 20% and the increase in width by 20% would affect the perimeter of the playground? Explain your answer.

② | **Mathematical Habit 4** Use mathematical models

Steven and his father are from Singapore, where the temperature is measured in degrees Celsius. While visiting downtown Los Angeles, Steven saw a temperature sign that read 72°F. He asked his father what the equivalent temperature was in °C.

His father could not recall the Fahrenheit-to-Celsius conversion formula, $C = \frac{5}{9}(F - 32)$. However, he remembered that water freezes at 0°C or 32°F and boils at 100°C or 212°F.

Using these two pieces of information, would you be able to help Steven figure out the above conversion formula? Explain.

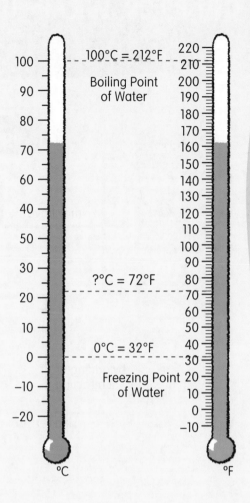

100°C = 212°F

Boiling Point of Water

?°C = 72°F

0°C = 32°F

Freezing Point of Water

°C

°F

How do you simplify, expand, or factor algebraic expressions?

Algebraic Expressions

Integral coefficients

Fractional coefficients

Decimal coefficients

may have

are written for

Word problems

can be

Simplified

by adding or subtracting

Like terms

Expanded

using

Distributive property

Factored

using

Greatest common factor

are used to help solve

Diagrams

Models

organize information for

Tables

is a way of solving

Algebraic reasoning

KEY CONCEPTS

- Algebraic expressions may contain more than one variable with rational coefficients and rational constants.

  Example: $\frac{1}{2}x + 1.2u - 3$.

- Algebraic expressions are written in simplest form by adding and subtracting the coefficients of the like terms.

- Algebraic expressions may be simplified using the commutative property of addition.

- Algebraic expressions are expanded using the distributive property.

- Algebraic expressions are factored using the greatest common factor (GCF) of the terms and the distributive property.

- You can use diagrams, models, or tables to help solve real-world problems algebraically.

Name: _____ Date: _____

Simplify each expression.

① $1.4w - 0.6w$

② $\frac{3}{4}m + \frac{4}{5}m$

③ $\frac{1}{6}y + \frac{1}{2}y + \frac{1}{3}y$

④ $1.8m + (-0.2m) - 7m$

⑤ $1.3a - 0.8b + 2.2b - a$

⑥ $1 + \frac{1}{5}a + \frac{3}{5}b - \left(-\frac{4}{5}a\right)$

Expand each expression. Then, simplify when you can.

⑦ $1.2(2p - 3)$

⑧ $\frac{1}{3}(12p + 9q)$

⑨ $\frac{1}{5}\left(\frac{t}{3} + \frac{1}{2}\right)$

⑩ $-4(-2q + 2.5)$

⑪ $-\frac{2}{3}(6x + 3)$

⑫ $-0.5(2m - 4n)$

⑬ $3(a + 3) + 2a$

⑭ $4(2p - 3) - 3(p + 2)$

⑮ $2.5(m - 2) + 5.6m$

⑯ $4(0.6n - 3) - 0.2(2n - 3)$

Factor each expression.

⑰ $4t - 20s$

⑱ $-6p - 21q$

⑲ $8i + 12 + 4j$

⑳ $6a + 10b - 20$

㉑ $-9m - 3n - 6$

㉒ $-15x - 6 - 12y$

Translate each verbal description into an algebraic expression. Then, simplify when you can.

23 One-fourth x less than the sum of 7 and $2x$.

24 4 times $5y$ divided by 18.

25 Five-ninths of $(3p + 1)$ subtracted from one-third of $(q + p)$.

Solve.

26 After 14 boys leave a concert, the ratio of boys to girls is 3 : 10. If there are p girls at the concert, write an algebraic expression for the number of boys at the beginning of the concert in terms of p.

27 40% of the fish in a pond are goldfish and the rest are Koi. The number of goldfish is g. The farmer then increases the number of Koi by 10%. How many Koi are there in the pond, in terms of g, now?

28 Three-fourths of the weight of a bunch of grapes is equivalent to three-fifths of the weight of a papaya. If the grapes weigh $(x + 28)$ pounds, what is the weight of a papaya in terms of x?

29 Mr. Lee ordered some pizzas to be delivered. The bill for the pizza was m dollars. Mr. Lee tipped the pizza delivery driver 15% of the bill.

a Write an expression for the total amount of money Mr. Lee paid.

b The bill for the pizza was $30. Find the amount of money Mr. Lee paid.

© 2020 Marshall Cavendish Education Pte Ltd

30 A box contains n quarters and some dimes. The ratio of quarters to dimes is 1 : 2.

a Write an expression for the total amount of money in the box.

b If there are 12 quarters, find the total amount of money in the box.

31 Ms. Smith is considering two cell phone plans that charge for each call made. The charges are shown below.

Cell Phone Plan	Monthly Subscription	Cost Per Minute
A	$10	21.4¢/min
B	$14	18.5¢/min

On average, Ms. Smith uses n minutes of calling time each month.

a Write an expression for the total charges for Ms. Smith's usage based on each cell phone plan.

b If $n = 100$, find the total cost for each cell phone plan. Which cell phone plan should Ms. Smith choose? Justify your choice.

32 The admission fee to a museum is $12.50 per nonsenior adult, $8 per child, and $6.50 per senior citizen. A tour group consists of m nonsenior adults, $\left(\frac{5}{4}m + 6\right)$ children, and $8n$ senior citizens.

a What is the total admission fee of the group?

b Write an expression for the admission fees of the children in the group subtracted from the combined admission fees of the nonsenior adults and senior citizens in the group.

c Evaluate your expression from b, when $m = 24$ and $n = 4$.

Assessment Prep

Answer each question.

33 Which expression is equivalent to $(4x + 3) + (-2x + 4)$?

(A) $-2x + 12$

(B) $-8x + 12$

(C) $6x + 7$

(D) $2x + 7$

34 Which expressions are equivalent to $-3.75 + 2(-4y + 6.1) - 3.25y$? Choose all that apply.

(A) $7y - 2y + 8.1$

(B) $8.45 - 8y - 3.25y$

(C) $-1.75 - 7.25y + 6.1$

(D) $-11.25y + 12.2 - 3.75$

35 What is the value of k when the expression $21.2x + k$ is equivalent to $5.3(4x + 2.6)$? Write your answer and your work or explanation in the space below.

36 A printer takes 2.4 seconds longer to print a page in color than a page in black and white. A page in black and white can be printed in 4 seconds. There are $\left(\frac{5}{8}w + 6\right)$ color pages and $(1.2w + 5)$ black and white pages to print. How long does it take to print all the pages? Write your answer and your work or explanation in the space below.

Name: _____   Date: _____

School Trip to National Park

1. A survey was conducted with x students. 10% of those surveyed said that they have been to a national park. Of the students who had never been to a national park, 50 of them planned to eventually visit a national park. Write an algebraic expression that represents the students who did not plan on visiting a national park.

2 y students went on a school trip to a national park. $\frac{1}{3}$ of the students had a parent accompanying them. 6 teachers also joined the trip. The cost of the trip was 9 dollars per person. Write an algebraic expression, in simplest form, to represent the total cost.

3 Of the total number of students who went for the school trip, 4 less than $\frac{1}{4}$ of them were girls. Do you agree or disagree that the expression $y - 4$, represents 4 times the number of students who were girls? Justify your reasoning with precise mathematical language. You can make use of expressions, equations, bar models or counters.

Rubric

Point(s)	Level	My Performance
7–8	4	• Most of my answers are correct. • I showed complete understanding of the concepts. • I used effective and efficient strategies to solve the problems. • I explained my answers and mathematical thinking clearly and completely.
5–6	3	• Some of my answers are correct. • I showed adequate understanding of the concepts. • I used effective strategies to solve the problems. • I explained my answers and mathematical thinking clearly.
3–4	2	• A few of my answers are correct. • I showed some understanding of the concepts. • I used some effective strategies to solve the problems. • I explained some of my answers and mathematical thinking clearly.
0–2	1	• A few of my answers are correct. • I showed little understanding of the concepts. • I used limited effective strategies to solve the problems. • I did not explain my answers and mathematical thinking clearly.

Teacher's Comments

STEAM

A Field Trip

Seventh-graders across the United States often take a special field trip as a class. Many students visit their state's capital or a state history museum. Where do seventh-graders at your school go on a class field trip? Where do you think they would like to go?

Task

Work in small groups to plan a class field trip.

1. Use the internet to learn more about field-trip possibilities in your community or state.

2. Select a destination. Then, examine the costs associated with the trip. Remember to consider the cost of transportation to and from your destination. Also, investigate the cost of entrance tickets, food, and special venues or activities at the site.

3. Calculate costs by hand, or use a digital tool. Write and solve equations identifying the total per-student cost, and the total amount your teacher will need to collect before the day of the trip.

4. To help students make the most of a new experience, prepare an activity guide. Draw or use digital tools to prepare a brochure. You can also plan something more original, like a scavenger hunt. Use your research to make a map of your destination. Then, provide clues that students must follow to locate specific objects, places, or information. Have students take photographs to record their discoveries.

5. Share your work with other teams.

How much can you raise?

There are many good causes that you can walk, run, or swim to support. Participating in a sport for charity is good for you, and good for the organizations that receive the money you raise.

The first step is to find a charity you want to support. Perhaps you see a sign or receive an online notice. You register, and the organization sends you volunteer materials, including a fundraising form. You explain the purpose of the event to friends and family members, and you invite them to donate money. Some supporters donate a specific amount. Others donate an amount for every mile you walk, run, or swim. You can use algebraic equations to calculate how much you will need to collect from each supporter after the event.

In this chapter, you will learn how to use algebraic equations and inequalities to represent and solve a variety of real-world problems similar to this one.

WALKATHON

How do you solve algebraic equations and inequalities?

Name: _____ Date: _____

Solving algebraic equations by balancing

You can use inverse operations to solve an equation. When you do, keep the equation balanced by performing addition, subtraction, multiplication, or division by the same nonzero number on both sides.

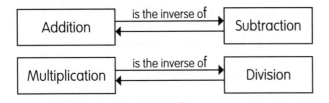

Solve each equation.

a $x + 2 = 9$

$$x + 2 = 9$$
$$x + 2 - 2 = 9 - 2 \quad \text{Subtract 2 from both sides.}$$
$$x = 7 \qquad\qquad \text{Simplify.}$$

b $\frac{2}{3}x = 2$

$$\frac{2}{3}x = 2$$

$$\frac{2}{3}x \div \frac{2}{3} = 2 \div \frac{2}{3} \quad \text{Divide both sides by } \frac{2}{3}.$$

$$\frac{2}{3}x \cdot \frac{3}{2} = 2 \cdot \frac{3}{2} \quad \text{Rewrite division as multiplication by the reciprocal of } \frac{2}{3}.$$

$$x = 3 \qquad\qquad \text{Simplify.}$$

▶ **Quick Check**

Solve each equation.

1 $x + 4 = 10$

2 $x - \frac{1}{2} = 2$

3 $\frac{1}{5}x = 3$

4 $1.2x = 2.4$

Solving algebraic equations by substitution

You can use substitution to solve an algebraic equation.

Solve $x + 6 = 8$.

If $x = 1$, $x + 6 = 1 + 6$ Substitute 1 for x.
                        $= 7$ ($\neq 8$)   1 is not the solution.

If $x = 2$, $x + 6 = 2 + 6$ Substitute 2 for x.
                        $= 8$ 2 is the solution.

The equation $x + 6 = 8$ is true when $x = 2$.
$x = 2$ gives the solution of the equation $x + 6 = 8$.

▶ **Quick Check**

State whether each statement is True or False.

5   $x = 1$ gives the solution of the algebraic equation $3x + 5 = 8$.

6   $y = 2$ gives the solution of the algebraic equation $6y - 3 = 8$.

7   $z = 6$ gives the solution of the algebraic equation $\frac{z}{3} = 3$.

8   $w = 3$ gives the solution of the algebraic equation $2w = 6$.

Graphing inequalities on a number line

You can represent an inequality on a number line using circles and arrows.

$p > 5.5$

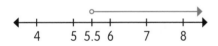

Use an empty circle to show that
5.5 is not a solution of the inequality.

$q \leq 11$

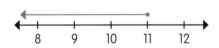

Use a shaded circle to show that
11 is a solution of the inequality.

▶ **Quick Check**

Draw a number line to represent each inequality.

9   $x \geq 3.5$ 10 $y < \frac{1}{2}$

Writing algebraic inequalities

Use >, >, ≥, ≤, or ≠ to compare unequal quantities or quantities that may not be equal.

Verbal Descriptions	Algebraic Inequality
The cost of an apple, a, is not $3.	$a \neq 3$
The cost of a greeting card, c, is less than $6.	$c < 6$
The mass of the strawberries, s, is more than 500 grams.	$s > 500$
The width of the pond, w, is at most 5 meters. OR The width of the pond, w, is no more than 5 meters. OR The width of the pond, w, is less than or equal to 5 meters.	$w \leq 5$
The length of the ribbon, r, is at least 10 inches. OR The length of the ribbon, r, is no less than 10 inches. OR The length of the ribbon, r, is greater than or equal to 10 inches.	$r \geq 10$

▶ **Quick Check**

Compare each pair of numbers or expressions using <, >, or =.

11 11 ◯ −12

12 −9 ◯ −7

13 25 · (−1) ◯ (−1) · 25

14 3 ÷ (−1) ◯ (−1) ÷ 3

Use x to represent the unknown quantity. Write an algebraic inequality for each statement.

15 The box can hold less than 70 pounds.

16 You have to be at least 17 years old to qualify for the contest.

17 The width of luggage that you can carry onto the plane is at most 17 inches.

18 There are more than 120 people standing in line for the roller coaster.

Identifying Equivalent Equations

Learning Objective:
• Identify equivalent equations.

> **New Vocabulary**
> equivalent equations

THINK

The width of a rectangle is 5 inches shorter than its length. Its perimeter is $39\frac{1}{2}$ inches. Chloe wrote "$l + (l - 5) + l + (l - 5) = 39\frac{1}{2}$" and David wrote "$2(l + l - 5) = 39\frac{1}{2}$" to represent the situation. Explain whether they are correct. What equation can you write to represent the situation? Explain.

ENGAGE

Consider the following equations:

a $7 + 3 - 1 = 10 - 1$

b $7 + 3 + 2 = 10 + 2$

c $(7 \cdot 3) + 3 = (7 \times 3) + (3 \times 3)$

d $(7 + 3) \div 5 = 10 \div 5$

What do you notice? Is there a pattern?
Share your observations.

LEARN Identify equivalent equations

① You have learned that factoring, simplifying, or expanding an expression produces an equivalent expression. Equivalent expressions have the same value for any given value of the variable.

Examples of equivalent expressions:
$4x + 3 + 3x = 7x + 3$ Group like terms.

$4x + 6 = 2(2x + 3)$ Factor. The common factor of $4x$ and 6 is 2.

$2(x - 5) = 2x - 10$ Use the distributive property to expand.

Equivalent equations are equations that have the same solution. Given an equation, use the operations of addition, subtraction, multiplication, or division to produce an equivalent equation. For example, you can subtract 2 from both sides of the equation $x - 1 = 7$ as shown.

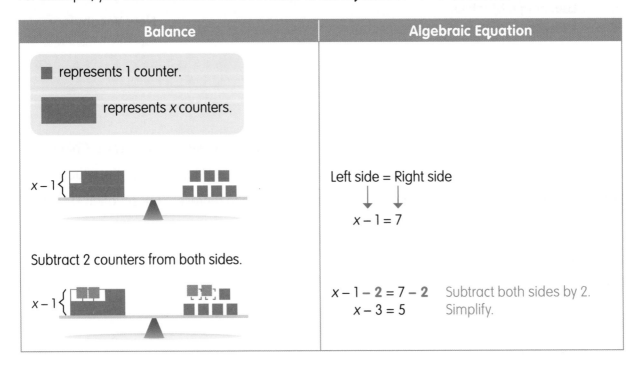

Compare the solutions of the original equation and the new equation:
$x = 8$ gives the solution of the equation $x - 1 = 7$.
$x = 8$ gives the solution of the equation $x - 3 = 5$.

Now suppose you add 3 to both sides of the equation $x - 3 = 5$.

Balance	Algebraic Equation
	$x - 3 + 3 = 5 + 3$ Add 3 to both sides.
	$x = 8$ Simplify.

Compare the solutions of the original equation and the new equation:
$x = 8$ gives the solution of the equation $x - 3 = 5$.
$x = 8$ gives the solution of the equation $x = 8$.

Then, suppose you multiply both sides of the equation $x = 8$ by 2.

Balance	Algebraic Equation
Multiply both sides by 2.	$x \cdot 2 = 8 \cdot 2$ Multiply both sides by 2. $2x = 16$ Simplify.

Compare the solutions of the original equation and the new equation:
$x = 8$ gives the solution of the equation $x = 8$.
$x = 8$ gives the solution of the equation $2x = 16$.

Finally, suppose you divide both sides of the equation $2x = 16$ by 4.

Balance	Algebraic Equation
Divide into four equal groups.	$2x \div 4 = 16 \div 4$ Divide both sides by 2. $\frac{1}{2}x = 4$ Simplify.

Compare the solutions of the original equation and the new equation:

$x = 8$ gives the solution of the equation $2x = 16$.

$x = 8$ gives the solution of the equation $\frac{1}{2}x = 4$.

So, performing the same operation on both sides of an equation may produce an equivalent equation with the same solution. You can use the fact that equivalent equations have the same solution to decide whether two equations are equivalent.

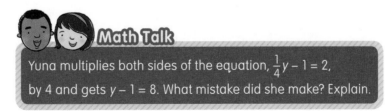

Math Talk

Yuna multiplies both sides of the equation, $\frac{1}{4}y - 1 = 2$, by 4 and gets $y - 1 = 8$. What mistake did she make? Explain.

2 Determine whether $x + 3 + 6x = 13$ and $7x + 3 = 13$ are equivalent equations. Explain your answer.

$x + 3 + 6x = 13$
$x + 6x + 3 = 13$ Use commutative property to group like terms.
$\quad 7x + 3 = 13$ Add like terms.

$x + 3 + 6x = 13$ can be rewritten as $7x + 3 = 13$ using familiar number properties.
So, the equations have the same solution and are equivalent.

3 Determine whether $5x - 4 = 6$ and $5x = 20$ are equivalent equations. Explain your answer.

Check if both equations have the same solution.
First, solve $5x = 20$.

$5x \div 5 = 20 \div 5$ Divide both sides by 5.
$\quad\quad x = 4$ Simplify.

Then, check if $x = 4$ is the solution for the equation, $5x - 4 = 6$.

If $x = 4$, $5x - 4 = 5 \cdot 4 - 4$ Substitute 4 for x.
$\quad\quad\quad\quad = 16$ $(\neq 6)$ 4 is not a solution.

Since the equations have different solutions, they are not equivalent equations.
So, $5x - 4 = 6$ and $5x = 20$ are not equivalent equations.

4 Determine whether $\frac{2}{3}x = 4$ and $x = 6$ are equivalent equations. Explain your answer.

Check if both equations have the same solution.

If $x = 6$, $\frac{2}{3}x = \frac{2}{3} \cdot 6$ Substitute 6 for x.
$\quad\quad\quad = 4$ 6 is a solution.

Since the equations have the same solution, 6, they are equivalent equations.
So, $\frac{2}{3}x = 4$ and $x = 6$ are equivalent equations.

TRY Practice identifying equivalent equations

Determine whether each pair of equations are equivalent. Explain your answer.

① $x - 3 + 4x = 5$ and $5x = 2$

> Check if $x - 3 + 4x = 5$ can be rewritten as $5x = 2$.

$$x - 3 + 4x = 5$$

$$x + 4x - 3 = 5 \qquad \text{Group the like terms.}$$

$$\underline{\hspace{1cm}} - 3 = 5$$

$$\underline{\hspace{1cm}} - 3 + \underline{\hspace{1cm}} = 5 + \underline{\hspace{1cm}} \qquad \text{Add } \underline{\hspace{1cm}} \text{ to both sides.}$$

$$\underline{\hspace{1cm}} = \underline{\hspace{1cm}} \qquad \text{Simplify.}$$

$x - 3 + 4x = 5$ _____ be rewritten as $5x = 2$.

So, the equations have _____ solutions and are _____.

② $x + 7 = 12$ and $2x = 10$

> Check if both equations have the same solution.

First, solve $2x = 10$.

$$2x = 10$$

$$2x \div \underline{\hspace{1cm}} = 10 \div \underline{\hspace{1cm}}$$

$$x = \underline{\hspace{1cm}}$$

Then, check if $x = \underline{\hspace{1cm}}$ is the solution for the equation, $x + 7 = 12$.

If $x = \underline{\hspace{1cm}}$, $x + 7 = \underline{\hspace{1cm}} + 7$

$$= \underline{\hspace{1cm}}$$

Since the equations have the _____ solution, they are _____.

③ $1.2x = 2.4$ and $x - 6 = 8$

④ $0.2x = 0.6$ and $3x + 1 = 10$

⑤ $\frac{2}{5}x = 4$ and $x = 10$

INDEPENDENT PRACTICE

Determine whether each pair of equations are equivalent. Explain your answer.

1 $2x = 4$ and $4x + 5 = 13$

2 $-2x + 9 = 7$ and $-2x = 2$

3 $5x - 4 + 3x = 8$ and $8x = 12$

4 $\frac{3}{4}x - 7 = 2$ and $x = 12$

Match each equation with an equivalent equation.

5 $0.5x + 1 = 1.5$

a $6x = 9$

6 $9 + 3.5x = 16$

b $\frac{3}{5}x = \frac{1}{15}$

7 $\frac{4}{5}x = 4$

c $\frac{3}{2}x = 3$

8 $2x + \frac{1}{2} = \frac{7}{2}$

d $\frac{2}{3}x = \frac{2}{3}$

9 $x - 8.3 = 1.3$

e $2x = 10$

10 $13.9 = 2.5x$

f $1.2 + x = 6.76$

11 $4x = \frac{4}{9}$

g $\frac{1}{2}x = 4.8$

Solve.

12 **Mathematical Habit 3** Construct viable arguments

Chris was asked to write an equation equivalent to $\frac{2}{3}x = 3 - x$. He wrote the following:

$$\frac{2}{3}x = 3 - x$$

$$\frac{2}{3}x \cdot 3 = 3 \cdot 3 - x$$

$$2x = 9 - x$$

Chris concluded that $\frac{2}{3}x = 3 - x$ and $2x = 9 - x$ are equivalent equations.

Do you agree with his conclusion? Give a reason for your answer.

2 Solving Algebraic Equations

Learning Objectives:
- Solve algebraic equations with variables on the same side of the equation.
- Solve algebraic equations in factored form.

THINK

Find in the blank in the equation, $2x + 2(2x - \text{\_\_\_\_\_}) = 8$, so that $x < 2$.
Show how you find the answer.

ENGAGE

Use to represent $2x + 6 = 12$.

Share how you find the value of x.

Now, consider this problem.
At the bowling alley, the total cost of bowling is $6 per game plus $3 for shoes. On one visit, Eric spent $21 altogether. How many games did Eric bowl? Explain your thinking.

LEARN Solve algebraic equations

① To solve an equation means to find the value of the variable that makes the equation true.
You can add, subtract, multiply, or divide both sides of the equation by the same nonzero number to solve an equation. Our goal is to produce an equivalent equation in which the variable is alone, or "isolated" on one side of the equation.

For example, to solve $2x + 6 = 9$,

Balance	Algebraic Equation
■ represents 1 counter. x represents x counters.	Solve the equation by isolating the variable, x. Left side Equals Right side ↓ ↓ ↓ $2x + 6$ $=$ 9

Remove 6 counters from both sides.

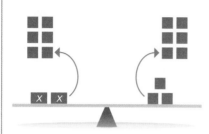

Divide each into two equal groups.

The counters on both sides are equal.

First, isolate the algebraic term, $2x$, on one side of the equation.

Decide which operation to use. Subtraction is the inverse of addition. To undo the addition of 6 to $2x$, subtract 6 from both sides of the equation.

$2x + 6 - 6 = 9 - 6$ Subtract 6 from both sides.
$2x = 3$ Simplify.

Then, isolate the variable, x. In other words, x will have a coefficient of 1.

Decide which operation to use. Division is the inverse of multiplication. To undo the multiplication of 2 and x, divide both sides of the equation by 2.

$2x \div 2 = 3 \div 2$ Divide both sides by 2.
$x = 1.5$ Simplify.

$x = 1.5$ gives the solution of the equation $2x + 6 = 9$.

Remember to keep an equation "balanced" by performing the same operation on both sides.

To check if $x = 1.5$ is the solution, substitute the value of $x = 1.5$ into the original equation.
$2x + 6 = 2 \cdot (1.5) + 6$
$= 9$

When $x = 1.5$, the equation $2x + 6 = 9$ is true.

When an expression in an algebraic equation involves more than one operation, you can use the order of operations "in reverse" to undo the operations and isolate the variable.

Steps for solving an equation:

 "Undo" addition or subtraction using inverse operations.

 "Undo" multiplication or division using inverse operations.

2 Solve $3x + 7 = 28$.

$$3x + 7 = 28$$
$3x + 7 - \mathbf{7} = 28 - \mathbf{7}$ Subtract 7 from both sides to undo addition.
$3x = 21$ Simplify.
$3x \div \mathbf{3} = 21 \div \mathbf{3}$ Divide both sides by 3 to undo multiplication.
$x = 7$ Simplify.

$x = 7$ gives the solution of the equation $3x + 7 = 28$.

Check
Substitute the value of $x = 7$ into the original equation.

$3x + 7 = 3 \cdot 7 + 7$
$= 28$

When $x = 7$, the equation $3x + 7 = 28$ is true.
$x = 7$ gives the solution.

3 Solve $0.5x + 1.5 = 4.5$.

$$0.5x + 1.5 = 4.5$$
$0.5x + 1.5 - \mathbf{1.5} = 4.5 - \mathbf{1.5}$ Subtract 1.5 from both sides.
$0.5x = 3$ Simplify.
$0.5x \cdot \mathbf{2} = 3 \cdot \mathbf{2}$ Multiply both sides by 2 to undo.
$x = 6$ Simplify.

$x = 6$ gives the solution of the equation $0.5x + 1.5 = 4.5$.

$0.5 = \dfrac{1}{2}$

$\dfrac{1}{2} \cdot 2 = 1$

Check
Substitute the value of $x = 6$ into the original equation.

$0.5x + 1.5 = 4.5 = 0.5 \cdot 6 + 1.5$
$= 4.5$

When $x = 6$, the equation $0.5x + 1.5 = 4.5$ is true.
$x = 6$ gives the solution.

④ Solve $\frac{1}{6}y - \frac{1}{3} = 2$.

> The term $\frac{1}{6}y$ can be written as $\frac{y}{6}$. There are two operations to undo: The subtraction of $\frac{1}{3}$ and the division by 6.

▶ **Method 1**
Solve by balancing the equation.

$$\frac{y}{6} - \frac{1}{3} = 2$$

$\frac{y}{6} - \frac{1}{3} + \frac{1}{3} = 2 + \frac{1}{3}$ Add $\frac{1}{3}$ to both sides.

$\frac{y}{6} = \frac{7}{3}$ Simplify.

$\mathbf{6} \cdot \left(\frac{y}{6}\right) = \mathbf{6} \cdot \left(\frac{7}{3}\right)$ Multiply both sides by 6, which is the reciprocal of the coefficient, $\frac{1}{6}$.

$y = 14$ Simplify.

▶ **Method 2**
Solve by balancing the equation.

$\mathbf{6} \cdot \left(\frac{y}{6} - \frac{1}{3}\right) = \mathbf{6} \cdot 2$ Multiply both sides by 6, the LCD of $\frac{1}{6}$ and $\frac{1}{3}$.

$6 \cdot \frac{y}{6} - 6 \cdot \frac{1}{3} = 6 \cdot 2$ Use the distributive property.

$y - 2 = 12$ Simplify.
$y - 2 + 2 = 12 + 2$ Add 2 to both sides.
$y = 14$ Simplify.

When $y = 14$, the equation $\frac{1}{6}y - \frac{1}{3} = 2$ is true.

$y = 14$ gives the solution of the equation $\frac{1}{6}y - \frac{1}{3} = 2$.

Math Note

When you multiply equations involving fractional coefficients by the LCD, the two sides of the equation will remain equal. This will result in equivalent equations that do not contain fractions.

Math Note

Multiplying and dividing rational numbers:

Two signs are the same:		Two signs are different:	
Multiplication	**Division**	**Multiplication**	**Division**
$(+) \cdot (+) = (+)$	$(+) \div (+) = (+)$	$(+) \cdot (-) = (-)$	$(+) \div (-) = (-)$
$(-) \cdot (-) = (+)$	$(-) \div (-) = (+)$	$(-) \cdot (+) = (-)$	$(-) \div (+) = (-)$
For example, $(-1) \cdot (-2) = 2$ and $1 \cdot 2 = 2$.		For example, $(-1) \cdot 2 = -2$, and $1 \cdot (-2) = -2$.	

TRY Practice solving algebraic equations

Solve.

1 $6x + 2 = 8$

$$6x + 2 = 8$$

$6x + 2 - \underline{\hspace{0.8cm}} = 8 - \underline{\hspace{0.8cm}}$ Subtract \underline{\hspace{0.8cm}} from both sides.

$\underline{\hspace{0.8cm}}x = \underline{\hspace{0.8cm}}$ Simplify.

$\dfrac{}{}x = \dfrac{}{}$ Divide both sides by \underline{\hspace{0.8cm}}.

$x = \underline{\hspace{0.8cm}}$ Simplify.

2 $3 - 7x = 10$

$$3 - 7x = 10$$

$3 - 7x - \underline{\hspace{0.8cm}} = 10 - \underline{\hspace{0.8cm}}$

$\underline{\hspace{0.8cm}} = \underline{\hspace{0.8cm}}$

$\underline{\hspace{0.8cm}} \div \underline{\hspace{0.8cm}} = \underline{\hspace{0.8cm}} \div \underline{\hspace{0.8cm}}$

$x = \underline{\hspace{0.8cm}}$

3 $5 - 3x = 20$

4 $4x - 3 + 0.5x = 1.5$

5 $\dfrac{9}{10}x - \dfrac{4}{5} = 1$

6 $\dfrac{9}{10} - \dfrac{4}{5}x = 1$

ENGAGE

Look at these equations.

a $2(x - 1)$ **b** $\dfrac{1}{2}(x + 1)$ **c** $3x + 4(x - 1)$

How do you expand the expressions? What do you get? Discuss.

Riley says using the above results, she can solve the following equations.

a $2(x - 1) = 5$ **b** $\dfrac{1}{2}(x + 1) = 3$ **c** $3x + 4(x - 1) = 10$

Do you agree or disagree? Explain your thinking.

LEARN Solve algebraic equations in factored form

① Solve $2(3x + 1) = 11$.

▶ **Method 1**
Use the distributive property and inverse operations.

First, use the distributive property to expand the expression.

$$2(3x + 1) = 11$$
$$2 \cdot 3x + 2 \cdot 1 = 11 \quad \text{Use the distributive property.}$$
$$6x + 2 = 11 \quad \text{Simplify.}$$

Then, isolate the algebraic term.

$$6x + 2 - \mathbf{2} = 11 - \mathbf{2} \quad \text{Subtract 2 from both sides.}$$
$$6x = 9 \quad \text{Simplify.}$$

Finally, isolate the variable.

$$6x \div \mathbf{6} = 9 \div \mathbf{6} \quad \text{Divide both sides by 6.}$$
$$x = 1.5 \quad \text{Simplify. Express in simplest form.}$$

▶ **Method 2**
Use inverse operations.

First, divide both sides by 2 to "undo" the multiplication.

$$2(3x + 1) = 11$$
$$\frac{2(3x + 1)}{\mathbf{2}} = \frac{11}{\mathbf{2}} \quad \text{Divide both sides by 2.}$$
$$3x + 1 = 5.5 \quad \text{Simplify.}$$

Then, isolate the algebraic term.

$$3x + 1 - \mathbf{1} = 5.5 - \mathbf{1} \quad \text{Subtract 1 from both sides.}$$
$$3x = 4.5 \quad \text{Simplify.}$$

Finally, isolate the variable.

$$3x \div \mathbf{3} = 4.5 \div \mathbf{3} \quad \text{Divide both sides by 3.}$$
$$x = 1.5 \quad \text{Simplify. Express in simplest form.}$$

> To simplify $\frac{2(3x + 1)}{2}$, think of $(3x + 1)$ as a single number. Just as $\frac{2x}{2} = x$, so does $\frac{2(3x + 1)}{2} = 3x + 1$.

② Solve $\frac{1}{6}(z + 1) = 6$.

▶ **Method 1**

Use the distributive property and inverse operations.

$$\frac{1}{6}(z + 1) = 6$$

$$\frac{1}{6} \cdot z + \frac{1}{6} \cdot 1 = 6 \qquad \text{Use the distributive property.}$$

$$\frac{1}{6}z + \frac{1}{6} = 6 \qquad \text{Simplify.}$$

$$\frac{1}{6}z + \frac{1}{6} - \frac{1}{6} = \frac{36}{6} - \frac{1}{6} \qquad \text{Subtract } \frac{1}{6} \text{ from both sides. Rewrite 6 as } \frac{36}{6}.$$

$$\frac{1}{6}z = \frac{35}{6} \qquad \text{Simplify.}$$

$$6 \cdot \frac{1}{6}z = 6 \cdot \frac{35}{6} \qquad \text{Multiply both sides by 6.}$$

$$z = 35 \qquad \text{Simplify.}$$

▶ **Method 2**

Use inverse operations.

$$\frac{1}{6}(z + 1) = 6$$

$$6 \cdot \frac{1}{6}(z + 1) = 6 \cdot 6 \qquad \text{Multiply both sides by 6.}$$

$$z + 1 = 36 \qquad \text{Simplify.}$$

$$z + 1 - 1 = 36 - 1 \qquad \text{Subtract 1 from both sides.}$$

$$z = 35 \qquad \text{Simplify.}$$

③ Solve $1.5(w + 2) + 2 = 8$.

$$1.5(w + 2) + 2 = 8$$

$$1.5 \cdot w + 1.5 \cdot 2 + 2 = 8 \qquad \text{Use the distributive property.}$$

$$1.5w + 5 = 8 \qquad \text{Simplify.}$$

$$1.5w + 5 - 5 = 8 - 5 \qquad \text{Subtract 5 from both sides.}$$

$$1.5w = 3 \qquad \text{Simplify.}$$

$$1.5w \div 1.5 = 3 \div 1.5 \qquad \text{Divide both sides by 1.5.}$$

$$w = 2 \qquad \text{Simplify.}$$

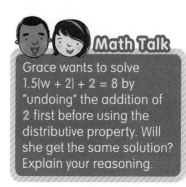

Math Talk

Grace wants to solve $1.5(w + 2) + 2 = 8$ by "undoing" the addition of 2 first before using the distributive property. Will she get the same solution? Explain your reasoning.

4 Solve $2x + 5(2 - x) = 40$.

> There is more than one way to solve this equation. Suppose you first divide each term by 5:
>
> $$2x \div 5 + 5(2 - x) \div 5 = 40 \div 5$$
>
> $$\frac{2}{5}x + (2 - x) = 8$$
>
> $$\frac{2}{5}x + 2 - x = 8$$
>
> $$-\frac{3}{5}x + 2 = 8$$
>
> Then, you have to solve an equation involving a variable with a negative fractional coefficient. A better method is to use the distributive property first.

$2x + 5(2 - x) = 40$	
$2x + 5 \cdot 2 - 5 \cdot x = 40$	Use the distributive property.
$2x + 10 - 5x = 40$	Simplify.
$10 - 3x = 40$	Subtract the like terms.
$10 - 3x - 10 = 40 - 10$	Subtract 10 from both sides.
$-3x = 30$	Simplify.
$-\dfrac{3x}{-3} = \dfrac{30}{-3}$	Divide both sides by -3.
$x = -10$	Simplify.

TRY **Practice solving algebraic equations in factored form**

Solve each equation. Check your solutions.

1 $1.5(p + 3) = 18$

2 $\frac{1}{4}(q + 1) = 9$

3 $2(x - 3) + 2 = 14$

4 $3(y - 1) + y = 1$

INDEPENDENT PRACTICE

Solve each equation with variables on the same side.

1 $4b - 2 = 6$

2 $5x + 4 = 24$

3 $7c - 11 = 17$

4 $18 = 3k - 3$

5 $\frac{a}{4} - 1 = 3$

6 $\frac{2}{3}v = 2 - \frac{4}{3}$

7 $\frac{5}{2}y + 8 = 18$

8 $\frac{3}{5}f - \frac{4}{5} = \frac{2}{5}$

9 $4.5 + 0.2p = 6.1$

10 $1.5d + 3.2 = 9.2$

11 $0.8w - 4 = 4$

12 $1.4z - 0.5 = 3.7$

Answer the question.

13 **Mathematical Habit 6** Use precise mathematical language

Tara was asked to solve the equation $-4p + 5 = 7$. Her solution is shown.

$$-4p + 5 = 7$$
$$-4p + 5 - 5 = 7 - 5$$
$$-4p = 2$$
$$p = \frac{1}{2}$$

Tara concluded that $p = \frac{1}{2}$ is the solution of the equation $-4p + 5 = 7$.

Describe and correct the error Tara made.

Solve each equation involving parentheses.

14 $7(2z + 1) = 35$

15 $18 = 6(5 - g)$

16 $\frac{1}{5}(3r - 4) = \frac{2}{5}$

17 $\frac{1}{8}(5x + 4) = \frac{3}{4}$

18 $0.3(k - 0.2) = 0.6$

19 $3(1.2b - 1) + 3.6 = 4.2$

20 $0.7(h + 2) + 1.6 = 17$

21 $2(a - 1) - 5a = 7$

22 $\frac{1}{4}(w - 4) - \frac{3}{4}w = 3$

23 $\frac{1}{6}s - \frac{1}{2}(s - 2) = \frac{45}{2}$

Answer the question.

24 **Mathematical Habit 6** Use precise mathematical language

Alex solved the algebraic equation $3(2x + 5) = 17$ as shown below:

$$3(2x + 5) = 17$$
$$3(2x + 5) - 5 = 17 - 5$$
$$3(2x) = 12$$
$$6x = 12$$
$$6x \div 6 = 12 \div 6$$
$$x = 2$$

Describe and correct the error Alex made.

3 Real-World Problems: Algebraic Equations

Learning Objective:
• Solve real-world problems algebraically.

THINK

Ethan ran at an average speed of 12 km/h for 15 minutes, and then continued to walk for half an hour at a certain average speed. If his average speed for the entire journey is 6 km/h, how can you find his average walking speed algebraically? How do you check your answer? Explain.

ENGAGE

A photo frame has a border of x inches. It surrounds a photograph that is placed within it. A photograph measuring 5 inches by 7 inches can fit in neatly without any white space. What are the dimensions of the frame? Draw a sketch to show your thinking.

If the outer perimeter of the frame is 28 inches, use an equation to model the situation. Share and explain how you find the width of the frame border.

LEARN Solve real-world problems algebraically

1 Evelyn framed a drawing as shown. The border of the frame is x inches wide. The dimensions of the drawing are 12 inches by 5 inches. If the outer perimeter of the frame is 58 inches, find the width of the frame border.

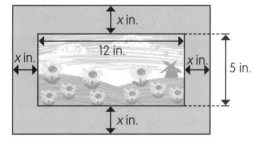

 STEP 1 Understand the problem.

What are the dimensions of the drawing?
What are the dimensions of the frame?
What is the outer perimeter of the frame?
What do I need to find?

STEP 2 Think of a plan.
I can use algebraic reasoning to translate the problem into algebraic expressions.

 STEP 3 Carry out the plan.
Using the diagram, write algebraic expressions for the dimensions of the frame.

Length of the frame: $12 + 2x$
Width of the frame: $5 + 2x$

Then, write an algebraic equation.

$2(\ell + w) = \text{Perimeter}$	Write a perimeter formula.
$2(12 + 2x + 5 + 2x) = 58$	Substitute.
$2(17 + 4x) = 58$	Add like terms.

Finally, solve the equation.

$2 \cdot 17 + 2 \cdot 4x = 58$	Use the distributive property.
$34 + 8x = 58$	Simplify.
$34 + 8x - 34 = 58 - 34$	Subtract 34 from both sides.
$8x = 24$	Simplify.
$\dfrac{8x}{8} = \dfrac{24}{8}$	Divide both sides by 8.
$x = 3$	Simplify.

The border of the frame is 3 inches wide.

 STEP 4 Check the answer.
I can substitute $x = 3$ into the dimensions of the frame to check my answer.

Length of frame $= 12 + 2x$ Width of frame $= 5 + 2x$
$\qquad\qquad\qquad = 12 + 2(3)$ $\qquad\qquad\qquad\quad = 5 + 2(3)$
$\qquad\qquad\qquad = 18$ in. $\qquad\qquad\qquad\qquad = 11$ in.

$2(18) + 2(11) = 36 + 22$
$\qquad\qquad\qquad = 58$ in.
$\qquad\qquad\qquad = \text{Outer perimeter of frame}$

My answer is correct.

2 Luis wrote a riddle: A positive number is $\frac{1}{3}$ of another positive number. If their difference is 48, find the two positive numbers.

Solve using algebraic reasoning.

Let one of the numbers be x.   Define the variable.

Then, the other number is $\frac{1}{3}x$.   Write the other number in terms of the variable.

Since $x > \frac{1}{3}x$ and their difference is 48, I can write $x - \frac{1}{3}x = 48$.

Find one of the numbers, x:

$x - \frac{1}{3}x = 48$ Write an equation.

$\frac{3}{3}x - \frac{1}{3}x = 48$ Rewrite x as $\frac{3}{3}x$.

$\frac{2}{3}x = 48$ Simplify.

$\frac{2}{3}x \cdot \frac{3}{2} = 48 \cdot \frac{3}{2}$ Multiply both sides by the reciprocal of $\frac{2}{3}$.

$x = 72$ Simplify.

Find the other number: $\frac{1}{3}x = \frac{1}{3} \cdot 72$ Evaluate $\frac{1}{3}x$ when $x = 72$.

$= 24$

The two positive numbers are 72 and 24.

Check:

$\frac{72}{3} = 24$

24 is $\frac{1}{3}$ of 72. ✓

$72 - 24 = 48$ ✓

The difference between the two numbers is 48.

The two positive numbers, 72 and 24, are correct.

3 A theater is divided into a red section and a blue section. The red section has 350 seats, and the rest of the seats are in the blue section. A ticket for a red section seat costs $75, and a ticket for a blue section seat costs $50.

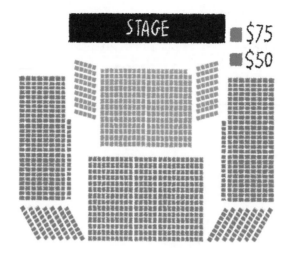

a Write an expression for the total amount collected from the sale of tickets for all the seats in the two sections.

Let x represent the number of blue section tickets.   Define the variable.

> Total sales from 350 red section tickets: $75 \cdot 350 = 26{,}250$
> Total sales from x blue section tickets: $50 \cdot x = 50x$
> Total sales equal sales of red section tickets plus sales of blue section tickets.

The total sales are $(26{,}250 + 50x)$ dollars.

b The total sales when all the tickets are sold are $68,750.
How many seats are in the blue section?

$$26{,}250 + 50x = 68{,}750 \qquad \text{Write an equation.}$$
$$26{,}250 + 50x - \mathbf{26{,}250} = 68{,}750 - \mathbf{26{,}250} \qquad \text{Subtract 26,250 from both sides.}$$
$$50x = 42{,}500 \qquad \text{Simplify.}$$
$$\frac{50x}{50} = \frac{42{,}500}{50} \qquad \text{Divide both sides by 50.}$$
$$x = 850 \qquad \text{Simplify.}$$

There are 850 seats in the blue section.

4   Ivan has 12 more comic books than Hana. If they have 28 comic books altogether, how many comic books does Ivan have?

Hana has **some** comic books. Ivan has **12 more than** Hana.
      ?   (? + 12)
They have **28 books altogether**.
      ? + (? + 12) = 28

Let the number of comic books that Hana has be x.
Then, the number of comic books that Ivan has is $x + 12$.

Define the variable.

Because they have 28 comic books altogether,

$$x + (x + 12) = 28$$
$$2x + 12 = 28$$
$$2x + 12 - 12 = 28 - 12$$
$$2x = 16$$
$$\frac{2x}{2} = \frac{16}{2}$$
$$x = 8$$

Write an equation.
Simplify.
Subtract 12 from both sides.
Simplify.

Divide both sides by 2.

Simplify.

Number of books that Ivan has: $x + 12 = 8 + 12$
$$= 20$$

Evaluate $x + 12$ when $x = 8$.

Ivan has 20 comic books.

Solve.

1 Matt wrote a riddle: A negative number is $\frac{2}{5}$ of another negative number. If the sum of the two negative numbers is -35, find the two negative numbers.

Let one of the numbers be x.

Then, the other number is $\frac{2}{5}x$.

> Since the sum of the numbers is -35, write
>
> _____ + _____ $= -35$. Then, solve the equation.

$$\text{\_\_\_\_} + \text{\_\_\_\_} = -35 \qquad \text{Write an equation.}$$

$$\text{\_\_\_\_} \, x = -35 \qquad \text{Add the like terms.}$$

$$\text{\_\_\_\_} x \cdot \text{\_\_\_\_} = \text{\_\_\_\_} \cdot \text{\_\_\_\_} \qquad \text{Multiply both sides by the reciprocal of \_\_\_\_.}$$

$$x = \text{\_\_\_\_} \qquad \text{Simplify.}$$

The other number: $\frac{2}{5}x = \frac{2}{5} \cdot$ _____   Evaluate $\frac{2}{5}x$ when $x =$ _____.

$$= \text{\_\_\_\_}$$

The two negative numbers are _____ and _____.

2 At an auditorium, tickets are sold for "circle seats" and "row seats." There are 220 circle seats, and the rest of the seats are row seats. Each circle seat ticket costs $100 and each row seat ticket costs $60.

a Write an expression for the total amount collected from the sale of all the seats at the auditorium.

Let x represent the number of row seat tickets.

Total sales from 220 circle seats $=$ _____ $\times$ _____

$$= \text{_____} \text{ dollars}$$

Total sales from x row seats $= x \cdot$ _____

$$= \text{_____} \, x \text{ dollars}$$

Total sales of all seats $= ($_____ $+$ _____ $x)$ dollars

The total amount collected from the sale of all the seats is _____ dollars.

b The total amount collected when all the tickets are sold is $68,800. How many row seat tickets are sold?

$$\underline{\hspace{1.5cm}} + \underline{\hspace{1.5cm}}\, x = 68{,}800$$

$$\underline{\hspace{1.5cm}} + \underline{\hspace{1.5cm}}\, x - \underline{\hspace{1.5cm}} = 68{,}800 - \underline{\hspace{1.5cm}}$$

$$\underline{\hspace{1.5cm}}\, x = \underline{\hspace{1.5cm}}$$

$$\underline{\hspace{1.5cm}}\, x \div \underline{\hspace{1.5cm}} = \underline{\hspace{1.5cm}} \div \underline{\hspace{1.5cm}}$$

$$x = \underline{\hspace{1.5cm}}$$

The number of row seat tickets sold is \underline{\hspace{1.5cm}}.

③ Fred has 16 more game cards than Sofia. If they have 48 game cards altogether, find the number of game cards Fred has.

Let the number of cards that Sofia has be x.

Then, the number of cards that Fred has is $x \bigcirc 16$.

Since they have 48 cards altogether,

$$x \bigcirc (x \bigcirc 16) = \underline{\hspace{1cm}}$$

$$\underline{\hspace{0.5cm}}\, x \bigcirc 16 = \underline{\hspace{1cm}}$$

$$\underline{\hspace{0.5cm}}\, x \bigcirc 16 \bigcirc \underline{\hspace{0.5cm}} = \underline{\hspace{0.5cm}} \bigcirc \underline{\hspace{0.5cm}}$$

$$\underline{\hspace{0.5cm}}\, x = \underline{\hspace{0.5cm}}$$

$$\underline{\hspace{0.5cm}}\, x \bigcirc \underline{\hspace{0.5cm}} = \underline{\hspace{0.5cm}} \bigcirc \underline{\hspace{0.5cm}}$$

$$x = \underline{\hspace{0.5cm}}$$

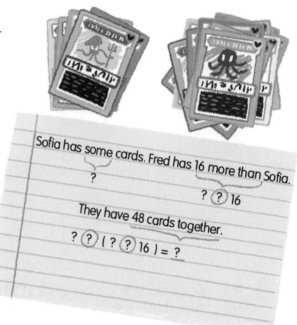

Sofia has some cards. Fred has 16 more than Sofia.

?

? ? 16

They have 48 cards together.

? ? (? ? 16) = ?

Number of cards that Fred has:

$$x \bigcirc 16 = \underline{\hspace{1cm}} \bigcirc 16$$

$$= \underline{\hspace{1cm}}$$

Fred has \underline{\hspace{1cm}} game cards.

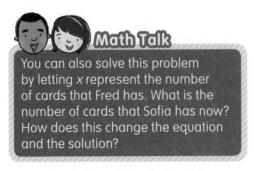

Math Talk

You can also solve this problem by letting x represent the number of cards that Fred has. What is the number of cards that Sofia has now? How does this change the equation and the solution?

4. A bike shop charges *x* dollars to rent a bike for half a day. It charges (*x* + 40) dollars to rent a bike for a full day. The table shows the shop's bike rentals for one day. On that day, the shop made a total of $600 from bike rentals.

Time Period	Amount ($)	Number of Bikes
Half day	x	5
Full day	x + 40	3

How much does it cost to rent a bike for a full day?

5. An artist is weaving a rectangular wall hanging. The wall hanging is already 18 inches long, and the artist plans to weave an additional 2 inches each day. The finished wall hanging will be 60 inches long. How many days will it take the artist to finish the wall hanging?

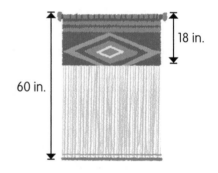

18 in.

60 in.

6. Ms. Lopez plans to buy a laptop for $1,345 in 12 weeks. She has already saved $145. How much should she save each week so she can buy the laptop?

INDEPENDENT PRACTICE

Solve.

1. Two sections of a garden are shaped like identical isosceles triangles. The base of each triangle is 50 feet, and the other two sides are each x feet long. If the combined perimeter of both gardens is 242 feet, find the value of x.

 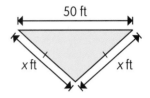

2. Mr. Carter has a rectangular plot of land that is 525 feet long and y feet wide. He decides to build a fence around the plot. If the perimeter of the plot is 1,504 feet, find the value of y.

3. The diagram shows an artificial lake. When Emma jogged twice around the lake, she jogged a distance of 2,700 meters. Find the value of x.

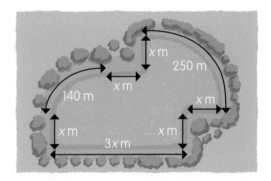

4. Sara wants to trim a lampshade with braid. The lampshade is shaped like a rectangular prism. The length of the base of the lampshade is 4 inches greater than its width. If the perimeter of the base is 54 inches, find the length of the base.

5 Demi was given a riddle to solve: The sum of two consecutive positive integers is 71. Find the two positive integers.

6 The sum of a negative number, $\frac{1}{4}$ of the negative number, and $\frac{7}{16}$ of the negative number is $-13\frac{1}{2}$. What is the negative number?

7 Kevin wrote a riddle: A positive number is 5 less than another positive number. 6 times the lesser number minus 3 times the greater number is 3. Find the two positive numbers.

8 At a charity basketball game, 450 tickets were sold to students at a school. The remaining x tickets were sold to the public. The prices of the two types of tickets are shown. When all the tickets were sold, $10,500 was collected. How many tickets were sold to the public?

9 Harry ordered pizzas for a party and organized the information into a table. If Harry paid a total of $93.65, how many mushroom pizzas did he order?

Type of Pizza	Number of Pizzas	Price of One Pizza
Mushroom	x	$13.95
Vegetarian	2	$11.95

10 Bruno saved some dimes and quarters to buy a gift for his mother. He counted his savings and organized the information in a table.

Type of Coins	Number of Coins	Value of One Coin
Dime	x	$0.10
Quarter	x – 12	$0.25

If Bruno saved $11, how many dimes and quarters did he have?

11 A plant grows at a rate of 4.5 centimeters per week. It is now 12 centimeters tall. Suppose that the plant continues to grow at the same rate. In how many weeks will it reach a height of 48 centimeters?

12 Mr. Evans is currently 4 times as old as his son, Dan. If Mr. Evans was 46 years old 2 years ago, how old is Dan now?

13 Mr. Martin drove from Townsville to Villaville and back again at the speeds shown. His total driving time was 12 hours. How far apart are the two towns?

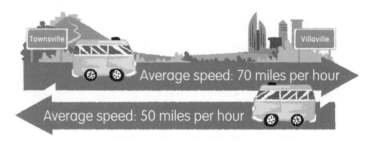

14 A factory made 845 pairs of shoes in January. These shoes were sent to 3 shoe stores and 1 outlet mall. The number of pairs of shoes sent to each shoe store was 4 times the number sent to the outlet mall. How many pairs of shoes were sent to the outlet mall in January?

15 The cost of seeing a weekday show is $\frac{2}{3}$ the cost of a weekend show. In one month, Alex spent $42.50 for 4 weekday shows and 3 weekend shows. Find the price of a weekday show and the price of a weekend show.

Solving Algebraic Inequalities

Learning Objectives:
- Solve algebraic inequalities.
- Graph the solution set of an inequality on a number line.
- Solve multi-step algebraic inequalities.

New Vocabulary
solution set
equivalent inequalities

THINK

Which of the following inequalities is equivalent to $8 + 2(1 - 4y) < 8$?
$8 - 4y > 7$ or $4y + 3 > 4$

ENGAGE

Draw a balance scale to represent $x > 2$.

What are the possible values of x? Draw a number line to support your answer.

What happens if you add 1 to both sides of the balance scale? What happens if you take away 1 from both sides of the balance scale? Explain your thinking.

If $x < -2$, what are the possible values of x? What operations could you carry out on both sides of the inequality so that it remains true? Substitute possible values of x to justify your answers.

LEARN   Solve and graph the solution sets of algebraic inequalities using addition and subtraction

1. An inequality is a mathematical statement that compares two numbers or expressions that are not equal or may not be equal. An inequality symbol such as >, <, ≥, ≤, or ≠ is used to make the comparison.

   Examples: $-3 < 5$, $-0.5 > -2$, $x < 6$, $3x \geq 12$, $x \neq 0$

   The solutions of an inequality are all of the values of the variable that make the inequality true. These values are also called the solution set of an inequality.

   Consider the inequality $x + 3 > 4$.

   ▶ **Method 1**
   Solve by substitution.

   When $x = 0$, $x + 3 = 0 + 3$
                    $= 3$
   The inequality $x + 3 > 4$ is false.

When $x = 1$,　　$x + 3 = 1 + 3$
　　　　　　　　　　　　$= 4$
The inequality $x + 3 > 4$ is false.

When $x = 1.1$,　　$x + 3 = 1.1 + 3$
　　　　　　　　　　　　$= 4.1$
$x + 3 > 4$ is true.

When $x = 2$,　　$x + 3 = 2 + 3$
　　　　　　　　　　　　$= 5$
$x + 3 > 4$ is true.

When $x = 3$,　　$x + 3 = 3 + 3$
　　　　　　　　　　　　$= 6$
$x + 3 > 4$ is true, and so on.

> The solutions of an inequality such as $x + 3 > 4$ always form a set of values. It is not just one value, unlike most equations.

So, when $x > 1$, the inequality $x + 3 > 4$ is true. The solution set is $x > 1$.

▶ **Method 2**

Solve by using inverse operations.

When you perform addition or subtraction on both sides of an inequality, the solution set of the inequality is still the same. You can use inverse operations to solve inequalities.

Solve the inequality $x + 3 > 4$.

Balance	Algebraic Equation
■ represents 1 counter. X represents x counters. *(balance diagrams)*	$x + 3 > 4$ Solve the inequality by using inverse operations to isolate the variable. Decide which operation to use. To undo the addition of 3 to x, you subtract 3 from both sides. $x + 3 - 3 > 4 - 3$　　Subtract 3 from both sides. $\qquad x > 1$　　　　Simplify.

The solution set is $x > 1$. The inequalities $x + 3 > 4$ and $x > 1$ are **equivalent inequalities** because the same set of values make both inequalities true.

2 When you solve an inequality such as $0 \geq y - 3$, you are finding the solution set that makes the inequality true. You can graph the solution set of the inequality on a number line after you have solved it.

$$0 \geq y - 3$$
$$0 + \mathbf{3} \geq y - 3 + \mathbf{3} \qquad \text{Add 3 to both sides.}$$
$$3 \geq y \qquad\qquad \text{Solution set.}$$

The solution set $3 \geq y$ means that the value of y is less than or equal to 3. You can rewrite $3 \geq y$ as $y \leq 3$. The inequality symbol still opens towards 3 and points to y. So, $y \leq 3$ and $3 \geq y$ are equivalent inequalities.

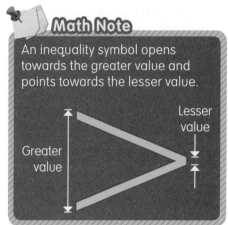

Math Note

An inequality symbol opens towards the greater value and points towards the lesser value.

Greater value

Lesser value

You can change the direction of the inequality symbol in the solution set $3 \geq y$ to help you graph the solution of the original inequality $0 \geq y - 3$.

$y \leq 3$ Switch sides and change direction.

The solution set is $y \leq 3$ and it can be represented on a number line as follows:

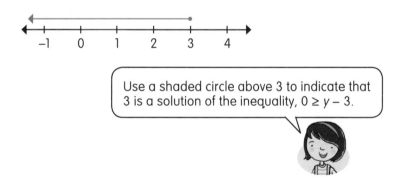

Use a shaded circle above 3 to indicate that 3 is a solution of the inequality, $0 \geq y - 3$.

To check the solution of an equation, you can substitute one value into the original equation to see if it is true. But you cannot check all the solutions of an inequality.

Instead, you can check the solution set by choosing some convenient values from the solution set, $y \geq 3$. You can substitute these values into the original inequality, $0 \geq y - 3$.

Check

When $y = 2.8$,

$y - 3 = 2.8 - 3$ Evaluate $y - 3$ when $y = 2.8$.
     $= -0.2$ (≤ 0) 2.8 is in the solution set.

When $y = 3$,

$y - 3 = 3 - 3$ Evaluate $y - 3$ when $y = 3$.
     $= 0$ (≤ 0) 3 is also in the solution set.

The original inequality, $0 \geq y - 3$, is true for any value of $y \leq 3$.

$y \leq 3$ is the correct solution set.

> If you substitute a value greater than 3, then the inequality $y - 3 \leq 0$ is not true. For example, if $y = 4$, then $4 - 3 = 1$. Since 1 is not less than or equal to 0, $y = 4$ is not in the solution set.

3   Solve the inequality $12 - y > 3$ and graph the solution set on a number line.

$\begin{aligned} 12 - y &> 3 \\ 12 - y + y &> 3 + y && \text{Add } y \text{ on both sides.} \\ 12 &> 3 + y && \text{Simplify.} \\ 12 - 3 &> 3 + y - 3 && \text{Subtract 3 on both sides.} \\ 9 &> y && \text{Simplify.} \\ y &< 9 && \text{Rewrite.} \end{aligned}$

The solution set is $y < 9$ and it can be represented on a number line as follows:

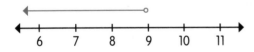

> Since $y < 9$, we use an empty circle above 9 to indicate that 9 is not a solution of the inequality. To check the solution set, substitute any value less than 9 into the original inequality. For example, you can choose $y = 0$, the most convenient number.

Check

Substitute the value of $y = 0$ into the original inequality.

$$12 - y = 12 - 0 \quad \text{Evaluate } 12 - y \text{ when } y = 0.$$
$$ = 12 \; (> 3) \quad \text{0 is in the solution set.}$$

The original inequality, $12 - y > 3$, is true for any value of $y < 9$.

$y < 9$ is the solution set.

TRY Practice solving and graphing the solution sets of algebraic inequalities using addition and subtraction

Solve each inequality and graph the solution set on a number line.

1 $x - 8 \geq 15$

2 $m + 11 < 26$

3 $6 + y \leq 2$

4 $13 < p - 5$

Consider the inequality 6 > 4.

What happens if you multiply both sides of the inequality by 2? What happens if you divide both sides of the inequality by 2? Explain your thinking.

Now, what happens if you multiply or divide both sides of the inequality by –2? Explain your thinking.

Write another inequality involving two numbers. Do the conclusions that you have drawn above apply to your inequality? Discuss.

LEARN **Solve and graph the solution sets of algebraic inequalities using multiplication and division**

Activity Exploring division and multiplication properties of an inequality

Work in pairs.

① Fill in the table. Use the symbols > or <.

Mathematical Operation	Number	Inequality Symbol	Number
You know that	16	>	8
Divide by – 2	$\frac{16}{-2} = -8$		$\frac{8}{-2} = -4$
Divide by 2	$\frac{16}{2} = 8$		$\frac{8}{2} = 4$
Divide by – 4	$\frac{16}{-4} = -4$		$\frac{8}{-4} = -2$
Divide by 4	$\frac{16}{4} = 4$		$\frac{8}{4} = 2$
Divide by – 8	$\frac{16}{-8} = -2$		$\frac{8}{-8} = -1$
Divide by 8	$\frac{16}{8} = 2$		$\frac{8}{8} = 1$

a **Mathematical Habit 8 Look for patterns**
What happens to the direction of the inequality symbol when you divide by a positive number? Based on your observation, write a rule for dividing both sides of an inequality by a positive number.

b **Mathematical Habit 8** Look for patterns

What happens to the direction of the inequality symbol when you divide by a negative number? Based on your observation, write a rule for dividing both sides of an inequality by a negative number.

② Fill in the table. Use the symbols > or <.

Mathematical Operation	Number	Inequality Symbol	Number
You know that	4	<	7
Multiply by – 2	$4 \cdot (-2) = -8$		$7 \cdot (-2) = -14$
Multiply by 2	$4 \cdot 2 = 8$		$7 \cdot 2 = 14$
Multiply by – 3	$4 \cdot (-3) = -12$		$7 \cdot (-3) = -21$
Multiply by 3	$4 \cdot 3 = 12$		$7 \cdot 3 = 21$
Multiply by – 5	$4 \cdot (-5) = -20$		$7 \cdot (-5) = -35$
Multiply by 5	$4 \cdot 5 = 20$		$7 \cdot 5 = 35$

a **Mathematical Habit 8** Look for patterns

What happens to the direction of the inequality symbol when you multiply by a positive number? Based on your observation, write a rule for multiplying both sides of an inequality by a positive number.

b **Mathematical Habit 8** Look for patterns

What happens to the direction of the inequality symbol when you multiply by a negative number? Based on your observation, write a rule for multiplying both sides of an inequality by a negative number.

1 When you multiply or divide both sides of an inequality by the **same positive number**, the inequality symbol remains in the **same direction** for the inequality to be true. When you multiply or divide both sides of an inequality by the **same negative number**, you **reverse the direction** of the inequality symbol for the inequality to be true.

You can apply these rules when we solve an algebraic inequality such as $6x < -24$.

$6x < -24$

$\dfrac{6x}{6} < \dfrac{-24}{6}$ Divide both sides by 6.

$x < -4$ Simplify.

The solution set of the inequality $6x < -24$ can be represented on a number line as shown:

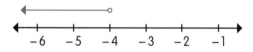

You can check that $x < -4$ is the solution by checking to see if values smaller than -4 make the original inequality $6x < -24$ true:
If $x = -5$, then $6 \cdot -5 < -24$ (true)
If $x = -6$, then $6 \cdot -6 < -24$ (true)

If you substitute a value more than or equal to -4, then the original inequality $6x < -24$ is not true.
For example, if $x = -3$, then $6 \cdot -3 = -18$.
-18 is greater than -24, not less than -24.

2 Solve the inequality $-5y \le -10$ and graph the solution set on a number line.

$-5y \le -10$

$\dfrac{-5y}{-5} \ge \dfrac{-10}{-5}$ Divide both sides by -5 and reverse the inequality symbol.

$y \ge 2$ Simplify.

The solution set of the inequality $-5y \le -10$ can be represented on a number line as follows:

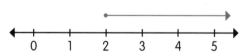

③ Solve the inequality $-\frac{1}{2}p \geq 3$ and graph the solution set on a number line.

$$-\frac{1}{2}p \geq 3$$

$$-\frac{1}{2}p \cdot (-2) \leq 3 \cdot (-2)$$ Multiply both sides by -2 and reverse the inequality symbol. Simplify.

$$p \leq -6$$

The solution set can be represented on a number line as shown:

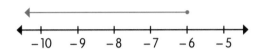

Math Note

The reciprocal of a negative number $-\frac{a}{b}$ is the negative number $-\frac{b}{a}$, because $\left(-\frac{a}{b}\right) \cdot \left(-\frac{b}{a}\right) = 1$. So, the reciprocal of $-\frac{1}{2}$ is $-\frac{2}{1}$, or simply -2.

TRY Practice solving and graphing the solution sets of algebraic inequalities using multiplication and division

Solve each inequality and graph the solution set on a number line.

① $8a \leq 48$

② $\frac{1}{5}w \geq 2$

③ $-7m > 21$

④ $6 > -0.3y$

ENGAGE

Consider the inequality $5 + 2x < 17$.

Make a list of numbers less than 17 and work backward to find the possible values of x. Share your method.

How is solving the equation $5 + 2x = 17$ similar to solving $5 + 2x < 17$? How is it different? Discuss.

LEARN Solve multi-step algebraic inequalities

1 You can use the same methods you use to solve multi-step equations to solve and then graph multi-step inequalities. Your goal is to isolate the variable on one side of the inequality.

Solve $3a - 7 > 26$ by using inverse operations.

First, isolate the algebraic term.

$$3a - 7 > 26$$
$$3a - 7 + 7 > 26 + 7 \quad \text{Add 7 to both sides.}$$
$$3a > 33 \quad \text{Simplify.}$$

Then, isolate the variable.

$$\frac{3a}{3} > \frac{33}{3} \quad \text{Divide both sides by 3.}$$
$$a > 11 \quad \text{Simplify.}$$

The solution set is $a > 11$.

The solution set can be represented on a number line as follows:

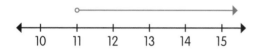

2 Solve the inequality $\frac{4}{5}x + 1 > 1\frac{3}{5}$ and graph the solution set on a number line.

$$\frac{4}{5}x + 1 > 1\frac{3}{5}$$
$$\frac{4}{5}x + 1 - 1 > 1\frac{3}{5} - 1 \quad \text{Subtract 1 from both sides.}$$
$$\frac{4}{5}x > \frac{3}{5} \quad \text{Simplify.}$$
$$\frac{4}{5}x \cdot \frac{5}{4} > \frac{3}{5} \cdot \frac{5}{4} \quad \text{Multiply both sides by } \frac{5}{4}, \text{ which is the reciprocal of } \frac{4}{5}.$$
$$x > \frac{3}{4} \quad \text{Simplify.}$$

The solution set can be represented on a number line as shown:

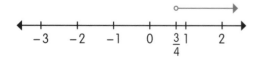

Remember to check your solution set. You can substitute any value within the solution set into the original inequality.

© 2020 Marshall Cavendish Education Pte Ltd

③ Solve the inequality $9 - 0.2a \geq 21$ and graph the solution set on a number line.

$$9 - 0.2a \geq 21$$
$$9 - 0.2a - \mathbf{9} \geq 21 - \mathbf{9} \qquad \text{Subtract 9 from both sides.}$$
$$-0.2a \geq 12 \qquad \text{Simplify.}$$
$$\frac{-0.2a}{-\mathbf{0.2}} \leq \frac{12}{-\mathbf{0.2}} \qquad \text{Divide both sides by } -0.2 \text{ and reverse the inequality symbol.}$$
$$a \leq -60 \qquad \text{Simplify.}$$

> Reverse the direction of the inequality symbol when you multiply or divide both sides of the inequality by the same negative number.

The solution set can be represented on a number line as shown:

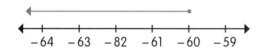

$$-64 \quad -63 \quad -82 \quad -61 \quad -60 \quad -59$$

④ Solve the inequality $2(3 - x) \leq 8$ and graph the solution set on a number line.

▶ **Method 1**
Use the distributive property and inverse operations.

$$2(3 - x) \leq 8$$
$$2 \cdot 3 - 2 \cdot x \leq 8 \qquad \text{Use the distributive property.}$$
$$6 - 2x \leq 8 \qquad \text{Simplify.}$$
$$6 - 2x - \mathbf{6} \leq 8 - \mathbf{6} \qquad \text{Subtract 6 from both sides.}$$
$$-2x \leq 2 \qquad \text{Simplify.}$$
$$\frac{-2x}{-\mathbf{2}} \geq \frac{2}{-\mathbf{2}} \qquad \text{Divide both sides by } -2 \text{ and reverse the inequality symbol.}$$
$$x \geq -1 \qquad \text{Simplify.}$$

The solution set can be represented on a number line as shown:

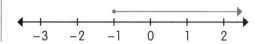

$$-3 \quad -2 \quad -1 \quad 0 \quad 1 \quad 2$$

▶ **Method 2**
Use inverse operations.

$$2(3 - x) \le 8$$
$2(3 - x) \div \mathbf{2} \le 8 \div \mathbf{2}$ Divide both sides by 2.
$3 - x \le 4$ Simplify.
$3 - x - \mathbf{3} \le 4 - \mathbf{3}$ Subtract 3 from both sides.
$-x \le 1$ Simplify.
$\dfrac{-x}{-1} \ge \dfrac{1}{-1}$ Divide both sides by -1 and reverse the inequality symbol.
$x \ge -1$ Simplify.

The solution set can be represented on a number line as shown:

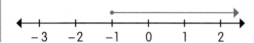

TRY Practice solving multi-step algebraic inequalities

Solve each inequality and graph the solution set on a number line.

① $4y + 7 < 27$

$$4y + 7 < 27$$

$4y + 7 - \underline{\hspace{0.5cm}} < 27 - \underline{\hspace{0.5cm}}$ Subtract _____ from both sides.

$4y < \underline{\hspace{0.8cm}}$ Simplify.

$4y \div \underline{\hspace{0.5cm}} < \underline{\hspace{0.5cm}} \div \underline{\hspace{0.5cm}}$ Divide both sides by _____.

$y < \underline{\hspace{0.8cm}}$ Simplify.

② $-5x - 9 \le 21$

③ $\dfrac{1}{2}r + \dfrac{3}{4} \ge 5$

④ $1.5 - 0.3p > 3.6$

⑤ $4(2 - m) \ge 20$

INDEPENDENT PRACTICE

Solve each inequality using addition and subtraction. Then, graph each solution set on a number line.

1 $x + 8 > 14$

2 $2 \geq x - 12$

3 $-7x + 5 + 8x > 3$

4 $-2x - 3 + 3x \geq 12$

5 $29 < \frac{2}{3}x + 14 + \frac{1}{3}x$

6 $\frac{1}{5}x + 9 + \frac{4}{5}x > -11$

7 $0.7x + 4 + 0.3x \leq 10$

8 $0.4x - 6 + 0.6x \geq 19$

9 **Mathematical Habit 2** Use mathematical reasoning

Solve the inequality $8 + 2x \geq 12$. What value is a solution of $8 + 2x \geq 12$ but is not a solution of $8 + 2x > 12$?

10   Mathematical Habit 6 Use precise mathematical language

Pedro solved the inequality $6y \leq -18$ as shown below:

$$6y \leq -18$$
$$6y \div 6 \geq -18 \div 6$$
$$y \geq -3$$

Describe and correct the error that Pedro made.

Solve each inequality using division and multiplication. Then, graph each solution set on a number line.

11 $3 \geq -3x$

12 $-4x > 12$

13 $-\dfrac{x}{5} \leq 2$

14 $-\dfrac{2}{3}x > 8$

15 $-0.2x \geq 6$

16 $9 > -0.5x$

Solve each inequality using the four operations. Then, graph each solution set on a number line.

17 $7y - 3 > 11$

18 $-3a + 5 < -7$

19 $\dfrac{x}{4} + \dfrac{3}{16} \geq 1$

20 $\dfrac{3}{5}a - \dfrac{4}{5} < \dfrac{7}{10}$

21 $7 - 0.3x > 4$

22 $2.4y + 5 < 29$

23 $5.4x + 4.2 - 3.8x > 9$

24 $6.6 + 1.3x - 5.2x \leq 14.4$

Solve each inequality with parentheses using the four operations.

25 $3(y + 2) \leq 18$

26 $8(y - 1) > 24$

27 $\frac{1}{2}(a + 1) \leq 4$

28 $\frac{2}{3}(3 - a) < 3$

29 $1.3(2 - x) > 3.9$

30 $3.6(5x - 1) < 5.4$

31 $4 + 2(1 - 3y) < 36$

32 $\frac{5}{9}(x + 1) \geq \frac{2}{3}$

33 $\frac{2}{3}(1 - 3x) > \frac{1}{6}$

34 $1.7 + 0.2(1 - x) \geq 2.7$

35 $2.5(3 - 2x) + 1 \geq 29$

36 $3.5(2x - 1) + 2x \leq 8.5$

Real-World Problems: Algebraic Inequalities

Learning Objective:
• Solve real-world problems involving algebraic inequalities.

THINK

Mr. Lee wants to rent a room for a private function. He approached two centers and here are the rates:

	Room Rental Per Hour	Set-Up Fee
Center A	$15	$40
Center B	$12	$80

Mr. Lee has $140. He wants to rent the room for at least 6 hours. Which center should he rent from? Formulate two inequalities to explain your answer.

ENGAGE

Look at these values: 10, 5, 18, 11, and x.

Show how you find the average of these values. If the average of these values is at least 10, what inequality can you write to represent the situation? If the average of these values is more than 10, how would the inequality change? How would the possible values of x change? Explain your reasoning.

 Solve real-world problems involving algebraic inequalities

1. Steven's scores for four math tests are 70, 75, 83, and 80. If he wants to get an average of at least 80 marks for 5 tests, what score should Steven get for his fifth test?

   You can use algebraic reasoning to translate the problem into an algebraic inequality.

   Let x be the score for the fifth test.   Define the variable.

$$\text{Average} \geq 80$$
$$\frac{70 + 75 + 83 + 80 + x}{5} \geq 80 \qquad \text{Write an inequality.}$$
$$\frac{308 + x}{5} \geq 80 \qquad \text{Simplify.}$$
$$5 \cdot \left(\frac{308 + x}{5}\right) \geq 5 \cdot 80 \qquad \text{Multiply both sides by 5.}$$
$$308 + x \geq 400 \qquad \text{Simplify.}$$
$$308 + x - 308 \geq 400 - 308 \qquad \text{Subtract 308 from both sides.}$$
$$x \geq 92 \qquad \text{Simplify.}$$

   Steven should get 92 marks or more for his fifth test.

2 Kaylee goes to an amusement park with her friends. The admission fee to the amusement park is $4 and each ride costs $0.80. If Kaylee has only $25 to spend, how many rides can she go on?

Let x be the number of rides that Kaylee can go on.   Define the variable.

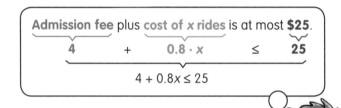

Admission fee plus cost of x rides is at most **$25**.

$$4 \quad + \quad 0.8 \cdot x \quad \leq \quad 25$$

$$4 + 0.8x \leq 25$$

$4 + 0.8x \leq 25$	Write an inequality.
$4 + 0.8x - 4 \leq 25 - 4$	Subtract 4 from both sides.
$0.8x \leq 21$	Simplify.
$\dfrac{0.8x}{0.8} \leq \dfrac{21}{0.8}$	Divide both sides by 0.8.
$x \leq 26.25$	Simplify.

Kaylee can go for at most 26 rides.

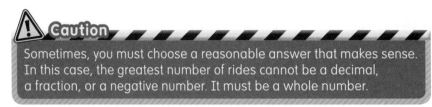

⚠ Caution

Sometimes, you must choose a reasonable answer that makes sense. In this case, the greatest number of rides cannot be a decimal, a fraction, or a negative number. It must be a whole number.

Solve.

1   The average length of four edges is at least 90 inches. The lengths of three of the edges are 87 inches, 90 inches, and 89 inches. Describe the length of the fourth edge.

Let x inches be the length of the fourth edge.

$$\text{Average} \geq \underline{\hspace{1cm}} \qquad \text{Define the variable.}$$

$$\frac{87 + 90 + 89 + x}{4} \geq \underline{\hspace{1cm}} \qquad \text{Write the inequality.}$$

$$\frac{266 + x}{4} \geq \underline{\hspace{1cm}} \qquad \text{Simplify.}$$

$$\underline{\hspace{1cm}} \cdot \left(\frac{266 + x}{4}\right) \geq \underline{\hspace{1cm}} \cdot \underline{\hspace{1cm}} \qquad \text{Multiply both sides by } \underline{\hspace{1cm}}.$$

$$266 + x \geq \underline{\hspace{1cm}} \qquad \text{Simplify.}$$

$$266 + x - \underline{\hspace{1cm}} \geq \underline{\hspace{1cm}} - \underline{\hspace{1cm}} \qquad \text{Subtract } \underline{\hspace{1cm}} \text{ from both sides.}$$

$$x \geq \underline{\hspace{1cm}} \qquad \text{Simplify.}$$

The length of the fourth edge is at least _____ inches.

2   Riley is at the bookstore with $75 to spend. She plans to buy a reference book that costs $18 and some novels that cost $12 each. Find how many novels Riley can buy along with the reference book.

Let x be the number of novels Riley can buy.   Define the variable.

$$\underline{\hspace{1cm}} + 12x \leq \underline{\hspace{1cm}} \qquad \text{Write the inequality.}$$

$$\underline{\hspace{1cm}} + 12x - \underline{\hspace{1cm}} \leq \underline{\hspace{1cm}} - \underline{\hspace{1cm}} \qquad \text{Subtract } \underline{\hspace{1cm}} \text{ from both sides.}$$

$$12x \leq \underline{\hspace{1cm}} \qquad \text{Simplify.}$$

$$12x \div \underline{\hspace{1cm}} \leq \underline{\hspace{1cm}} \div \underline{\hspace{1cm}} \qquad \text{Divide both sides by } \underline{\hspace{1cm}}.$$

$$x \leq \underline{\hspace{1cm}} \qquad \text{Simplify.}$$

Riley can buy at most _____ novels.

③ Ms. Cooper pays $200 in advance on her account at a health club. Each time she visits the club, $8 is deducted from the account. If she needs to maintain a minimum amount of $50 in the account, how many visits can Ms. Cooper make before she needs to top up the account again?

④ Carlos has at most 7 hours to spend in an amusement park, in which he uses 1 hour for lunch and the rest of the time on park rides. What is the maximum number of rides Carlos can complete if each ride takes 15 minutes?

INDEPENDENT PRACTICE

Solve.

1. The perimeter of an equilateral triangle is at most 45 centimeters. Find the possible length of each side.

2. Robert scored 1,800 points in four rounds of a debate competition. His opponent, Audrey, scored 324 points in the first round, 530 points in the second round, and 619 points in the third round. How many points must Audrey score in the final round to surpass Robert's score?

3. Blake plans to sign up for a language class that will cost at least $195. His father gives him $75 and he earns $28 from mowing the lawn for his neighbors. Write and solve an inequality to find out how much more money he needs to save before he can sign up for the class.

④ In her last basketball game, Carla scored 46 points. In the current game, she has scored 24 points so far. How many more two-point baskets must she make if she wants her total score in her current game to be at least as great as her score in the last game?

⑤ At Middleton Middle School, Maya must score an average of at least 80 points on 4 tests before she can apply for a scholarship. If she scored 79, 81, and 77 for the first three tests, what must she score on her last test?

⑥ At the movies, a bag of popcorn costs $3.50 and a bottle of water costs $2.75. If Jessica has $18 and bought only 2 bottles of water, how many bags of popcorn can she buy at most?

7 Party favors are on sale for $2.40 each. You have $380 to spend on the decorations and gifts, and you have already spent $270 on decorations. Write and solve an inequality to find the number of party favors you can buy.

 8 Evelyn can either take her lunch or buy it at school. It costs $1.95 to buy lunch. If she wants to spend no more than $30 each month, how many lunches can she buy at most?

 9 Bryan always likes to have at least $150 in his savings account. Currently he has $800 in the account. If he withdraws $35 each week, after how many weeks will the amount in his savings account be less than $150?

10 A cab company charges $0.80 per mile plus $2 for tolls. Rachel has at most $16 to spend on her cab fare. Write and solve an inequality for the maximum distance she can travel. Can she afford to take a cab from her home to an airport that is 25 miles away?

11 Nine subtracted from four times a number is less than or equal to fifteen. Write an inequality and solve it.

MATH JOURNAL

Mathematical Habit 6 Use precise mathematical language

Compare the inequality $-5(x + 6) < 10$ with solving the equation $-5(x + 6) = 10$. Describe the similarities and differences between solving the inequality and solving the equation. How does the solution set of the inequality $-5(x + 6) < 10$ differ from the solution of the equation $-5(x + 6) = 10$?

Similarities:

Differences:

Problem Solving with Heuristics

1 **Mathematical Habit 1** **Persevere in solving problems**

Jamar is five times as old as Kylie. Larissa is five times as old as Jamar.
Mitchell is twice as old as Larissa. The sum of their ages is the age of Nora.
Nora just turned 81. How old is Jamar?

② **Mathematical Habit** 4 Use mathematical models

Sara can buy 40 pens with a sum of money. She can buy 5 more pens if each pen costs $0.05 less.

a How much does each pen cost?

b If Sara wants to buy at least 10 more pens with the same amount of money, how much can each pen cost at most?

? How do you solve algebraic equations and inequalities?

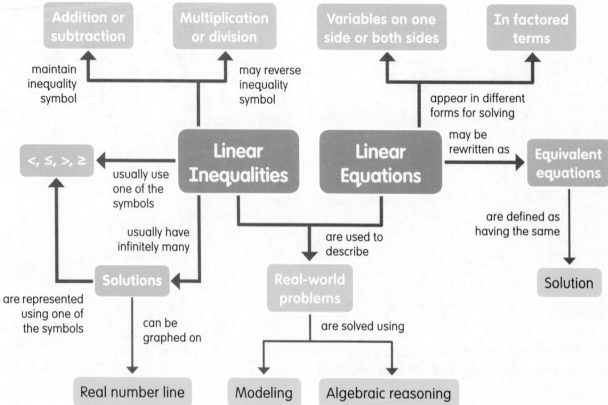

KEY CONCEPTS

- Equations with the same solution are called equivalent equations.
- Solving an equation involves isolating the variable on one side of the equation by writing a series of equivalent equations.
- An inequality symbol is used to compare two quantities that are not equal or may not be equal.
- The orientation of the inequality symbol must be reversed when both sides of an inequality are multiplied or divided by the same negative number.

Solve each equation.

① $8x - 7 = 17$

② $4 - 6x = 8$

③ $6 - \dfrac{y}{3} = 0$

④ $3 - 3.6x = 4.2$

⑤ $3.4y - 5.2 - 3y = 2$

⑥ $15y - 4(2y - 3) = -2$

⑦ $\dfrac{1}{4}(x + 3) + \dfrac{3}{8}x = \dfrac{13}{4}$

⑧ $0.4(x + 0.7) - 0.6x = -4.2$

Solve each inequality. Graph each solution set.

⑨ $4x - 3 > 1$

⑩ $6 \le 1 - 5x$

⑪ $\dfrac{2}{3} - \dfrac{x}{6} \ge -\dfrac{1}{2}$

⑫ $-6.9 < 8.1 - 1.5x$

⑬ $12.9 < 0.3(5.3 - x)$

⑭ $3(x + 1) - 5x > 7$

Write an equation for each question. Then, solve.

15 Mia is 6 years older than her sister Natalie. The sum of their ages is 48. How old is Natalie?

16 The sum of the page numbers of two facing pages in a book is 145. What are the page numbers?

17 The perimeter of an equilateral triangle is $6\frac{3}{4}$ inches. Find the length of each side of the equilateral triangle.

18 The sum of the interior angle measures of a quadrilateral is 360°. The measure of angle A is 3 times the measure of angle D. The measure of angle B is 4 times that of angle D. The measure of angle C is 24° more than angle B. Find the measure of each angle of the quadrilateral.

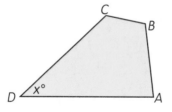

The diagram may not be drawn to scale.

© 2020 Marshall Cavendish Education Pte Ltd

Write an inequality for each question. Then, solve.

19 Julia wants the average amount of money she spends each day on her four-day vacation to be no more than $64. On the first three days, she spends $71, $62, and $59. What is the greatest amount of money she can spend on the fourth day?

20 Mr. Jones has found a job in a computer store. As shown below, he has two options for how he will be paid. The commission he makes for Option B is based on his weekly sales. For example, if his sales total $1,000 a week, he receives his base salary of $250 plus 8% of $1,000.

Option A	Option B
Fixed salary of $600 per week with no commission	Fixed salary of $250 per week plus commission of 8% of his weekly sales

Mr. Jones is thinking about Option B. What would his weekly sales need to be for him to make at least as much as he would for Option A?

21 The school events committee is planning to buy a banner and some helium balloons for graduation night. A store charges them $35 for the banner and $3.50 for each helium balloon. If the committee has at most $125 to spend, how many helium balloons can they buy?

22 The coach of the field hockey team can spend at most $475 on new team uniforms. The coach will order the uniforms online and pay a mailing cost of $6.50. If each uniform costs $29, how many uniforms can the coach order?

Assessment Prep

Answer each question.

23 Solve the equation for y.
$5(3 - 2y) = 18$
Write your answer and your work or explanation in the space below.

24 The width of a rectangular wall panel is 3 feet shorter than its length. The perimeter of the panel is 54 feet.

PART A

Which equation can be used to determine x, the length of the panel, in feet?

Ⓐ $x + x + 3 = 54$

Ⓑ $x + 3x = 54$

Ⓒ $2x + 2(x - 3) = 54$

Ⓓ $2x + 2(x + 3) = 54$

PART B

What is the length of the panel, in feet? Write your answer and your work or explanation in the space below.

25 Which is the solution of the inequality, $-4a + 3 < -13$?

Ⓐ $a > 4$

Ⓑ $a < 4$

Ⓒ $a > -4$

Ⓓ $a < -4$

Name: _____   Date: _____

Walkathon

1 Alma, Brooklyn, Carla, and Diana had collected donations following a walkathon. Alma had collected 3 times as much as Brooklyn. Carla had collected $25 less than Alma. Diana had collected twice as much as Alma. Then, Diana received a check of $55 from her grandmother.

a Write an expression to represent the amount Alma collected in terms of the amount Brooklyn collected.

b Write an expression to represent the amount Carla collected in terms of the amount Brooklyn collected.

c Write an expression to represent the amount Diana collected in terms of the amount Brooklyn collected.

2 Their teacher also took part in the walkathon and collected $1,070. The amount that their teacher collected had the same combined total amount that Alma, Brooklyn, Carla, and Diana had collected.

a Find the amount that Brooklyn collected.

b How much in donations did Alma, Carla, and Diana each collect?

Rubric

Point(s)	Level	My Performance
7–8	4	• Most of my answers are correct. • I showed complete understanding of the concepts. • I used effective and efficient strategies to solve the problems. • I explained my answers and mathematical thinking clearly and completely.
5–6	3	• Some of my answers are correct. • I showed adequate understanding of the concepts. • I used effective strategies to solve the problems. • I explained my answers and mathematical thinking clearly.
3–4	2	• A few of my answers are correct. • I showed some understanding of the concepts. • I used some effective strategies to solve the problems. • I explained some of my answers and mathematical thinking clearly.
0–2	1	• A few of my answers are correct. • I showed little understanding of the concepts. • I used limited effective strategies to solve the problems. • I did not explain my answers and mathematical thinking clearly.

Teacher's Comments

Proportion and Percent of Change

What Do Muralists Do?

Some artists think big. Visit almost any large American city, and you are likely to find the work of muralists, fine artists who paint directly onto walls, ceilings, or both. While some of their paintings may be life-sized, others are much larger. And while some are decorative, others serve a different purpose. They may advertise products or deliver social messages.

Muralists are concerned with proportional relationships. Before they begin painting, muralists sketch their designs. An object only 3 inches tall in a sketch, for example, may ultimately be 100 times taller on a wall. The length of each object in the sketch increases proportionately by a certain percent. Muralists use the percent proportion to turn a sketch drawn on a piece of paper into art that covers walls. In this chapter, you will learn about proportional relationships to solve real-world problems.

What happens to the proportion when variables in direct or inverse proportion change?

Comparing quantities using a ratio

A ratio compares two or more numbers or quantities. You can write a ratio of two quantities, such as 7 and 8, in three ways: 7 to 8, 7 : 8, or $\frac{7}{8}$. The numbers 7 and 8 are the terms of the ratio. You can express a ratio in simplest form by dividing its terms by their greatest common factor (GCF).

▶ **Quick Check**

Write a ratio in simplest form to compare each of the following.

A store sells 60 headphones, 45 sets of earbuds, and 80 speakers.

① The number of speakers to the number of sets of earbuds.

② The number of headphones to the number of speakers.

Recognizing equivalent ratios

Equivalent ratios show the same comparison of numbers and quantities. They have the same ratio in simplest form. You can obtain equivalent ratios by multiplying or dividing both terms of a ratio by the same number.

× 2 ⟮ 3 : 20 ⟯ × 2
= 6 : 40

÷ 5 ⟮ 15 : 100 ⟯ ÷ 5
= 3 : 20

So, 3 : 20, 6 : 40, and 15 : 100 are equivalent ratios.
Since 3 and 20 have no common factors except 1, the ratio 3 : 20 is in simplest form.

▶ **Quick Check**

State whether each pair of ratios are equivalent.

③ 9 : 11 and 18 : 22

④ $\frac{1}{33}$ and $\frac{33}{1}$

⑤ 3 to 6 and 9 to 18

State whether each ratio is in simplest form. Then, write two ratios that are equivalent to the given ratio.

⑥ 4 : 5

⑦ $\frac{15}{100}$

⑧ 7 to 14

Finding rates and unit rates

A rate compares two quantities with different units.
A unit rate compares a quantity to one unit of another quantity. For example, speed is a unit rate that compares distance traveled to a given unit of time.

Mia reads 7 books in two weeks. Find her reading speed in books per day.

14 days $\longrightarrow$ 7 books

    1 day $\longrightarrow$ $\frac{7}{14} = \frac{1}{2}$ book

Mia reads $\frac{1}{2}$ book per day.

▶ Quick Check

Find the unit rate.

9 The winner of the first Tour de France bicycle race in 1903 was Maurice Garin. It took him over 94 hours to complete 2,428 kilometers. Find his approximate average speed. Round your answer to the nearest whole number.

Find and compare the unit rate for each item.

The cost of a food item at two different stores is shown. Find the unit price at each store and state where the item costs less.

10 Store A: $3.20 for 16 oz of walnuts.
Store B: $2.30 for 10 oz of walnuts.

11 Store C: $2.13 for 3 lb of potatoes.
Store D: $3.35 for 5 lb of potatoes.

Identifying and plotting coordinates

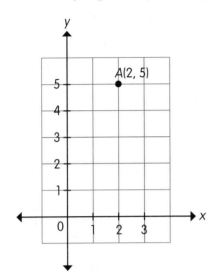

An ordered pair (x, y) is used to represent the location of a point on a graph.

Point A $(2, 5)$ represents the location of a point that is 2 units to the right of the origin, and 5 units up from the origin. The x-coordinate of point A is 2 and the y-coordinate is 5.

The coordinates of the origin are $(0, 0)$.

▶ **Quick Check**

Use the coordinate plane below.

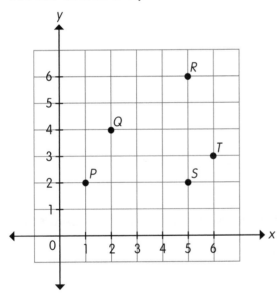

12 Give the coordinates of points P, Q, R, S, and T.

Solving percent problems

At an art exhibition, 80% of the people were adults, and the rest were children. Given that there were 600 children, how many people were at the art exhibition?

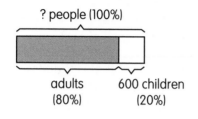

? people (100%)

adults
(80%)

600 children
(20%)

From the bar model,

20% ⟶ 600

1% ⟶ $\frac{600}{20}$ = 30

100% ⟶ 30 · 100 = 3,000

There were 3,000 people at the art exhibition.

▶ **Quick Check**

Solve.

13 45% of the beads in a box are blue. Given that there are 36 blue beads in the box, how many beads are there in all?

14 Taylor bought a model car priced at $72. She also had to pay a 5% sales tax. What was the total amount she paid?

1 Identifying Direct Proportion

Learning Objectives:
- Identify direct proportion.
- Recognize that a constant of proportionality can be a unit rate.

New Vocabulary
direct proportion
proportion
constant of proportionality

THINK

p is directly proportional to q, and $p = 12$ for a particular value of q.
Find the new value of p if the value of q is doubled.

ENGAGE

Study the given table.

Number of Tourists (x)	1	2	3
Cost of Admission Tickets (y dollars)	15	30	45

What do you notice about the relationship between the number of tourists and the cost of admission tickets? Explain the relationship in two ways.

LEARN Identify direct proportion from a table

Strawberries
$2/lb

1. At a store, each pound of strawberries costs $2.
   So, 2 pounds of strawberries cost: $2 · 2 = $4,
   3 pounds of strawberries cost: $2 · 3 = $6, and so on.

   The table shows the cost, y dollars, for x pounds
   of strawberries.

Increasing weight →

Weight of Strawberries (x pounds)	1	2	3
Cost (y dollars)	2	4	6

Increasing cost →

Notice what happens when you compare the costs of the strawberries to the number of pounds:

$$\frac{\$2}{1\,\text{lb}} = \frac{\$4}{2\,\text{lb}} = \frac{\$6}{3\,\text{lb}}$$ The rates, cost per pound, are equivalent.

These rates can be associated with ratios: $\frac{2}{1} = \frac{4}{2} = \frac{6}{3}$.

An equation that says two ratios are equivalent is called a **proportion**.

$\frac{2}{1} = \frac{4}{2}$ and $\frac{4}{2} = \frac{6}{3}$ are examples of proportions.

You read the proportion $\frac{4}{2} = \frac{6}{3}$ as "4 is to 2 is as 6 is to 3." Since the first term is two times the second term in each ratio, the ratios are equivalent.

$4 = \mathbf{2} \cdot 2$

$6 = \mathbf{2} \cdot 3$

You can see that the cost of strawberries is always **two times** the number of pounds:

Cost for 1 pound: $2 $\mathbf{2} \cdot 1 = \$2$

Cost for 2 pounds: $4 $\mathbf{2} \cdot 2 = \$4$

Cost for 3 pounds: $6 $\mathbf{2} \cdot 3 = \$6$

The cost of strawberries and the number of pounds are said to be in direct proportion. If you let y be the cost of strawberries and x be the number of pounds, you can write two equivalent equations:

$\frac{y}{x} = 2$ and $y = 2x$

If $\frac{y}{x} = k$ or $y = kx$, where k is a constant value, then y is said to be directly proportional to x. The constant value, k, in a direct proportion is called the **constant of proportionality**.

Math Note

Direct proportion is sometimes called direct variation, and the constant of proportionality is sometimes called the constant of variation. You can say that the value of y varies directly with the value of x.

2. A store owner uses a table to decide how many fish to put in an aquarium. Determine whether the number of fish, f, is directly proportional to the volume of water, g gallons. If so, find the constant of proportionality and state what it represents in this situation. Then, write a direct proportion equation.

Volume of Water (g gallons)	4	10	20
Number of Fish (f)	6	15	30

For each pair of values, f and g:

$\dfrac{6 \text{ fish}}{4 \text{ gal}} = \dfrac{15 \text{ fish}}{10 \text{ gal}} = \dfrac{30 \text{ fish}}{20 \text{ gal}}$ The rates are equivalent and can be associated with the ratio 3 : 2.

So, the number of fish is directly proportional to the volume of water.

The constant of proportionality is $\frac{3}{2}$, and it represents the number of fish per gallon of water. The direct proportion equation is $f = \frac{3}{2}g$.

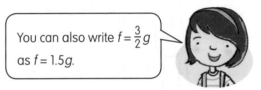

You can also write $f = \frac{3}{2}g$ as $f = 1.5g$.

3. The table shows the distance traveled by a snail, d centimeters, after t hours. Determine whether d is directly proportional to t. If so, find the constant of proportionality and state what it represents in this situation. Then, write a direct proportion equation.

Time (t hours)	1	2	3
Distance Traveled (d centimeters)	9	18	21

For each pair of values, d and t:

$\dfrac{9 \text{ cm}}{1 \text{ h}} = 9 \qquad \dfrac{18 \text{ cm}}{2 \text{ h}} = 9 \qquad \dfrac{21 \text{ cm}}{3 \text{ h}} = 7$

Since the speeds of the snail are not constant, d and t are not in direct proportion.

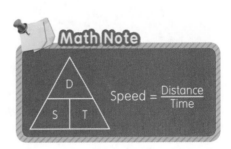

Math Note

Speed = $\dfrac{\text{Distance}}{\text{Time}}$

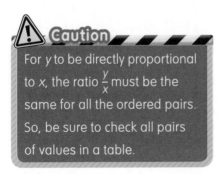

⚠ **Caution**

For y to be directly proportional to x, the ratio $\frac{y}{x}$ must be the same for all the ordered pairs. So, be sure to check all pairs of values in a table.

Work in pairs.

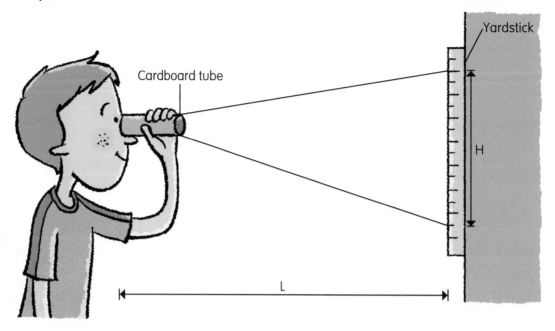

Cardboard tube

Yardstick

H

L

① Tape a yardstick to the wall. Stand 1 foot away from the wall. Look at the yardstick through a cardboard tube. How many inches of the yardstick can you see? Record in the first column of the table below.

Distance from the Wall (L feet)	1	2	3	4	5
Length of Yardstick Seen (H inches)					
$\dfrac{H}{L}$	$\dfrac{\square}{1}$	$\dfrac{\square}{2}$	$\dfrac{\square}{3}$	$\dfrac{\square}{4}$	$\dfrac{\square}{5}$

Repeat for other values of L shown. Then, fill in the table.

② **Mathematical Habit 2** Use mathematical reasoning

What happens to H as L increases? Based on your observations, do you think H is directly proportional to L? Explain your reasoning.

Determine whether y is directly proportional to x.

1 The table shows the distance traveled by a school bus, y miles, after x hours.

Time (x hours)	2	3	4
Distance Traveled (y miles)	100	150	200

For each pair of values, x and y:

$\dfrac{\_\_\_\text{mi}}{\_\_\text{h}} = \_\_\_$ $\dfrac{\_\_\_\text{mi}}{\_\_\text{h}} = \_\_\_$ $\dfrac{\_\_\_\text{mi}}{\_\_\text{h}} = \_\_\_$

So, the distance traveled by the school bus is _____ to the number of hours it has traveled.

The constant of proportionality is _____ and it represents the speed of the bus.

The direct proportion equation is _____ .

2 The table shows the number of pitches made, y, in x innings of a baseball game.

Number of Innings (x)	1	2	3
Number of Pitches (y)	15	30	50

For each pair of values, x and y:

$\dfrac{\_\_\_\text{pitches}}{\_\_\text{innings}} = \_\_\_$ $\dfrac{\_\_\_\text{pitches}}{\_\_\text{innings}} = \_\_\_$ $\dfrac{\_\_\_\text{pitches}}{\_\_\text{innings}} = \_\_\_$

So, the number of pitches made is _____ to the number of innings of a baseball game.

ENGAGE

Look at the two tables below.

a

x	1	2	3
y	4	8	22

b

x	1	2	3
y	5	9	13

In which of these tables is y directly proportional to x? What is the direct proportion equation? Write two more equations that are equivalent to the direct proportion equation. What can you say about the two equations that you have written? Explain your answer.

LEARN Identify direct proportion from an equation

1. When y is directly proportional to x, you can write $\frac{y}{x} = k$. You can use algebra to write another form of this equation, giving y in terms of x. For example, when $k = 2$, multiply both sides of the equation $\frac{y}{x} = 2$ by x to get the equivalent equation $y = 2x$.

$\frac{y}{x} = 2$ Write an equation.

$x \cdot \frac{y}{x} = x \cdot 2$ Multiply both sides by x to undo the division of y by x.

$y = 2x$ Simplify.

You can also use algebra to decide if an equation represents a direct proportion.

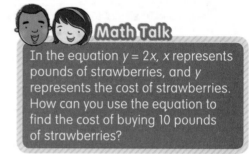

Math Talk

In the equation $y = 2x$, x represents pounds of strawberries, and y represents the cost of strawberries. How can you use the equation to find the cost of buying 10 pounds of strawberries?

2. Determine whether $\frac{1}{2}y = 3x$ represents a direct proportion. If so, state the constant of proportionality.

$\frac{1}{2}y = 3x$

$2 \cdot \frac{1}{2}y = 2 \cdot 3x$ Multiply both sides by 2.

$y = 6x$ Simplify.

Try to rewrite the equation as an equivalent equation in the form $y = kx$.

Since the original equation $\frac{1}{2}y = 3x$ can be rewritten as an equivalent equation in the form $y = kx$, it represents a direct proportion. The constant of proportionality is **6**.

3. Determine whether $y - 2 = 5x$ represents a direct proportion. If so, state the constant of proportionality.

$y - 2 = 5x$

$y - 2 + 2 = 5x + 2$ Add 2 to both sides.

$y = 5x + 2$ Simplify.

Since the original equation $y - 2 = 5x$ cannot be rewritten as an equivalent equation in the form $y = kx$, it does not represent a direct proportion.

TRY Practice identifying direct proportion from an equation

Determine whether each equation represents a direct proportion. If so, state the constant of proportionality.

1 $0.4y = x$

$0.4y = x$

$\dfrac{0.4y}{\rule{1cm}{0.4pt}} = \dfrac{x}{\rule{1cm}{0.4pt}}$ Divide both sides by _____ .

$y = \underline{\hspace{1cm}}$ Simplify.

Since the original equation $0.4y = x$ _____ be rewritten as an equivalent equation in the form $y = kx$, it _____ a direct proportion. The constant of proportionality is _____ .

2 $x = 1 - 2y$

$x = 1 - 2y$

$x + 2y = 1 - 2y + 2y$ Add $2y$ to both sides.

$x + 2y - \underline{\hspace{1cm}} = 1 - \underline{\hspace{1cm}}$ Subtract _____ from both sides.

$2y = 1 - \underline{\hspace{1cm}}$ Simplify.

$\dfrac{2y}{\rule{1cm}{0.4pt}} = \dfrac{1}{\rule{1cm}{0.4pt}} - \dfrac{\ }{\rule{1cm}{0.4pt}}$ Divide both sides by _____ .

$y = \underline{\hspace{2cm}}$ Simplify.

Since the original equation $x = 1 - 2y$ _____ be rewritten as an equivalent equation in the form $y = kx$, it _____ a direct proportion.

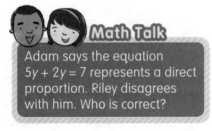

Math Talk

Adam says the equation $5y + 2y = 7$ represents a direct proportion. Riley disagrees with him. Who is correct?

ENGAGE

Solve each part.

a The cost of a bag of popcorn is $4. The total cost of x bags of popcorn is y dollars. What is an equation that represents this direct proportion?

b The table shows the total cost (y dollars) of x bags of popcorn. y is directly proportional to x.

Number of Bags of Popcorn (x)	1	2	3
Total Cost (y dollars)	4	8	12

What is an equation that represents this direct proportion?

c y is directly proportional to x, and $y = 20$ when $x = 5$. What is an equation that represents this direct proportion?

How are these parts the same? How are they different? Explain your thinking.

LEARN Identify a constant of proportionality from a table, in a verbal description, or in an equation

1. The constant of proportionality in a direct proportion often represents a unit rate. In the example on page 283, the constant of proportionality **2** represents the unit cost of the strawberries. The total cost of the strawberries, y dollars, is the product of the unit cost and the weight of the strawberries purchased, x pounds.

So, the equation of the direct proportion is: y dollars $= \dfrac{\$2}{1 \text{ pound}} \cdot x$ pounds

$$y = 2x$$

2. The table shows the price, P dollars, for x cans of soup. P is directly proportional to x. Find the constant of proportionality and state what it represents in this situation. Then, write a direct proportion equation.

Number of Cans (x)	1	2	3
Price (P dollars)	1.60	3.20	4.80

Constant of proportionality: $\dfrac{\$1.60}{1 \text{ can}} = 1.6$

The constant of proportionality is **1.6** and it represents the cost, in dollars, per can of soup. The direct proportion equation is $P = 1.6x$.

③ Ana is buying some baseball caps. Each cap costs $8. The amount Ana pays for the caps is directly proportional to the number of caps she buys. Write an equation that represents the direct proportion.

Let x be the number of baseball caps Ana buys. Define the variables.
Let y dollars be the amount she pays.

Cost per baseball cap: $\mathbf{8}$ per cap.

The direct proportion equation is $y = \mathbf{8}x$.

First, define the variables. Then, identify the constant of proportionality. Finally, write a direct proportion equation.

④ y is directly proportional to x, and $y = 3$ when $x = 9$. Find the constant of proportionality. Then, write a direct proportion equation.

Since y is directly proportional to x, use $\frac{y}{x} = k$ to find the constant of proportionality, k.

Constant of proportionality: $\dfrac{y}{x} = \dfrac{3}{9}$

$\qquad\qquad\qquad\quad = \dfrac{1}{3}$ Write in simplest form.

The constant of proportionality is $\dfrac{1}{3}$.

The direct proportion equation is $y = \dfrac{1}{3}x$.

TRY Practice identifying a constant of proportionality from a table, in a verbal description, or in an equation

Solve.

① The table shows the number of baseballs, y, made in x days. The number of baseballs made is directly proportional to the number of days of production. Find the constant of proportionality and state what it represents in this situation. Then, write a direct proportion equation.

Number of Days (x)	1	2	3
Number of Baseballs (y)	56	112	168

Constant of proportionality: _____

The constant of proportionality is _____ and it represents

the _____.

The direct proportion equation is _____.

2 A cafeteria sells sandwiches for $4 each. The amount Robert pays for some sandwiches is directly proportional to the number he buys. Write an equation that represents the direct proportion.

Let _____ be the number of sandwiches.

Let _____ be the amount Robert pays.

Cost per sandwich: $_____ per sandwich

The direct proportion equation is _____.

3 q is directly proportional to p, and $p = 12$ when $q = 24$. Find the constant of proportionality. Then, write a direct proportion equation.

Constant of proportionality: $\dfrac{q}{p} = \dfrac{}{}$

$ = \underline{}$ Write in simplest form.

The constant of proportionality is _____ .

The direct proportion equation is _____ .

4 w is directly proportional to h, and $w = 18$ when $h = 3$. Find the constant of proportionality. Then, write a direct proportion equation.

INDEPENDENT PRACTICE

Determine whether y is directly proportional to x. If so, find the constant of proportionality. Then, write a direct proportion equation.

1

x	1	2	3
y	5	10	15

2

x	2	4	6
y	130	100	70

3

x	3	6	9
y	20	40	50

4

x	2	4	6
y	50	100	150

Determine whether each equation represents a direct proportion. If so, identify the constant of proportionality.

5 $3y = \frac{1}{2}x$

6 $2y - 5 = x$

7 $p = 0.25q$

8 $4.5a = b + 12$

Solve.

9 The table shows the distance traveled, *d* miles, and the amount of gasoline used, *n* gallons. Determine whether *d* is directly proportional to *n*. If so, find the constant of proportionality and state what it represents in this situation. Then, write a direct proportion equation.

Amount of Gasoline (*n* gallons)	1	2	3
Distance Traveled (*d* miles)	20	40	60

10 The table shows the number of points scored, *y*, in *x* basketball games. Determine whether *y* is directly proportional to *x*. If so, find the constant of proportionality and state what it represents in this situation. Then, write a direct proportion equation.

Number of Games (*x*)	1	2	3
Number of Points (*y*)	24	48	80

11 The table shows the number of tennis balls produced, *y*, by *x* machines. Determine whether *y* is directly proportional to *x*. If so, find the constant of proportionality and state what it represents in this situation. Then, write a direct proportion equation.

Number of Machines (*x*)	1	3	5
Number of Tennis Balls (*y*)	20	60	100

12 **Mathematical Habit 6** Use precise mathematical language

Describe how you can tell whether two quantities are in direct proportion.

13 **Mathematical Habit 2** Use mathematical reasoning

An equilateral triangle with a side length of c inches has a perimeter of P inches. The perimeter of the equilateral triangle is described by the equation $P = 3c$. Determine whether P is directly proportional to c. Explain your reasoning.

14 Pablo rode his bike at a steady rate of 20 miles per hour. Given that the distance, d miles, is directly proportional to the duration he rides, t hours, state the constant of proportionality and write a direct proportion equation.

15 Emily worked in a florist shop and earned $12 per hour. Given that the amount she earned, w dollars, is directly proportional to the time she worked, t hours, state the constant of proportionality and write a direct proportion equation.

16 y is directly proportional to x, and $y = 10$ when $x = 15$. Write a direct proportion equation that relates x and y.

17 y is directly proportional to x, and $y = 33$ when $x = 11$. Write a direct proportion equation that relates x and y.

18 Owen hikes 3 miles in 45 minutes. Given that the distance is directly proportional to the duration he walks, find the constant of proportionality and write an equation to represent the direct proportion.

19 Pedro pays $20 to download 16 songs. Given that the amount he pays is directly proportional to the number of songs he downloads, find the constant of proportionality and write a direct proportion equation.

20 Mathematical Habit 3 Construct viable arguments

Each table shows the cost of placing an advertisement in a newspaper, C dollars, for t days. Describe how the two tables are alike, and how they are different. Use direct proportion to explain your answer.

The Daily Post

Number of Days (t)	1	2	3	4	5
Total Cost of Advertisement (C dollars)	20	40	60	80	100

The Evening Star

Number of Days (t)	1	2	3	4	5
Total Cost of Advertisement (C dollars)	20	40	60	70	80

2 Representing Direct Proportion Graphically

Learning Objective:
• Use a graph to interpret direct proportion.

 THINK

A graph that shows a direct proportion between two variables passes through (2, 12), (5, a), and (b, 48). What is a possible value of a and b? How many possible values are there? Explain your answer.

ENGAGE

The mass of a cup is 100 grams. What is the mass of 2 cups and 3 cups respectively? Use a table to show this information. What can you say about the table? Use the table to plot a graph. What does the graph look like? Share your ideas.

LEARN Use a graph to interpret direct proportion

① Each time the wheel on Nathan's unicycle goes around, the unicycle moves forward 2 meters. The distance the unicycle moves forward is directly proportional to the number of revolutions.

The table and the graph show the relationship between the number of revolutions and distance the wheel moves.

Revolutions (x)	1	2	3
Distance (y meters)	2	4	6

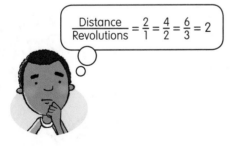

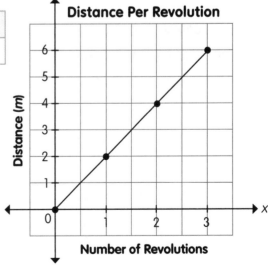

The graph of a direct proportion is always a straight line through the origin, (0, 0), and does not lie along the horizontal or vertical axis.

For the graph on page 297, each point (x, y) means that in x revolutions, the unicycle wheel moves y meters. For example, the point (0, 0) means that in 0 revolution, the wheel moves 0 meter. The point (1, 2) means that in 1 revolution, it moves 2 meters.

The point (1, **2**) can be used to find the constant of proportionality: $\frac{2}{1} = 2$

In general, you can use the point (1, **y**) on a direct proportion graph to find a constant of proportionality.

You can use the constant of proportionality to write a direct proportion equation, $y = 2x$.

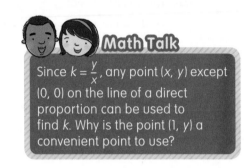

Math Talk

Since $k = \frac{y}{x}$, any point (x, y) except (0, 0) on the line of a direct proportion can be used to find k. Why is the point (1, y) a convenient point to use?

2 State whether the graph represents a direct proportion. If so, find the constant of proportionality. Then, write a direct proportion equation.

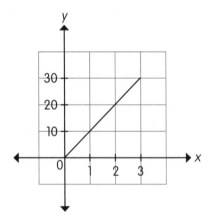

The graph is a straight line through the origin, and it does not lie along the x- or y-axis. So, it represents a direct proportion.

Since the graph passes through (1, **10**), the constant of proportionality is **10**.

The direct proportion equation is $y = 10x$.

Use (1, **10**) to find the constant of proportionality.

③ State whether the graph represents a direct proportion. If so, find the constant of proportionality. Then, write a direct proportion equation.

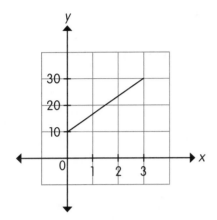

Although the graph is a straight line that does not lie along the *x*- or *y*-axis, it does not pass through the origin. So, the graph does not represent a direct proportion.

④ State whether the graph represents a direct proportion. If so, find the constant of proportionality. Then, write a direct proportion equation.

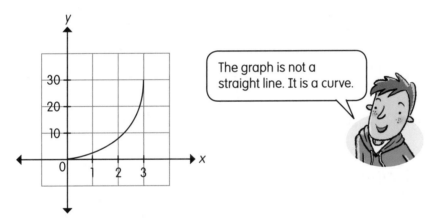

The graph is not a straight line. It is a curve.

Although the graph passes through the origin and does not lie along the *x*- or *y*-axis, it is not a straight line. So, it does not represent a direct proportion.

5 Kevin works at a bookstore. The amount of money he earns is directly proportional to the number of hours he works. The graph shows the amount of money, w dollars, he earns in t hours.

a Find the constant of proportionality. How much does Kevin earn per hour?

Since the graph passes through (1, **15**), the constant of proportionality is **15**.

In this case, the constant of proportionality is the amount of money earned per hour.
So, Kevin earns money at a rate of $**15** per hour.

b Write a direct proportion equation.

The direct proportion equation is $w = **15**t$.

c Explain what the point (2, 30) represents in this situation.

It means that Kevin earns $30 in 2 hours.

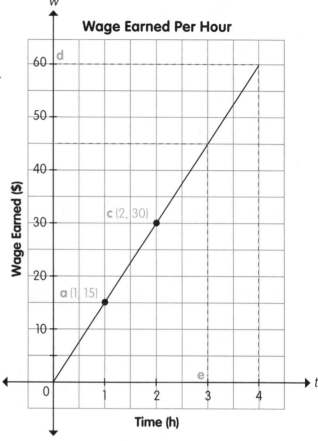

Wage Earned Per Hour

d If Kevin works 4 hours, how much will he earn?

From the graph, Kevin will earn $60 in 4 hours.

e If Kevin wants to earn $45, how long should he work?

From the graph, Kevin should work for 3 hours.

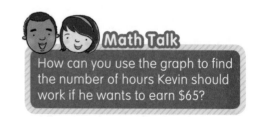

Math Talk

How can you use the graph to find the number of hours Kevin should work if he wants to earn $65?

State whether each graph represents a direct proportion. If so, find the constant of proportionality. Then, write a direct proportion equation.

1

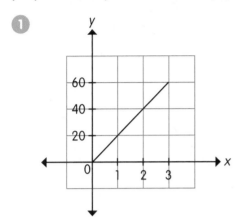

2

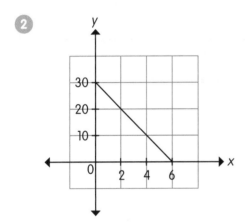

3

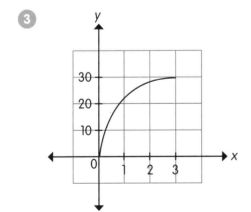

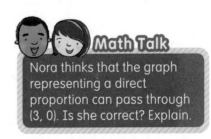

Math Talk

Nora thinks that the graph representing a direct proportion can pass through (3, 0). Is she correct? Explain.

Solve.

4 Ms. Garcia is driving on a long distance trip. The distance she travels is directly proportional to time she travels. The graph shows the distance she travels, y miles, after t hours.

a Find the constant of proportionality. What is Ms. Garcia's driving speed in miles per hour?

Constant of proportionality:

$$\underline{} = \underline{}$$

The constant of proportionality is _____. So, Ms. Garcia's driving speed is _____ miles per hour.

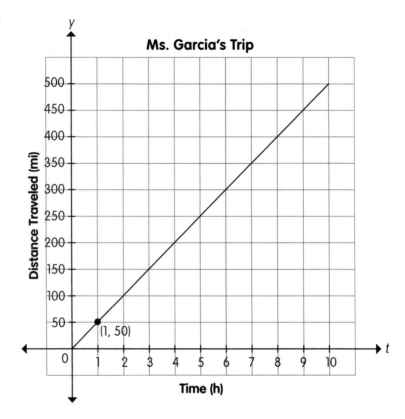

Ms. Garcia's Trip

b Write a direct proportion equation.

The direct proportion equation is $y =$ _____ t.

c Explain what the point (7, 350) represents in this situation.

It means that Ms. Garcia travels _____ miles in _____ hours.

d Find the distance traveled in 3 hours.

From the graph, the distance traveled is _____ miles.

e How long does it take Ms. Garcia to travel 400 miles?

From the graph, it takes her _____ hours to travel 400 miles.

INDEPENDENT PRACTICE

State whether each graph represents a direct proportion. If so, find the constant of proportionality. Then, write a direct proportion equation.

 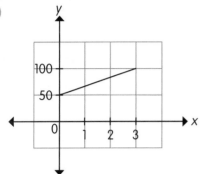

 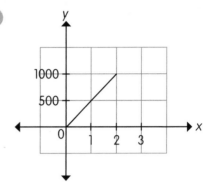

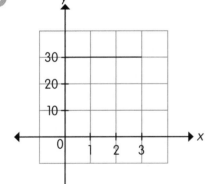 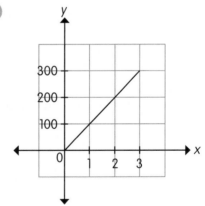

Solve.

5 The cost of staying at a motel is directly proportional to the number of nights you stay. The graph shows the cost of staying at a motel, y dollars, for x nights.

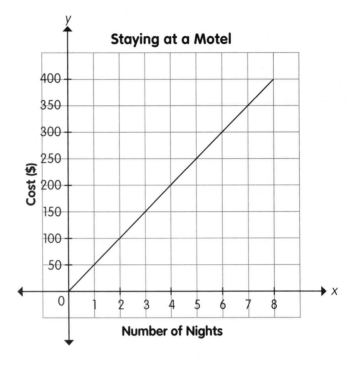

a Find the constant of proportionality. What does this value represent in this situation?

b How much does it cost to stay at the motel for one week?

6 [Mathematical Habit 6] Use precise mathematical language

Explain how you can determine whether a line represents a direct proportion.

7. When you travel to another country, you can exchange U.S. dollars for the currency of that country. The amount of the new currency you get for your dollars depends on the exchange rate. The graph shows the amount of Mexican pesos, y, you could get if you were to exchange x U.S. dollars for pesos.

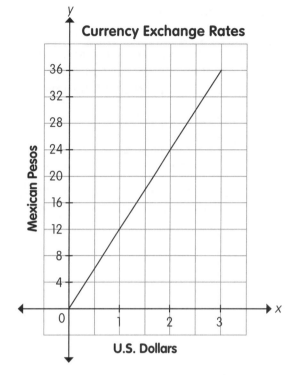

a Is the amount of pesos directly proportional to the amount of U.S. dollars? Explain.

b How many pesos do you get for 3 U.S. dollars?

c Convert 24 pesos to U.S. dollars.

d What is the exchange rate when you convert dollars to pesos?

e Write the direct proportion equation.

Use graph paper. Solve.

8 Haley works at a pottery studio. She is making ceramic pots to sell at a craft fair. Graph the relationship between the number of ceramic pots she makes, y, and the number of days she works at the studio, x. Use 1 unit on the horizontal axis to represent 1 day and 1 unit on the vertical axis to represent 5 ceramic pots.

Number of Days (x)	0	1	2	3	4	5	6
Number of Pots (y)	0	5	10	15	20	25	30

a Determine whether the graph represents a direct proportion. If so, find the constant of proportionality and write the direct proportion equation.

b Explain what the point (4, 20) represents in this situation.

c How many ceramic pots can Haley make in 3 days?

d Haley will not start selling ceramic pots until she has made at least 30. How long will it take her to make that many ceramic pots?

3 Real-World Problems: Direct Proportion

Learning Objective:
• Solve real-world direct proportion problems.

New Vocabulary
cross product

THINK

1. Discuss with your partner which of the following real-world scenarios are direct proportions.

   a   The relation between the total cost of books and the number of books bought, where all the books bought are the same.

   b   The relation between the volume of water in a tank and time, where the tank is being filled up at a steady rate.

   c   The relation between the total cost of shirts and the number of shirts bought, where all the shirts bought are the same and there is a buy-two-get-one-free offer.

   d   The relation between the distance a ball rolls and time, where the ball is rolling in a straight line on horizontal ground.

2. For the scenarios that are direct proportions, describe what is the constant of proportionality. For the scenarios that are not direct proportions, explain why.

ENGAGE

The cost of 5 mats is $50. The cost of the mats is directly proportional to the number of mats. If Nathaniel wants to buy 12 mats, how do you find the total cost of the mats? Show at least two different methods to explain your thinking.

Create a real-world direct proportion problem. Trade your problem with your partner and solve it. Share your method.

Solve real-world direct proportion problems

① Since the ratios $\frac{2}{5}$ and $\frac{4}{10}$ are equivalent, you can use them to write a proportion.

Notice what happens when you find the cross products of the proportion.

$$\frac{2}{5} = \frac{4}{10}$$

Cross products:

2 · 10 = 4 · 5   Multiply the numerator of the left fraction by the denominator of the right fraction.
Multiply the numerator of the right fraction by the denominator of the left fraction.

   20 = 20   Simplify.

If you find the cross products of other proportions, you will see that the cross products of a proportion are always equal.

> **Cross products property:**
> If $\frac{a}{b} = \frac{c}{d}$, where $b \neq 0$ and $d \neq 0$, then $ad = bc$.

You can use the cross products property to solve problems that involve quantities that are in direct proportion.

② Julia pays $40 for 8 T-shirts at a store. Given that the cost of T-shirts is directly proportional to the number of T-shirts she buys, use proportionality reasoning to find the cost of 5 T-shirts.

STEP 1 Understand the problem.

> How many T-shirts does Julia buy? How much do the T-shirts cost? Is the cost of the T-shirts in direct proportion to the number of T-shirts? What do I need to find?

STEP 2 Think of a plan.
I can use a proportion or a direct proportion equation.

STEP 3 Carry out the plan.

▶ **Method 1**

Use a proportion.

Let y be the cost of 5 T-shirts.   Define the variable.

$$\frac{40 \text{ dollars}}{8 \text{ T-shirts}} = \frac{y \text{ dollars}}{5 \text{ T-shirts}}$$ Write a proportion.

$$\frac{40}{8} = \frac{y}{5}$$ Write ratios as fractions.

$$8 \cdot y = 40 \cdot 5$$ Write cross products.

$$8y = 200$$ Simplify.

$$\frac{8y}{8} = \frac{200}{8}$$ Divide both sides by 8.

$$y = 25$$ Simplify.

The cost of 5 T-shirts is $25.

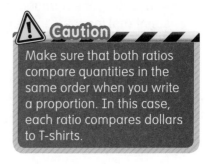

Caution

Make sure that both ratios compare quantities in the same order when you write a proportion. In this case, each ratio compares dollars to T-shirts.

▶ **Method 2**

Use a direct proportion equation.

Let x be the number of T-shirts.   Define the variables.
Let y be the cost of the T-shirts.

Constant of proportionality:

$$\frac{y}{x} = \frac{40}{8}$$ Substitute $y = 40$ and $x = 8$.

$$= 5$$ Simplify.

In this situation, the constant of proportionality is the cost per T-shirt. Since the cost is directly proportional to the number of T-shirts, translate the verbal description into a direct proportion equation in the form $y = kx$.

Then, write a direct proportion equation.

Direct proportion equation: $y = 5x$ Write an equation.

Finally, find the cost of 5 T-shirts.

When $x = 5$ and $y = 5x$, $y = 5 \cdot 5$ Evaluate $y = 5x$ when $x = 5$.

$$y = 25$$ Simplify.

The cost of 5 T-shirts is $25.

 STEP 4 Check the answer.
I can use the unitary method to check my answer.

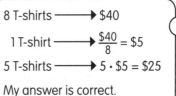

8 T-shirts ⟶ $40

1 T-shirt ⟶ $\frac{\$40}{8} = \$5$

5 T-shirts ⟶ $5 \cdot \$5 = \$25$

My answer is correct.

Solve.

1. At a factory, the number of cars produced is directly proportional to the number of hours spent making the cars. It takes 45 hours to make 60 cars. How long does it take to make 250 cars?

▶ **Method 1**
Use a proportion.

Let x be the number of hours it takes to make 250 cars.　Define the variable.

$$\frac{60 \text{ cars}}{\boxed{} \text{ hours}} = \frac{\boxed{} \text{ cars}}{x \text{ hours}}$$　Write a proportion.

$$\frac{60}{\boxed{}} = \frac{\boxed{}}{x}$$　Write ratios as fractions.

$$x \cdot 60 = \underline{} \cdot \underline{}$$　Write cross products.

$$60x = \underline{}$$　Simplify.

$$\frac{60x}{\boxed{}} = \frac{\boxed{}}{}$$　Divide both sides by _____.

$$x = \underline{}$$　Simplify.

It takes _____ hours to make 250 cars.

▶ **Method 2**
Use a direct proportion equation.

Let x be the number of hours.　Define the variables.
Let y be the number of cars.

Constant of proportionality: $\dfrac{y}{x} = \dfrac{\boxed{}}{\underline{}} = \underline{}$　Substitute $y = $ _____ and $x = $ _____ and simplify.

Direct proportion equation: $y = \underline{}\, x$　Write an equation.

When $y = 250$ and $y = \underline{}\, x,\ 250 = \underline{} \cdot x$　Evaluate $y = $ _____ x when $y = 250$.

$$\underline{} \cdot x = 250$$　Write an equivalent equation.

$$x \cdot \frac{\underline{}}{\underline{}} = 250 \cdot \frac{\underline{}}{\underline{}}$$　Multiply both sides by _____.

$$x = \frac{\underline{}}{}$$　Simplify.

It takes _____ hours to produce 250 cars.

a Study the given table.

Time (x hours)	3	?	12
Amount of Money (y dollars)	45	75	?

What do you think the data represents? Given that x is directly proportional to y, how do you find the missing values? Share your ideas.

b Two more data were recorded as follows:

Time (x hours)	8	10
Amount of Money (y dollars)	90	140

Which of the data is incorrect? Explain your answer.

LEARN Solve real-world direct proportion problems involving a table

1 The number of peaches for sale at an orchard, P, is directly proportional to the number of crates used to pack the peaches, C. The table shows the relationship between the total number of peaches for sale and the number of crates.

Number of Crates (C)	15	?	56
Number of Peaches (P)	600	1,000	?

a Write a direct proportion equation that relates P and C.

Number of peaches per crate:

$\frac{600}{15} = 40$

> The constant of proportionality is the number of peaches per crate.

The direct proportion equation is $P = 40C$.

b Find the missing values in the table.

When $P = 1,000$ and $P = 40C$, $1,000 = 40C$ Evaluate $P = 40C$ when $P = 1,000$.

$\frac{1,000}{40} = \frac{40C}{40}$ Divide both sides by 40.

$25 = C$ Simplify.

$C = 25$ Write an equivalent equation.

1,000 peaches are packed into 25 crates.

When $C = 56$ and $P = 40C$, $P = 40 \cdot 56$ Evaluate $P = 40C$ when $C = 56$.

$P = 2,240$ Simplify.

There are 2,240 peaches in 56 crates.

Practice solving real-world direct proportion problems involving a table

Solve.

1 The number of eggs used, *E*, is directly proportional to the number of cakes baked, *C*.

Number of Cakes (*C*)	3		80
Number of Eggs (*E*)	12	60	

a Write a direct proportion equation that relates *E* and *C*.

Constant of proportionality:

$$\frac{E}{C} = \frac{}{}$$

$$= \underline{}$$

The direct proportion equation is *E* = _____ *C*.

b Find the missing values in the table.

When *E* = 60 and *E* = _____ *C*, 60 = _____ *C*

$$C = \underline{}$$

60 eggs are used to bake _____ cakes.

When *C* = 80 and *E* = _____ *C*, *E* = _____ · 80

$$= \underline{}$$

_____ eggs are used to bake 80 cakes.

2 The number of pears for sale at an orchard, *P*, is directly proportional to the number of crates used to pack the pears, *C*. The table shows the relationship between the total number of pears for sale and the number of crates.

Number of Crates (*C*)	8	10	
Number of Pears (*P*)		200	500

a Write a direct proportion equation that relates *P* and *C*.

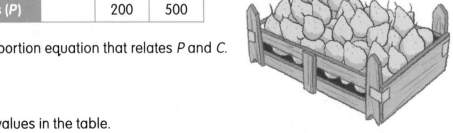

b Find the missing values in the table.

INDEPENDENT PRACTICE

Write a direct variation equation and find each indicated value.

1 m varies directly as n, and $m = 14$ when $n = 7$.

   a Write an equation that relates m and n.

   b Find m when $n = 16$.

   c Find n when $m = 30$.

2 p varies directly as q, and $p = 6$ when $q = 30$.

   a Write an equation that relates p and q.

   b Find q when $p = 10$.

   c Find p when $q = 7$.

In each table, b is directly proportional to a. Fill in each table.

3

a	4		19
b	12	15	

4

a	4		16
b	10	25	

Solve.

5 The amount of blood in a person's body, *b* quarts, is directly proportional to his or her body weight, *w* pounds. A person who weighs 128 pounds has about 4 quarts of blood.

   a Find the constant of proportionality.

   b Write an equation that relates the amount of blood in a person's body to his or her body weight.

   c Find the weight of a person whose body has about 5 quarts of blood.

6 The height of a stack of books, *H* inches, is directly proportional to the number of books, *n*. The height of a stack of 10 books is 12 inches.

   a Find the constant of proportionality.

   b Write an equation that relates *H* and *n*.

   c Find the height of a stack of 24 books.

7 The total weight of *n* beach balls is *m* ounces. *m* is directly proportional to *n*, and *n* = 12 when *m* = 54.

   a Find the weight per beach ball.

   b Write an equation that relates *n* and *m*.

   c Find the value of *m* when *n* = 30.

8 The cost of plastic cups, *C* dollars, is directly proportional to the number of plastic cups, *n*. The cost of 6 plastic cups is $2.34.

   a Find the cost per plastic cup.

   b Write an equation that relates *C* and *n*.

   c Find the value of *C* when *n* is 7.

Use a proportion to solve each question.

9 5 oranges cost $2. Find the cost of 2 dozen oranges.

10 It costs $180 to rent a car for 3 days. Find the cost of renting a car for 1 week.

11 James drove 48 miles and used 2 gallons of gasoline. How many gallons of gasoline will he use if he drives 78 miles?

12 A caterer knows that the ratio of the number of glasses of juice to the number of people at a party should be 3 : 1. If 15 people are coming to a party, how many glasses of juice should there be?

13 A recipe for meatloaf requires 10 ounces of ground beef. The recipe serves 5 people, and you would like to make enough for 8. How much ground beef should you use?

14 Paula donates $30 to charity for every $100 she earns. Last summer, she earned $3,680. How much did she donate to charity?

15 Ali mixes cans of yellow and blue paint to make green paint. The ratio of the number of cans of yellow paint to the number of cans of blue paint is 4 : 3. Ali needs to make more paint. He has 2 cans of yellow paint to use. How many cans of blue paint does he need to make the same shade of green?

16 The area, A square feet, of the wall Ivan is painting is directly proportional to the time he spends painting the wall, T hours. It takes Ivan 4 hours to paint 113.6 square feet of the wall. How long will he take to paint 227.2 square feet of the wall?

17 It takes Karina 2 hours to paint 5 model boats.

  a How long will it take her to paint 10 model boats?

  b How many model boats can she paint in 10 hours?

18 An initial amount of money deposited in a bank account that earns interest is called the principal. In the table below, P stands for principal, and I stands for the interest earned by that principal for a period of one year at a particular bank. At this bank, the interest earned for a period of one year is directly proportional to the principal amount deposited.

Principal (P dollars)	600	1,000	
Interest Earned (I dollars)	15		56

  a Write a direct proportion equation that relates I and P.

  b Fill in the table.

19 **Mathematical Habit 6** Use precise mathematical language
y varies directly as x. Describe how the value of y changes when the value of x is tripled.

20 **Mathematical Habit 3** Construct viable arguments
Laila wants to buy some blackberries. Three stores sell blackberries at different prices:

Store A   Store B   Store C

$2.40/lb $1.28/8 oz $1.08/6 oz

Which store has the best deal? Explain.

4 Identifying Inverse Proportion

Learning Objectives:
- Identify inverse proportion.
- Use a graph to interpret inverse proportion.
- Solve inverse proportion problems.

> **New Vocabulary**
> inverse proportion

THINK

In a bottled water factory, 5 machines can fill 100 bottles in 1 hour. There are 100 such machines in the factory. Assume that all the machines fill the bottles at the same rate.

a   In the scenario above, identify one direct proportion and one inverse proportion. Explain your answer.

b   The factory received an order of 2500 bottles that needs to be completed within a day. Give three possible ways the manager of the factory can meet the order, and the number of hours each way will take.

ENGAGE

Form a rectangle with 8 square tiles in as many ways as you can. What do you observe about the lengths and widths of the rectangles? Share your observations.

 Identify inverse proportion from a table

Activity Recognizing inverse proportion

Work in pairs.

There are 6 ways of forming a rectangle with 12 square tiles. The diagram shows two possible ways.

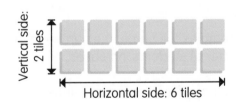
Vertical side: 2 tiles
Horizontal side: 6 tiles

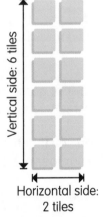
Vertical side: 6 tiles
Horizontal side: 2 tiles

① Form different rectangles by rearranging the 12 square tiles. Record your results in the table below.

Vertical Side (v)		2			6	
Horizontal Side (h)		6			2	
$v \cdot h$		12				

② **Mathematical Habit 6 | Use precise mathematical language**
Write down your observations about the values of $v \cdot h$. Describe the relationship between v and h.

①

A group of students share some game cards so that each of them gets the same number of cards. The table shows the relationship between the number of students, x, and the number of game cards each student gets, y.

Increasing number of students →

Number of Students (x)	1	2	3
Number of Game Cards (y)	120	60	40

← Decreasing number of cards

Since the total number of game cards remains the same, the number of game cards each student receives decreases as the number of students increases.

In this case, you can say that the number of game cards each student receives is inversely proportional to the number of students.

From the table, you can see that the product of x and y is always a constant value.

$xy = 1 \cdot 120$ $xy = 2 \cdot 60$ $xy = 3 \cdot 40$
   $= 120$ $= 120$ $= 120$

For any two quantities (x, y) that are in an inverse proportion relationship, their product, xy, is a constant value called the constant of proportionality.

 **Math Note**

Inverse proportion is sometimes called inverse variation. You can say that the number of game cards varies inversely with the number of students, or the number of game cards and the number of students are in inverse variation.

② The table shows the time it takes, t hours, for n construction workers to pave a road. Determine whether t is inversely proportional to n. If so, find the constant of proportionality.

Number of Workers (n)	1	2	3
Time (t hours)	36	18	12

For each pair of values, n and t:

$$nt = 1 \cdot 36 \qquad nt = 2 \cdot 18 \qquad nt = 3 \cdot 12$$
$$= 36 \qquad\qquad = 36 \qquad\qquad = 36$$

Check whether the product of n and t is a constant value.

The value of n increases as the value of t decreases, and the product of n and t is a constant value. So, t is inversely proportional to n. The constant of proportionality is 36.

③ The table shows the time taken, y hours, by x students to put a jigsaw puzzle together. Determine whether y is inversely proportional to x. If so, find the constant of proportionality.

Number of Students (x)	1	2	3
Time (y hours)	2	1	0.4

For each pair of values, x and y:

$$xy = 1 \cdot 2 \qquad xy = 2 \cdot 1 \qquad xy = 3 \cdot 0.4$$
$$= 2 \qquad\qquad = 2 \qquad\qquad = 1.2$$

If any product of x and y is different, then y is not inversely proportional to x.

The value of x increases as the value of y decreases but the product of x and y is not a constant value. So, y is not inversely proportional to x.

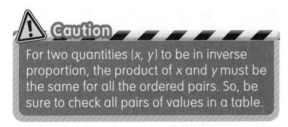

Caution

For two quantities (x, y) to be in inverse proportion, the product of x and y must be the same for all the ordered pairs. So, be sure to check all pairs of values in a table.

TRY Practice identifying inverse proportion from a table

Solve.

1 Some friends want to share the cost of buying a present. The table shows the amount of money that each person has to contribute, y dollars, and the number of people sharing the cost, x. Determine whether y is inversely proportional to x. If so, find the constant of proportionality.

Number of People (x)	1	2	3
Amount Contributed (y dollars)	180	90	60

For each pair of values, x and y:

1 · 180 = _____   _____ · 90 = _____   _____ · _____ = _____

The value of x increases as the value of y decreases, and the product of x and y is

_____ value. So, y is _____ to x.

The constant of proportionality is _____ .

2 Hugo drove from Town A to Town B. The table shows the time he took, y hours, if he traveled at various speeds, x miles per hour. Determine whether x and y are in inverse proportion. If so, find the constant of proportionality.

Speed (x miles per hour)	40	50	60
Time (y hours)	9	$7\frac{1}{3}$	6

For each pair of values, x and y:

40 · 9 = _____   50 · $\dfrac{}{}$ = _____   _____ · _____ = _____

The value of x increases as the value of y decreases, but the product of x and y is

_____ value. So, y is _____ to x.

For each of the following equations, draw a table of values. Use your table to explain which of these equations are equations of inverse proportion.

a $p = -2q$

b $rs = 2$

c $v = \dfrac{2}{w}$

d $\dfrac{x}{y} = \dfrac{1}{2}$

If m and n are in inverse proportion and the constant of proportionality is $\dfrac{1}{2}$, what possible equations can you write? Explain your thinking.

LEARN Identify inverse proportion from an equation

1   When two quantities, such as y and x, are inversely proportional, their product is a constant value. You can write an algebraic equation relating y and x:

$$xy = k \quad \text{or} \quad y = \dfrac{k}{x}$$

To determine whether the two variables in a given equation are inversely proportional, you can use algebra to rewrite the equation in one or both of the forms.

2   Determine whether the equation $\dfrac{1}{2}y = \dfrac{5}{x}$ represents an inverse proportion. If so, state the constant of proportionality.

$$\dfrac{1}{2}y = \dfrac{5}{x}$$

$\dfrac{1}{2}y \cdot 2 = \dfrac{5}{x} \cdot 2$ Multiply both sides by 2.

$y = \dfrac{10}{x}$ Simplify.

$y \cdot x = \dfrac{10}{x} \cdot x$ Multiply both sides by x.

$xy = 10$ Simplify.

Try to rewrite the equation as an equivalent equation in the form $xy = k$ or $y = \dfrac{k}{x}$.

The original equation can be rewritten as two equivalent equations in the form $xy = k$ and $y = \dfrac{k}{x}$: $xy = 10$ and $y = \dfrac{10}{x}$. So, the equation represents an inverse proportion.

The constant of proportionality is **10**.

TRY Practice identifying inverse proportion from an equation

Determine whether each equation represents an inverse proportion. If so, state the constant of proportionality.

① $\frac{3}{5}y = \frac{6}{x}$

$$\frac{3}{5}y = \frac{6}{x}$$

$\frac{3}{5}y \cdot \underline{\hspace{1cm}} = \frac{6}{x} \cdot \underline{\hspace{1cm}}$ Multiply both sides by _____.

$y = \dfrac{\blacksquare}{x}$ Simplify.

$y \cdot x = \dfrac{\blacksquare}{x} \cdot x$ Multiply both sides by x.

$xy = \underline{\hspace{1cm}}$ Simplify.

The original equation _____ be rewritten as two equivalent equations in the form

$y = \dfrac{k}{x}$ and $xy = k$. So, the equation _____ an inverse proportion. The constant

of proportionality is _____.

② $y - 3x = 5$

$$y - 3x = 5$$

$y - 3x + \underline{\hspace{1cm}} = 5 + \underline{\hspace{1cm}}$ Add _____ to both sides.

$\underline{\hspace{1cm}} = \underline{\hspace{1cm}}$ Simplify.

The original equation _____ be rewritten as two equivalent equations in the form

$y = \dfrac{k}{x}$ and $xy = k$. So, the equation _____ an inverse proportion.

ENGAGE

Study the given table.

x	10	20	40	50	80
y	40	20	10	8	5

Give an example of a real-world scenario that might result in this set of data. What do you notice about the relationship between the x and y? What does the graph look like? Share your ideas.

LEARN Use a graph to interpret inverse proportion

1. As you saw earlier, the number of game cards each student gets, y, is inversely proportional to the number of students sharing 120 game cards, x. The graph shows this relationship.

Number of Students (x)	1	2	3
Number of Game Cards (y)	120	60	40

The graph of an inverse proportion is a curve.

Since one variable decreases as the other increases, and the product of the variables is a constant value, neither value can be 0. So, the graph of an inverse proportion never crosses the horizontal and vertical axes.

Use the coordinates of any point (x, y) to find the constant of proportionality.

For example:

$(2, 60) \longrightarrow 2 \cdot 60 = 120$

$(3, 40) \longrightarrow 3 \cdot 40 = 120$

$(4, 30) \longrightarrow 4 \cdot 30 = 120$

$(6, 20) \longrightarrow 6 \cdot 20 = 120$

So, the constant of proportionality is 120.

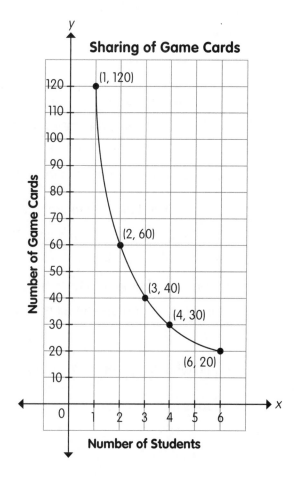

2 The time it takes to clean the windows in an office building is inversely proportional to the number of window cleaners. The graph shows the amount of time, *y* hours, that it takes *x* window cleaners to clean the windows.

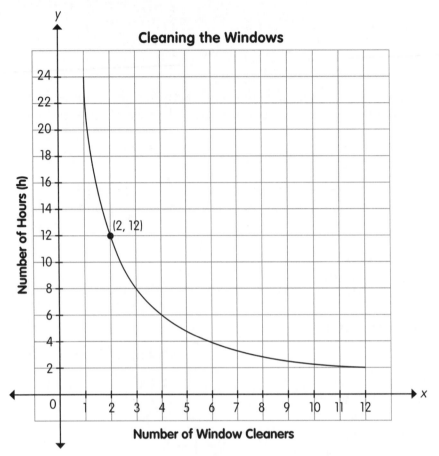

a Find the constant of proportionality graphically. Then, write an inverse proportion equation.

Use (2, 12) to find the constant of proportionality:

$x \cdot y = 2 \cdot 12$ Choose the point (2, 12).

$xy = 24$ Multiply.

The constant of proportionality is 24.

The inverse proportion equation is $xy = 24$.

> Choose a point on the graph to find the constant of proportionality. You can choose any point.

b Explain what the point (2, 12) represents in this situation.

It means that it will take 2 window cleaners 12 hours to clean the windows.

TRY Practice using a graph to interpret inverse proportion

Solve graphically.

1 The amount of time needed for volunteers to pick up trash on a beach is inversely proportional to the number of volunteers. The graph shows the amount of time, y hours, needed by x volunteers.

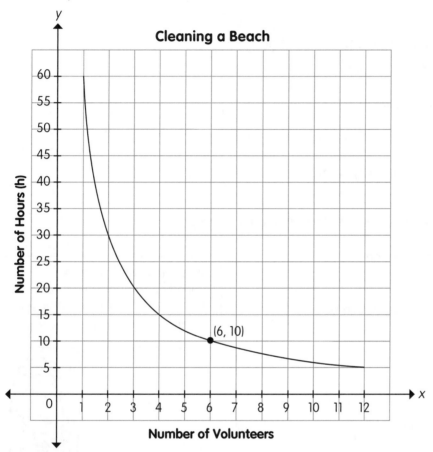

Cleaning a Beach

(6, 10)

Number of Hours (h)

Number of Volunteers

a Find the constant of proportionality graphically. Then, write an inverse proportion equation.

Use the point (_____ , _____) from the graph to find the constant
of proportionality:

$x \cdot y =$ _____ · _____   Choose the point (_____ , _____).

$xy =$ _____   Multiply.

The constant of proportionality is _____ .

The inverse proportion equation is _____ .

b Explain what the point (6, 10) represents in this situation.

It means that _____ volunteers can clean the beach in _____ hours.

ENGAGE

When driving across a certain distance, the speed of the car is inversely proportional to the time it took to travel. If a car traveled for 4 hours at a speed of 50 mph, how long would it travel for if it was driving at a speed of 30 mph?

LEARN Solve inverse proportion problems

1. y is inversely proportional to x, and $y = 20$ when $x = 8$.

   a Find the constant of proportionality.

   Constant of proportionality:

   $x \cdot y = 20 \cdot 8$
   $ = 160$

   The constant of proportionality is 160.

   b Write an inverse proportion equation that relates x and y.

   Inverse proportion equation:

   $xy = 160$ or $y = \dfrac{160}{x}$

   The inverse proportion equation is
   $xy = 160$ or $y = \dfrac{160}{x}$.

   > Since x and y are in inverse proportion, translate the verbal description into an inverse proportion equation in the form of $xy = k$ or $y = \dfrac{k}{x}$.

   c Find the value of y when $x = 5$.

   When $x = 5$ and $y = \dfrac{160}{x}$, $y = \dfrac{160}{5}$ Evaluate $y = \dfrac{160}{x}$ when $x = 5$.

   $\phantom{When x = 5 and y = \dfrac{160}{x},} y = 32$ Simplify.

   The value of y is 32.

2 At an auto repair garage, the number of hours, it takes to repair a car is inversely proportional to the number of workers. It takes 2 workers 6 hours to repair a car. How long will it take 4 workers to repair the same car if they work at the same rate?

Let x be the number of workers.   Define the variables.
Let y be the number of hours.

Constant of proportionality:

$x \cdot y = 2 \cdot 6$
$\quad\quad = 12$

> Translate the verbal description into an inverse proportion equation in the form $xy = k$.

Inverse proportion equation:

> Evaluate $xy = 12$ when $x = 4$ to find the number of hours 4 workers take to repair a car.

$xy = 12$ Write an equation.

When $x = 4$ and $xy = 12$,

$4 \cdot y = 12$ Evaluate $xy = 12$ when $x = 4$.
$4y = 12$ Simplify.
$\dfrac{4y}{4} = \dfrac{12}{4}$ Divide both sides by 4.
$y = 3$ Simplify.

It will take 4 workers 3 hours to repair a car.

TRY Practice solving inverse proportion problems

Solve.

1 y is inversely proportional to x, and $y = 3$ when $x = 5$.

a Find the value of the constant of proportionality.

Constant of proportionality:

$x \cdot y = \underline{\quad\quad} \cdot \underline{\quad\quad}$

$ = \underline{\quad\quad}$

The constant of proportionality is _____.

b Write an inverse proportion equation that relates x and y.

Inverse proportion equation:

$$\underline{\quad\quad} = \underline{\quad\quad} \quad \text{or} \quad \underline{\quad\quad} = \underline{\quad\quad}$$

The inverse proportion equation is $\underline{\quad\quad} = \underline{\quad\quad}$ or $\underline{\quad\quad} = \underline{\quad\quad}$.

c Find the value of y when $x = 10$.

When $x = 10$ and $y = \dfrac{\quad}{x}$, $\quad y = \dfrac{\quad}{\quad}$ Evaluate $y = \dfrac{\quad}{x}$ when $x = 10$.

$$y = \underline{\quad\quad} \quad\quad \text{Simplify.}$$

The value of y is $\underline{\quad\quad}$.

2 Trucks are used to paint dividing lines on a long highway. The number of hours the trucks take to paint the lines is inversely proportional to the number of trucks. 15 trucks can paint the highway in 28 hours. How many trucks are needed to paint the same highway in 20 hours?

Let x be the number of trucks.
Let y be the number of hours.

Constant of proportionality:

$$x \cdot y = \underline{\quad\quad} \cdot \underline{\quad\quad}$$

$$= \underline{\quad\quad}$$

Inverse proportion equation:

$$xy = \underline{\quad\quad} \quad\quad \text{Write an inverse equation.}$$

When $y = 20$ and $xy = \underline{\quad\quad}$,

$20 \cdot x = \underline{\quad\quad}$ Evaluate $xy = \underline{\quad\quad}$ when $y = 20$.

$20x = \underline{\quad\quad}$ Simplify.

$\dfrac{20x}{\quad} = \dfrac{\quad}{\quad}$ Divide both sides by $\underline{\quad\quad}$.

$x = \underline{\quad\quad}$ Simplify.

$\underline{\quad\quad}$ trucks are needed to paint the highway in 20 hours.

INDEPENDENT PRACTICE

Determine whether two quantities are in inverse proportion. If so, find the constant of proportionality.

1

x	25	10	5
y	2	5	10

2

x	7	5	3
y	30	60	70

3

x	4	6	8
y	16	24	32

4

x	6	3	1
y	2	4	12

Determine whether each equation represents an inverse proportion. If so, find the constant of proportionality.

5 $10x = \dfrac{5}{y}$

6 $\dfrac{y}{20} = x$

7 $y + \dfrac{1}{7}x = \dfrac{1}{2}$

8 $0.1x = \dfrac{5}{y}$

Each graph represents an inverse proportion. Find the constant of proportionality.

9

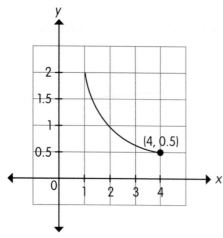

(4, 0.5)

10

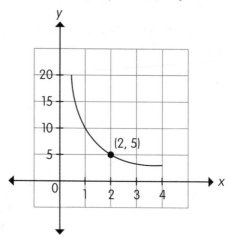

(2, 5)

11

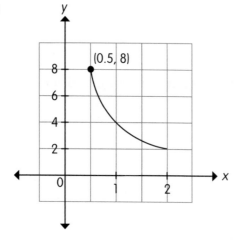

(0.5, 8)

12

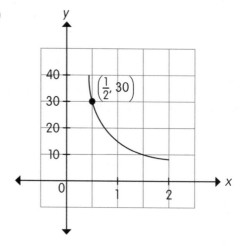

$\left(\frac{1}{2}, 30\right)$

Solve.

13 | **Mathematical Habit** 2 | **Use mathematical reasoning**

Describe how you can determine whether two quantities are in inverse proportion.

14 The workers at a bakery must mix 12 batches of bagel dough every hour to meet the needs of customers. The number of batches of bagel dough, b, that each worker needs to mix in one hour is inversely proportional to the number of workers, n. The graph shows the relationship between b and n.

a Find the constant of proportionality from the graph. Then, write an inverse proportion equation.

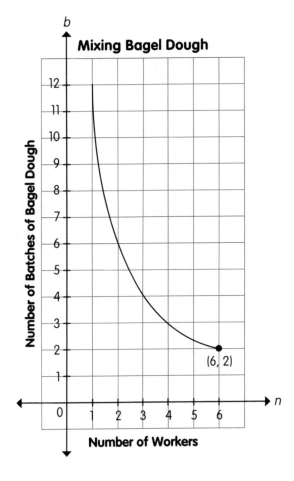

b Explain what the constant of proportionality represents in this situation.

c Explain what the point (6, 2) represents in this situation.

15 A rectangle has a fixed area that does not change. The length, ℓ, of the rectangle is inversely proportional to its width, w. The graph shows the relationship between ℓ and w.

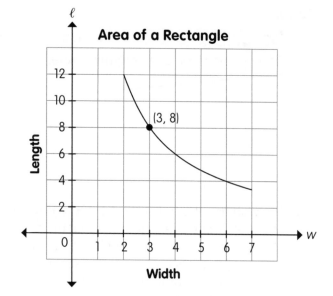

a Find the constant of proportionality from the graph. Then, write an inverse proportion equation.

b Explain what the constant of proportionality represents in this situation.

c Explain what the point (3, 8) represents in this situation.

16 y is inversely proportional to x, and $y = 2$ when $x = 5$.

a Find the constant of proportionality.

b Write an inverse equation relating x and y.

c Find the value of x when $y = 4$.

17 y is inversely proportional to x, and $y = \frac{1}{3}$ when $x = \frac{1}{2}$.

a Find the constant of proportionality.

b Write an inverse proportion equation relating x and y.

c Find the value of y when $x = \frac{1}{5}$.

18 **Mathematical Habit 2** Use mathematical reasoning

y is inversely proportional to x. Describe how the value of y changes if the value of x is halved.

19 The number of hours it takes to mow nine lawns is inversely proportional to the number of gardeners. It takes 3 gardeners 4 hours to mow nine lawns. How many hours would it take 1 gardener to mow the same nine lawns?

20 The number of minutes it takes to download a file is inversely proportional to the download speed. It takes Rachel 12 minutes to download a file when the download speed is 256 kilobytes per second. How long will it take her to download the same file if the download speed is 512 kilobytes per second?

21 **Mathematical Habit 2** Use mathematical reasoning

Each table shows the price, y dollars, that x people have to pay to rent a guest house for one day. Describe how the two tables are alike, and how they are different. Use inverse proportion to explain your answer.

Guest House A

Number of People (x)	1	2	3	4
Price (y dollars)	240	120	80	60

Guest House B

Number of People (x)	1	2	3	4
Price (y dollars)	240	120	85	65

In questions 22 to 25, determine whether each relationship represents a direct or inverse proportion. Explain your answer.

22 A rectangle with length, x inches, and width, y inches, has an area of 50 square inches. Its area is given by the equation $xy = 50$.

23 The density of a substance is the mass of the substance per unit of volume. A particular substance with a mass of m grams and a volume of v cubic centimeters has a density of 3 grams per cubic centimeter. An equation for the density of the substance is $3 = \frac{m}{v}$.

24 The music director at a school wants x students to sell 200 tickets to the spring musical. The 200 tickets are distributed to the students in equal amounts so that each student gets y tickets to sell. The number of tickets each student gets is given by the equation $y = \frac{200}{x}$.

25 The amount of sales tax that you pay when you buy a new shirt is based on the price of the shirt.

5 Percent Increase and Decrease

Learning Objectives:
• Find a quantity given a percent increase or decrease.
• Find percent increase or decrease.

> **New Vocabulary**
> discount
> markup

THINK

The cost price of a bag was $100. A seller marked up the price by 10%, and then sold it at a discount of 11% during a sale. Can we say that the final price of the bag decreased by 1%? Why do you say so? Explain.

ENGAGE

a   A cake cost $20. Its price increased by $5. Express this increase as a percent of the original price. What can you say about the percent increase of the price of the cake?

b   Using your answer in (a), what do you think is the percent decrease in price if the cake originally cost $25 and had its price reduced by $5?

LEARN Find a quantity given a percent increase or decrease

1   The price of a pair of running shoes increased by 15% since last year. If the price of the running shoes cost $60 last year, how much does it cost now?

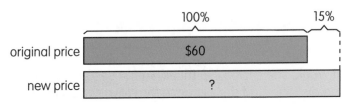

▶ **Method 1**

100% + 15% = 115%

100% ⟶ $60

1% ⟶ $60 ÷ 100 = $0.60

115% ⟶ $0.60 · 115 = $69

The pair of shoes costs $69 now.

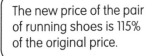

The new price of the pair of running shoes is 115% of the original price.

▶ **Method 2**

15% of $\$60 = \dfrac{15}{100} \cdot \$60$

$= \$9$

$\$60 + \$9 = \$69$

The pair of shoes costs $69 now.

First, find the increase in the price. The increase is 15% of the original price.

2 There is a 20% discount on all items in a store. Mateo bought a computer that costs $1,585.75 before discount. Find the price of the computer after discount.

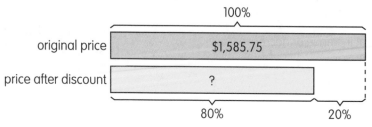

▶ **Method 1**

100% − 20% = 80%

100% ⟶ $1,585.75

1% ⟶ $\frac{\$1,585.75}{100}$

80% ⟶ $\frac{\$1,585.75}{100} \cdot 80 = \$1,268.60$

> The price of the computer after discount is 80% of the original price.

The price of the computer after discount is $1,268.60.

▶ **Method 2**

80% of $1,585.75 $= \frac{80}{100} \cdot \$1,585.75$

$= \$1,268.60$

The price of the computer after discount is $1,268.60.

TRY Practice finding a quantity given a percent increase or decrease

Solve.

1 Mya is training for a race. In the first week, she cycled 195 miles. In the second week, she increased the distance she cycled by 20%. Find the distance that Mya cycled in the second week.

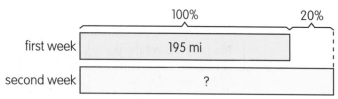

▶ **Method 1**

100% + _____% = _____%

100% ⟶ _____ mi

1% ⟶ _____ ÷ 100 = _____ mi

120% ⟶ _____ · 120 = _____ mi

Mya cycled _____ miles in the second week.

▶ Method 2

$$20\% \text{ of } 195 \text{ mi} = \frac{}{100} \cdot \underline{\hspace{2cm}}$$

$$= \underline{\hspace{2cm}} \text{ mi}$$

$195 + \underline{\hspace{1.5cm}} = \underline{\hspace{1.5cm}}$

Mya cycled _____ miles in the second week.

2. A farmer harvested 2,215 pounds of apples last year. Due to poor weather, the farmer harvested 8% fewer apples this year compared to the last. How many pounds of apples did the farmer harvest this year?

What percent does 2,215 pounds represent?

%

| harvested last year | _____ lb |
| harvested this year | ? |

% %

$100\% - \underline{\hspace{1.5cm}}\% = \underline{\hspace{1.5cm}}\%$

The amount of apples harvested this year was _____% of the amount harvested last year.

$$\underline{\hspace{1.5cm}}\% \text{ of } \underline{\hspace{1.5cm}} \text{ lb} = \frac{}{100} \cdot \underline{\hspace{1.5cm}}$$

$$= \underline{\hspace{2cm}} \text{ lb}$$

The farmer harvested _____ pounds of apples this year.

Given the original cost and the selling price of an item, how do you know if there is a percent increase or decrease? Draw bar models to explain your thinking. Use examples to justify your thinking. Discuss with your partner how you find the percent change in your examples.

LEARN Find percent increase or decrease

1. The original cost of a bicycle is $450. The selling price of the bicycle at a retail store is $585. Find the percent markup.

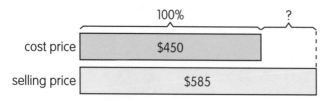

The markup is the rate at which a seller raises the price of goods over their cost.

Increase in price = $585 − $450
           = $135

Percent markup = $\frac{\$135}{\$450} \cdot 100\%$

           = 30%

Percent change = $\frac{\text{Change}}{\text{Original quantity}} \cdot 100\%$

The percent markup is 30%.

2. Last year, there were 2,176 members in a club. The number of members dropped to 1,980 this year. Find the percent decrease in the membership of the club. Round your answer to a whole number.

Decrease in members = 2,176 − 1,980
             = 196

Percent decrease = $\frac{196}{2,176} \cdot 100\%$

           ≈ 9%

The percent decrease in the membership of the club is about 9%.

Work in pairs.

(1) Each person takes eight cards and writes a different 4-digit number on each card. Shuffle all the cards and place them face down in a pile. Take turns to each draw a card from the pile. Then, use a calculator to find the percent increase or decrease of the second number from the first. Round your answers to the nearest tenth of a percent.

Example:

First card

2,176

Second card

1,751

Difference = 2,176 − 1,751

= 425 (decrease)

Percent decrease = $\frac{425}{2,176} \cdot 100\%$

≈ 19.5%

Record your results in the table as shown.

First Card	2,176				
Second Card	1,751				
Increase/Decrease	425				
Percent Change	19.5%				

(2) Repeat by drawing other number cards. Record your results in the same table.

TRY **Practice finding percent increase or decrease**

Solve.

(1) The original price of a remote control car was $80. During a sale, its price became $64. Find the percent discount.

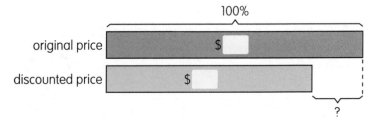

100%

original price $☐

discounted price $☐

?

Discount = $_____ − $_____

= $_____

Percent discount = $\dfrac{}{} \cdot 100\%$

= _____%

The percent discount was _____%.

2 Alex deposited $1,200 into a savings account. At the end of the first year, the amount of money in the account increased to $1,260. What was the percent interest?

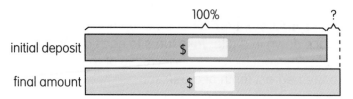

100%   ?

initial deposit $_____

final amount $_____

Interest = $_____ − $_____

= $_____

Percent interest = ———— · 100%

= _____%

The percent interest was _____%.

Interest is the amount of money earned from savings, or the amount charged by banks for borrowing money.

ENGAGE

A bag cost $50. How much is 90% and 80% of the bag respectively? Think of more percents and fill up the table below.

Percent	100%	90%	80%		
Cost	$50				

Look at the values in your table. What do you notice about the relationship between percent and cost?

LEARN Solve direct proportion problems involving percent

1 The regular price of a phone was $228. During a sale, its price was marked down by $45.60. Use a proportion to find the percent discount.

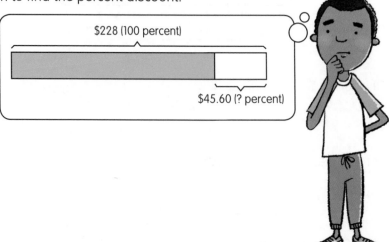

$228 (100 percent)

$45.60 (? percent)

Let x be the percent discount.

▶ **Method 1**

$$\frac{100 \text{ percent}}{\$228} = \frac{x \text{ percent}}{\$45.60}$$ Write a proportion.

$$\frac{100}{228} = \frac{x}{45.60}$$ Write ratios as fractions.

$$x \cdot 228 = 100 \cdot 45.6$$ Write cross products.

$$228x = 4{,}560$$ Simplify.

$$228x \div \mathbf{228} = 4{,}560 \div \mathbf{228}$$ Divide both sides by 228.

$$x = 20$$ Simplify.

The percent discount was 20%.

▶ **Method 2**

Ratio of percents = Ratio of dollar amounts

x percent : 100 percent = \$45.60 : \$228   Write a proportion.

$$\frac{x}{100} = \frac{45.60}{228}$$ Write ratios as fractions.

$$\mathbf{100} \cdot \frac{x}{100} = \frac{45.60}{228} \cdot \mathbf{100}$$ Multiply both sides by 100.

$$x = 20$$ Simplify.

The percent discount was 20%.

Math Talk

Diego uses a different proportion to solve this problem.

$$\frac{\$45.60}{\$228} = \frac{100 \text{ percent}}{x \text{ percent}}$$

Will he get the correct answer if he uses this proportion? Explain your reasoning.

Solve.

1 A store owner bought some handbags for $32 each from the manufacturer. Later, the store owner marked up the price of each handbag by $8. Use a proportion to find the percent increase in the price of the handbags.

▶ Method 1

$$\frac{100 \text{ percent}}{\$\rule{1cm}{0.4pt}} = \frac{x \text{ percent}}{\$\rule{1cm}{0.4pt}}$$ Write a proportion.

$$\frac{100}{\rule{1cm}{0.4pt}} = \frac{x}{\rule{1cm}{0.4pt}}$$ Write ratios as fractions.

$$x \cdot \rule{1cm}{0.4pt} = 100 \cdot \rule{1cm}{0.4pt}$$ Write cross products.

$$\rule{1cm}{0.4pt} \, x = \rule{1cm}{0.4pt}$$ Simplify.

$$\rule{1cm}{0.4pt} \, x \div \rule{1cm}{0.4pt} = \rule{1cm}{0.4pt} \div \rule{1cm}{0.4pt}$$ Divide both sides by _____.

$$x = \rule{1cm}{0.4pt}$$ Simplify.

The percent increase was _____%.

▶ Method 2

Ratio of percents = Ratio of dollar amounts

x percent : 100 percent = $_____ : $_____   Write a proportion.

$$\frac{x}{100} = \frac{\rule{1cm}{0.4pt}}{\rule{1cm}{0.4pt}}$$ Write ratios as fractions.

$$100 \cdot \frac{x}{100} = \frac{\rule{1cm}{0.4pt}}{\rule{1cm}{0.4pt}} \cdot 100$$ Multiply both sides by 100.

$$x = \rule{1cm}{0.4pt}$$ Simplify.

The percent increase was _____%.

MATH SHARING

Mathematical Habit 3 Construct viable arguments

Caleb has 40 magnets. Zara has 50 magnets. Zara says that she has 25% more magnets than Caleb; hence, Caleb has 25% fewer magnets than her. Do you agree with Zara? Discuss.

Name: _____ Date: _____

INDEPENDENT PRACTICE

Solve.

1. Steven bought an antique coin for $25. He sold it for 30% more than what he paid. How much did Steven sell the coin for?

2. The cost price of a bottle of juice is $1.25. It is sold at a 40% markup in a store. Find the selling price of the bottle of juice.

3. The original price of a toy was $110. There was a storewide discount of 25%. Find the discounted price of the toy.

4. The price of a pound of grapes was $3.20 last year. This year, the price of grapes fell by 15% due to a better harvest. Find the price of a pound of grapes this year.

5. The original price of a television set was $850. At a sale, the television set was sold for $680. Find the percent discount.

6 The regular price of roses is $1.20 a stem. During festive occasions, the price of a stem of rose is $2.10. Find the percent increase during festive occasions.

7 The weight of a cub was 1.2 pounds at birth. At 3 months, its weight was 2.4 pounds and at 6 months, its weight was 4.2 pounds. What was the percent increase in its weight at 6 months compared to

   a its weight at birth?

   b its weight at 3 months?

8 The membership at a fitness club was 250. A year later, the membership dropped by 35. Use a proportion to find the percent decrease in the membership of the fitness club.

9 **Mathematical Habit 3** Construct viable arguments

   In an experiment, Anna and Jason monitored the changes in temperature of water heated by a burner. The temperature of the water was 70°F at first. After 5 minutes, the temperature increased to 140°F. After another 5 minutes, the temperature increased to 210°F. Anna and Jason were told to find the percent increase in temperature from 5 minutes to 10 minutes after the water was heated.

Anna's answer:	Jason's answer:
210°F − 140°F = 70°F	210°F − 140°F = 70°F
$\frac{70}{70} \cdot 100\% = 100\%$	$\frac{70}{140} \cdot 100\% = 50\%$
The percent increase in temperature was 100%.	The percent increase in temperature was 50%.

   Who is correct, Anna or Jason? Explain why.

6 Real-World Problems: Percent Increase and Decrease

Learning Objectives:
• Solve real-world problems involving percent increase or decrease.
• Solve real-world problems involving a quantity represented by a percent.
• Solve real-world problems involving fractions and percents.
• Solve real-world problems involving the concept of "percent of percent."

THINK

A liquid soap dispenser was fully filled in the morning. By noon, 10% of the liquid soap was used. By evening, 20% of the remaining soap was used. At night, liquid soap was poured into the dispenser so that it reached its original volume. What is the percent increase of the liquid soap in the dispenser from evening to night?

ENGAGE

A container has 4 quarts of water.

a Kylie pours more water into the container and the volume of water increases by 25%. How much water is there in the container now?

b Kylie then uses some water from the container to make juice for a party and the volume decreases by 40%. How much water is left in the container?

Discuss with your partner how you can use bar models to represent and solve this problem.

LEARN Solve real-world problems involving percent increase or decrease

① The volume of water in a tank was 20 gallons at first. After two hours, the volume of water decreased by 33%. Another two hours later, the volume increased by 20%.

a Find the volume of water after two hours.

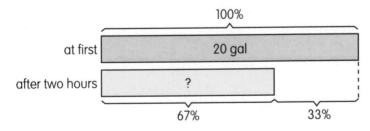

100% − 33% = 67%

The volume of water in the tank after two hours was 67% of the volume at first.

67% of 20 gal = $\frac{67}{100} \cdot 20$

            = 13.4 gal

There were 13.4 gallons of water after two hours.

b Find the volume of water after four hours.

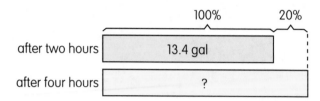

after two hours [13.4 gal]

after four hours [?]

Here, the original quantity (100%) is the volume after the first two hours.

20% of 13.4 gal = $\frac{20}{100}$ · 13.4

= 2.68 gal

13.4 + 2.68 = 16.08

There were 16.08 gallons of water after four hours.

TRY Practice solving real-world problems involving percent increase or decrease

Solve.

1 Jordan saved for three months. He saved $50 in the first month. His savings increased by 20% in the second month. In the third month, Jordan's savings decreased by 75%.

a Find the amount that Jordan saved in the second month.

first month [$ ____]

second month [?]

_____% of $_____ = $\frac{}{100}$ · $_____

= $_____

$_____ + $_____ = $_____

Jordan saved $_____ in the second month.

b Find the amount that Jordan saved in the third month.

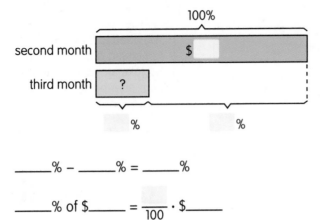

_____% − _____% = _____%

_____% of $_____ = $\frac{}{100}$ · $_____

 = $_____

Jordan saved $_____ in the third month.

ENGAGE

Madeline has a collection of seashells. 60% of her seashells is 75. Discuss with your partner how you can make use of this information to find out how many seashells Madeline has. How many methods can you think of?

LEARN Solve real-world problems by finding a quantity represented by a percent

1 Ms. Turner had some flour. She used 20% of the flour to bake cakes and had 16 pounds of flour left. She then used 25% of the remaining flour to bake muffins.

a How much flour did Ms. Turner have at first?

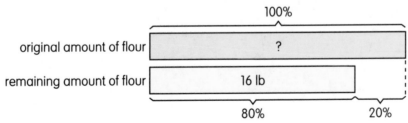

80% ⟶ 16 lb

1% ⟶ 16 ÷ 80 = 0.2 lb

100% ⟶ 100 · 0.2 = 20 lb

Ms. Turner had 20 pounds of flour at first.

b How much flour did Ms. Turner have left after baking muffins?

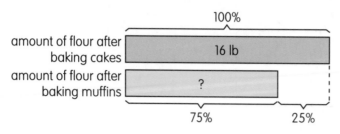

100%

amount of flour after baking cakes | 16 lb

amount of flour after baking muffins | ?

75%   25%

You need to find 75% of the remaining amount of flour. So, take the remaining amount of flour after baking cakes as 100%.

$100\% - 25\% = 75\%$

$75\% \cdot 16 \text{ lb} = \dfrac{75}{100} \cdot 16$

$\phantom{75\% \cdot 16 \text{ lb}} = 12 \text{ lb}$

Ms. Turner had 12 pounds of flour left after baking muffins.

TRY **Practice solving real-world problems by finding a quantity represented by a percent**

Solve.

1 Jacob had some savings. He spent 15% of his savings on a storybook and had $14.45 left. He then spent 20% of the remaining amount of money on snacks.

a How much was Jacob's savings?

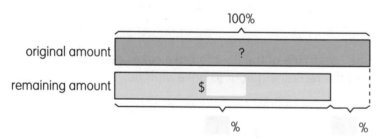

100%

original amount | ?

remaining amount | $

____%   ____%

$100\% - \underline{}\% = \underline{}\%$

$\underline{}\% \longrightarrow \$\underline{}$

$1\% \longrightarrow \$\underline{} \div \underline{} = \$\underline{}$

$100\% \longrightarrow 100 \cdot \$\underline{} = \$\underline{}$

Jacob's savings was $_____.

b How much did Jacob have left after buying snacks?

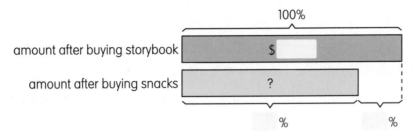

100% − _____% = _____%

_____% · $_____ = $\frac{}{100}$ · $_____

= $_____

Jacob had $_____ left after buying snacks.

ENGAGE

a Sebastian has a collection of cards. $\frac{1}{3}$ of the cards are baseball cards, $\frac{1}{2}$ of the remaining cards are football cards, and the rest are basketball cards. How many cards does he have in total if he has 28 basketball cards?

b Discuss with your partner how you can use your methods for (a) to solve the following question:

Emily has a collection of stamps. 20% of her stamps are triangle stamps, $\frac{1}{3}$ of the remaining stamps are square stamps, and the rest are rectangle stamps. How many triangle stamps does she have if she has 40 rectangle stamps?

LEARN Solve real-world problems involving fractions and percents

① Jada has a box of 2,000 beads. 25% of the beads are red. $\frac{3}{5}$ of the remaining beads are blue and the rest are green. Find the number of green beads.

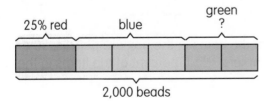

100% − 25% = 75%

75% of 2,000 = $\frac{75}{100}$ · 2,000 = 1,500

1,500 beads are either blue or green.

$1 - \frac{3}{5} = \frac{2}{5}$

Number of green beads = $\frac{2}{5}$ · 1,500

= 600

There are 600 green beads.

Solve.

1. Mr. Nelson's monthly salary is $2,500. His salary is 15% more than that of Mr. Parker's. Each month, Mr. Parker saves $\frac{2}{5}$ of his salary. Find the amount of money Mr. Parker spends each month.

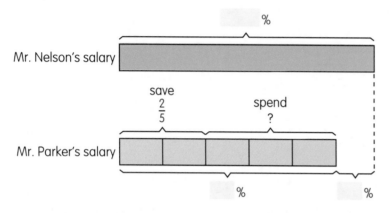

_____% – _____% = _____%

_____% of $_____ = $\frac{}{100}$ · $_____

$ = $_____

1 – $\frac{}{}$ = $\frac{}{}$

Amount Mr. Parker spends = $\frac{}{}$ · _____

$ = $_____

Mr. Parker spends $_____ each month.

ENGAGE

a   What is $\frac{1}{4}$ of $\frac{2}{3}$? Explain how you can use your method to find 50% of 80%.

b   A box contains pencils, pens, and markers. 20% of the items in the box are pencils, 50% of the remaining items are pens, and the rest are markers. What percent of the items in the box are markers?

1 Students in a class were asked to pick their favorite sport from basketball, football, and hockey. 40% of the students chose basketball, 75% of the remaining students chose football, and the rest chose hockey.

a What percent of the students chose football?

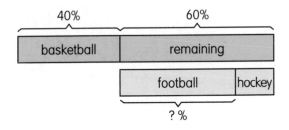

$100\% - 40\% = 60\%$

60% of the students chose football or hockey.

$$75\% \text{ of } 60\% = \frac{75}{100} \cdot 60\%$$
$$= 45\%$$

45% of the students chose football.

b Given that 6 students chose hockey, how many students were there in the class?

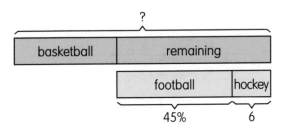

$60\% - 45\% = 15\%$

$15\% \longrightarrow 6$

$1\% \longrightarrow 6 \div 15 = 0.4$

$100\% \longrightarrow 0.4 \cdot 100 = 40$

There were 40 students in the class.

TRY Practice solving real-world problems involving the concept of "percent of percent"

Solve.

1. Some fruit were delivered to a stall. 20% of the fruit were oranges. 35% of the remaining fruit were apples, and the rest were pears.

   a What percent of the fruit were apples?

   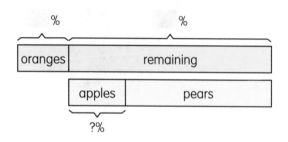

   _____% − _____% = _____%

   _____% of the fruit were apples and pears.

   _____% of _____% = $\frac{}{100}$ · _____%

   = _____%

   _____% of the fruit were apples.

   b Given that there were 65 pears, how many pieces of fruit were delivered to the stall?

   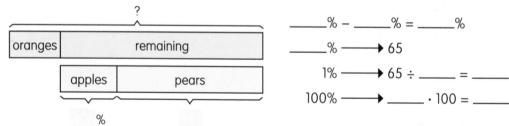

   _____% − _____% = _____%

   _____% ⟶ 65

   1% ⟶ 65 ÷ _____ = _____

   100% ⟶ _____ · 100 = _____

   _____ pieces of fruit were delivered to the stall.

MATH SHARING

Mathematical Habit 6 Use precise mathematical language
Find examples of percent increase or decrease by examining bills or receipts for discount, service charge, or other taxes. Discuss with your classmates how percent changes are calculated.

Name: _____ Date: _____

INDEPENDENT PRACTICE

Solve.

1 Mai had 120 game cards. She bought 25% more cards. Mai then gave 40% of the cards to her brother.

a Find the number of cards after she bought more.

b Find the number of cards Mai had left after she gave some to her brother.

2 In an experiment, Carter found that the amount of water in a container decreased by 20% every two minutes. Find the amount of water left after four minutes if he started with 8 gallons of water.

3 Diego had 12 meters of rope. After using some rope for an activity, he had 45% of rope left. How many meters of rope did Diego use?

4 Lola had a bag of tokens. After a game, she lost 30% of her tokens and had 28 tokens left. Find the number of tokens Lola had at first.

5 Aisha had a roll of ribbon. She used 15% of the ribbon to decorate cards and had 17 feet of ribbon left. She then used 20% of the remaining ribbon to wrap gifts.

a What was the original length of the roll of ribbon?

b What was the remaining length of ribbon after Aisha used them to wrap gifts?

6 Miguel opened a savings account with a bank. The interest rate on his savings was 1% for the first year. For the second year, the interest rate will be 2%.

   a Miguel had $1,515 in his savings account at the end of the first year. What was the initial deposit he made?

   b How much will Miguel have in his account at the end of the second year?

7 Mia won $200 in a race. She saved 15% of the money and spent the rest. Of the amount of money she spent, $\frac{1}{5}$ were spent on socks and the remaining on a pair of running shoes. Find the amount of money Mia spent on the pair of running shoes.

8 At a florist's shop, 60% of the flowers are roses and the rest are lilies and daisies. The number of daisies is $\frac{2}{3}$ of the number of lilies. There are 270 roses. How many lilies are there?

9 A school sold 200 tickets for its summer musical. 40% of the tickets were sold to students, and the rest were sold to adults. 20% of these tickets were sold to teachers and the rest to the students' parents. Find the number of tickets that were sold to parents.

10 A charity carnival raised funds from food, games, and book stalls. 30% of the amount was from the sale of food. 25% of the remaining amount was from the sale of books. $2,100 was collected from the game stalls. Find the total amount of money raised by the carnival.

Mathematical Habit 3 Construct viable arguments

Amelia has a box of 150 beads that are either red, purple, or yellow. 20% of the beads are red and $\frac{2}{5}$ of the remaining beads are yellow. Amelia worked out the number of yellow beads as follows:

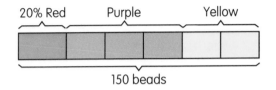

20% Red   Purple   Yellow

150 beads

$100\% - 20\% = 80\%$

$\frac{2}{5} \cdot 150 = 60$

There were 60 yellow beads.

Explain to Amelia her mistake and show her the correct solution.

Explanation:

Correct solution:

Problem Solving with Heuristics

1 **Mathematical Habit 1** **Persevere in solving problems**

Ms. Davis plans to drive from Town P to Town Q, a distance of 350 miles. She hopes to use only 12 gallons of gasoline. After traveling 150 miles, she checks her gauge and estimates that she has used 5 gallons of gasoline. At this rate, will Ms. Davis arrive at Town Q before stopping for gasoline? Justify your answer.

② **Mathematical Habit 1** Persevere in solving problems

In the figure, the area of Square Y is 40% of the area of the whole figure. The area of the shaded part is 60% of the area of Square Y. What percent of Rectangle X is shaded? Round your answer to the nearest hundredth.

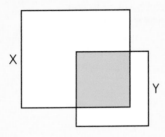

CHAPTER WRAP-UP

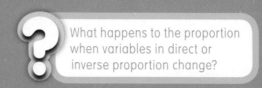

? What happens to the proportion when variables in direct or inverse proportion change?

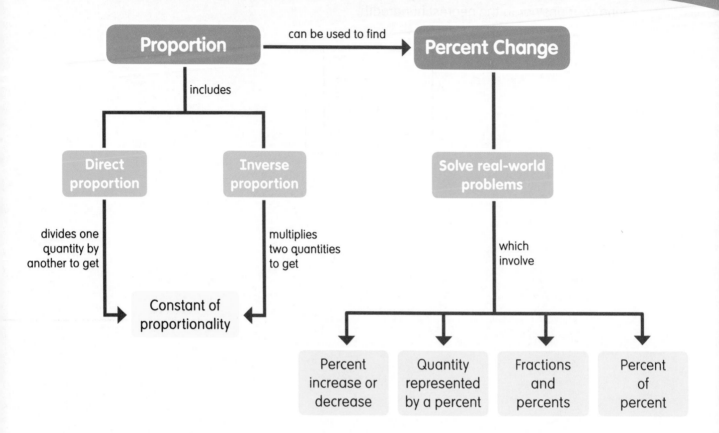

KEY CONCEPTS

- When y is directly proportional to x, and they have a constant of proportionality, k, you can write an algebraic equation relating y and x:

  $y = kx$ or $\dfrac{y}{x} = k$

- The graph of a direct proportion is always a straight line that passes through the origin, (0, 0), but does not lie along the horizontal or vertical axis.

- When two quantities, such as y and x, are in inverse proportion, and their product is a constant of proportionality, k, you can write an algebraic equation relating y and x:

  $xy = k$ or $y = \dfrac{k}{x}$

- The graph of an inverse proportion is a curve that never crosses the horizontal and vertical axes.

- You can find percent change using this formula:

  Percent change $= \dfrac{\text{Change}}{\text{Original quantity}} \cdot 100\%$

State whether each table, graph, or equation represents a direct proportion, an inverse proportion, or neither.

1️⃣

x	3	5	7
y	4.5	7.5	10.5

2️⃣

x	2	4	8
y	50	25	12.5

3️⃣

x	6	8	24
y	12	9	3.5

4️⃣

x	5	10	15
y	2.5	5	7.5

5️⃣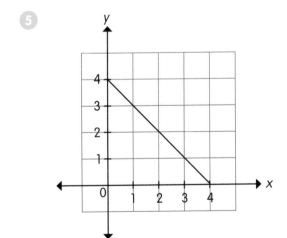

6️⃣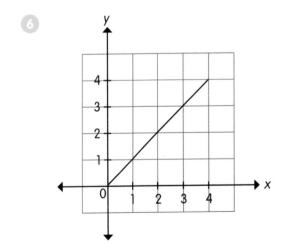

7
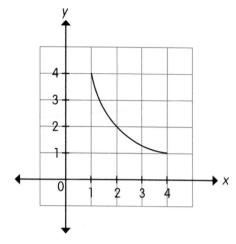

8
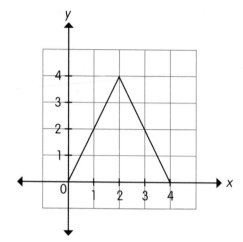

9 $y = \frac{1}{2}x + 5$

10 $\frac{y}{4} = 7x$

11 $-3 + x = y$

12 $\frac{y}{2} = \frac{3}{x}$

In each table, *y* is directly proportional to *x*. Find the constant of proportionality. Then, fill in each table.

13

x	2	4	
y		16	25

14

x	3	5	
y		2.5	3

In each table, *y* is inversely proportional to *x*. Find the constant of proportionality. Then, fill in each table.

15

x	2	4	
y	30		10

16

x	2.5		5
y		2	1.6

Use proportionality reasoning to solve each question.

17 *y* is directly proportional to *x*, and *y* = 56 when *x* = 7. Find the value of *y* when *x* = 4.

18 *y* is inversely proportional to *x*, and *y* = 12 when *x* = 4. Find the value of *x* when *y* = 8.

Use a proportion to solve each question.

19 The graph shows that the cost of gasoline, *y* dollars, is directly proportional to *x* gallons of gasoline.

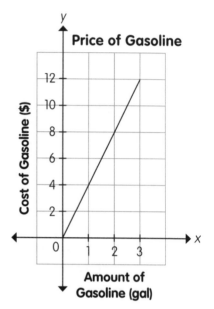

Price of Gasoline

a Find the constant of proportionality. What does this value represent in the context of the problem?

b Write a direct proportion equation.

c If Luis spent $24 for gasoline, how many gallons of gasoline did he buy?

20 Out of every $100 that Taylor earns at her part-time job, she saves $25 for college. The amount she saves is directly proportional to the amount she earns. If she earns $3,880 in one year, how much will she save for college?

21 Yong made fruit punch using 2 parts orange juice to 3 parts soda water. The amount of soda water that Yong used is directly proportional to the amount of orange juice he used. How many cups of orange juice should Yong use with 18 cups of soda water?

Use graph paper. Solve.

22 In the table below, *P* stands for the amount of money deposited in a bank account, and *I* stands for the interest earned for a period of one year at a bank. *P* is directly proportional to *I*. Graph the direct proportion relationship between *P* and *I*. Use 1 unit on the horizontal axis to represent $1 and 1 unit on the vertical axis to represent $50.

Interest Earned (*I* dollars)	2	4	6
Amount of Money Deposited (*P* dollars)	100	200	300

a Using the graph, find the interest earned when the amount of money deposited is $350.

b Write an equation relating *P* and *I*. Then, find the amount of money deposited when the interest earned is $15.

Use a proportion to solve each question.

23 The time taken by some students to deliver 500 flyers, *t* hours, is inversely proportional to the number of students, *n*. The graph shows the relationship between *n* and *t*.

a Find the constant of proportionality graphically.

b Write an equation relating *n* and *t*.

c Describe the relationship between the number of students and the time needed to deliver the flyers.

d Explain what the point (6, 2) represents in this situation.

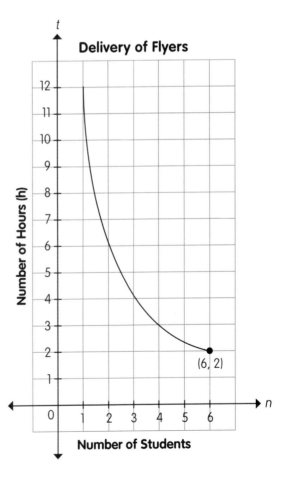

Delivery of Flyers

(6, 2)

Number of Hours (h)

Number of Students

24 Jesse has set aside a certain amount of money to download applications for his new smart phone. The number of applications he can afford to download is inversely proportional to the cost of each download. With his money, he can afford to download 12 applications that cost $2 each. How many applications can he afford to download if he finds less expensive applications that cost only $1.50 each?

25 A company begins a new product line and needs to increase the number of employees by 16%. The current number of employees is 650. How many employees does the company need?

26 Maria had 120 bookmarks at first. Her uncle gave her 25% more bookmarks. Then, she sold 20% of all the bookmarks.

a Find the total number of bookmarks Maria had after her uncle gave her some.

b Find the number of bookmarks Maria had in the end.

27 A grocery store received a shipment of 2,000 pounds of fruit. 15% of the fruit were rotten. $\frac{3}{5}$ of the remaining fruit were sold that week. Find the amount of fruit left at the end of the week.

28 Ms. Evans earns $6,000 each month. Ms. Walker earns 65% of what Ms. Evans earns. Ms. Walker spends 80% of her salary and saves the rest. Find the amount of money Ms. Walker saves each month.

 29 To encourage healthy eating at school, Ms. Garcia brought carrot sticks, apple slices, and celery sticks to share with her class. 40% of the snacks were carrot sticks. 40% of the remaining snacks were apple slices, and the rest were celery sticks. There were 90 celery sticks. How many carrot sticks and apple slices were there in all?

Answer each question.

(30) Which of these represents inverse proportion? Choose all that apply.

(A) The time taken for a car to travel a distance of 50 miles at different speeds.

(B) The weight of 1 block of concrete when 12 blocks of concrete weigh 80 pounds.

(C) The time taken for 6 men to paint a house, when one man takes 3 days.

(D) $xy = k$ (where k is a constant)

(E) The total cost of apples bought, when one apple costs 80 cents.

This question has two parts.

(31) In a particular year, the cost of producing a batch of magazines comprises the following costs:

Paper: $4,000

Printing: $1,500

The costs of paper and printing will increase by 8% and 12%, respectively, in the following year.

PART A

What are the new costs for paper and printing? Write your answers and your work or explanation in the space below.

PART B

What is the percent change in the costs of producing the same batch of magazines in the following year? Round your answer to the nearest hundredth. Write your answers and your work or explanation in the space below.

© 2020 Marshall Cavendish Education Pte Ltd

Name: _____ Date: _____

Trip to the Art Gallery

1 While on a visit to an art gallery, Mr. Williams sees a replica of a famous painting he likes. The painting is 8 feet long by 6 feet wide. However, Mr. Williams wants the painting to be 10 feet long, so that he can display it on a wall at home. The gallery is able to increase the size of the painting if Mr. Williams can provide them with the percent increase in dimensions.

    a Find the percent increase in length if Mr. Williams wants the painting to be 10 feet long.

    b Find the new width of the painting if the increase in length is proportional to the increase in width.

    c Find the percent increase in the area of the painting.

2 The cost of the painting is $1,800. However, there is a promotion and Mr. Williams will enjoy a 15% discount after adding a tax of 7%. Mr. Williams chooses to pay for the painting over 12 monthly instalments, and he needs to pay an additional 5% of the final cost.

a Find the tax payable for the painting.

b Find the cost of the painting after discount.

c Find the final cost of the painting with the additional 5% charge. Round your answer to the nearest cent.

Rubric

Point(s)	Level	My Performance
7–8	4	• Most of my answers are correct. • I showed complete understanding of the concepts. • I used effective and efficient strategies to solve the problems. • I explained my answers and mathematical thinking clearly and completely.
5–6	3	• Some of my answers are correct. • I showed adequate understanding of the concepts. • I used effective strategies to solve the problems. • I explained my answers and mathematical thinking clearly.
3–4	2	• A few of my answers are correct. • I showed some understanding of the concepts. • I used some effective strategies to solve the problems. • I explained some of my answers and mathematical thinking clearly.
0–2	1	• A few of my answers are correct. • I showed little understanding of the concepts. • I used limited effective strategies to solve the problems. • I did not explain my answers and mathematical thinking clearly.

Teacher's Comments

STEAM

Domestic Migration

Birds, butterflies, and other animals are not the only living things that migrate, or move from one geographic location to another. People migrate, too. The U.S. Census Bureau collects and analyzes data to determine how state populations change from year to year.

Task

Work in pairs or small groups to investigate domestic migration within the United States.

1. Search the U.S. Census Bureau to find the most recent report of percent changes in population for the 50 states.

2. Construct two graphs, one to display ten states experiencing the greatest percent of population change and one to display ten states experiencing the least percent of population change.

3. Continue your research to learn more about how domestic migration is affecting your state. Use art materials or digital tools to create an infographic illustrating the impact of population change in your state. For example, how have population changes affected the job market, housing, transportation, social services, and natural resources?

4. Share your work. As a class, discuss and list possible advantages and disadvantages of migrating domestically.

MIGRATION
Straight Ahead ↑↑

Glossary

A

- **additive inverse**
  The additive inverse of a number x is the number that, when added to x, yields zero. Example: 2 and -2 are additive inverses.

C

- **complex fraction**
  A fraction in which the numerator, the denominator, or both the numerator and the denominator contain a fraction.

  Examples: $\dfrac{\left(\frac{2}{7}\right)}{8}$, $\dfrac{3}{\left(-\frac{5}{2}\right)}$, and $\dfrac{\left(4\frac{1}{2}\right)}{\left(-1\frac{5}{16}\right)}$

  are complex fractions.

- **constant of proportionality**
  The constant value of the ratio of two quantities x and y that are in direct proportion. When x and y are inversely proportional, the constant of proportionality is the product of x and y.

  Example: In the direct proportion equation $y = 2x$, 2 is the constant of proportionality. In the inverse proportion equation $y = 4$, 4 is the constant of proportionality.

- **cross product**
  A product found by multiplying the numerator of one fraction by the denominator of another fraction. If two fractions are equal, then their cross products are also equal.

  Example: $\dfrac{3}{4} = \dfrac{9}{12}$, so $3 \cdot 12 = 4 \cdot 9$.

D

- **direct proportion**
  A relationship between two quantities in which both quantities increase or decrease by the same factor.

- **discount**
  The amount by which an original price of something is reduced.

E

- **equivalent equations**
  Algebraic equations with the same solution Example: $2(6 - x) = 0$ and $12 - 2x = 0$ are equivalent equations.

- **equivalent inequalities**
  Algebraic inequalities with the same solution set.
  Example: $2x < 8$ and $x - 1 < 3$ are equivalent inequalities.

I

- **inverse proportion**
  A relationship between two quantities in which one quantity decreases as the other increases and vice versa so that the product of the two quantities remains constant.

L

- **least common denominator**
  The common multiple of the denominators of two or more fractions that has the least value.
  Example: The least common denominator of

  $\dfrac{1}{2}$ and $\dfrac{1}{5}$ is 10.

M

- **markup**
  The rate at which a seller raises the price of goods over their cost.

N

- **negative fraction**
  A fraction to the left of 0 on a number line.
  Examples: $-\frac{1}{2}$, $-\frac{13}{5}$, and $-\frac{10}{3}$ are negative fractions.

- **negative integer**
  An integer to the left of 0 on a number line.
  Examples: -5, -17, and -98 are negative integers.

P

- **positive integer**
  An integer to the right of 0 on a number line.
  Examples: 2, 10, and 51 are positive integers.

- **proportion**
  An equation that says two ratios are equivalent.
  Examples: $\frac{5}{2} = \frac{10}{4}$ and $\frac{8}{3} = \frac{24}{9}$ are proportions.

R

- **rational number**
  A number that can be written as $\frac{m}{n}$, where m and n are integers with n being a nonzero integer.
  Examples: 8, $\frac{7}{11}$, and $-\frac{63}{253}$ are rational numbers.

repeating decimal

- **repeating decimal**
  A decimal that has a group of one or more digits that repeat endlessly.
  Examples: 0.111..., 0.030303..., and 0.16333... are repeating decimals.

S

- **set of integers**
  The set of negative integers, 0, and positive integers: ..., -4, -3, -2, -1, 0, 1, 2, 3, 4, ...

- **solution set**
  A set of values that make an inequality true.
  Example:
  $$x + 3 > 4$$
  $$x + 3 - 3 > 4 - 3$$
  $$x > 1$$

  $x > 1$ is the solution set.

T

- **terminating decimal**
  A decimal that has a finite number of nonzero decimal places.
  Examples: 0.5, 0.28, and 0.75 are terminating decimals.

Z

- **zero pair**
  A pairing of the integers 1 and -1, whose sum is 0.
  Example: $2 + (-3)$ has two zero pairs:

  $$2 + (-3) = 1 + 1 + (-1) + (-1) + (-1)$$
  $$= [1 + (-1)] + [1 + (-1)] + (-1)$$

Index

Pages in **boldface** type show where a term is introduced.

Properties
    associative, *see* Associative property
    commutative, *see* Commutative property
    distributive, *see* Distributive properpty

Proportion, **284**
    constant of proportionality, *see* Constant
        of proportionality
    cross products of, 307
    direct, *see* Direct proportion
    inverse, *see* Inverse proportion

Quantities
    combined to make zero, 36
    comparing unequal, 212

Quotient of rational numbers, 88

Rate(s)
    finding, 280
    unit, 280, 290

Rational numbers, **12**, 113
    adding, 79–80, 82, 91–92
        with different denominators, 79
        with same denominators, 79
    classifying, 24
    comparing, 26, 28
    dividing, 88, 90–92
    multiplying, 86–87, 91–92
    on number line, 14–16
    as repeating decimals, **23**–25
    subtracting, 83–85, 91–92
        with different denominators, 83
        with same denominator, 83
    as terminating decimals, **21**–22
    writing, using long division, 21–25

Ratios
    comparing quantities using, 278
    equivalent, 278
    in simplest form, 278

Real-world problems
    solving
        algebraically, 231–232, 234, 236
        algebraic expressions, 191
        algebraic inequalities, 259–261

        algebraic reasoning for, 187–188, 190
        direct proportion, 307–308, 310
        fractions, 349–350
        percent, 347–350
        percent increase/decrease, 345–346
        "percent of percent" concept, 351–352
    tables to organize information for, 178
    translate into algebraic expressions, 175–176,
        178–180, 182
    using a table, 311–312

Reciprocal, 7, 88–90

Recognizing
    equivalent expressions, 128
    parts of algebraic expression, 126

Repeated addition, 63–64
    multiplication rules using, 63

Repeating decimals, **23**
    rational numbers as, 23–25

Set(s)
    of integers, **9**
    solution, *see* Solution set
    of whole numbers, 9

Simplest form, *throughout, see for example,* 7, 17–18,
    93–94, 200, 226
    ratio in, 278

Simplify
    expressions, throughout, see for example, 5, 127,
        135–152, 159–160, 162–164
        by adding like terms, 129–133
        with more than two terms, 145–148
        by subtracting like terms, 139–142
        with two variables, 149–150
    numerical expressions, using order of
        operations, 5

Solution set, **243**
    of algebraic inequalities, 243–248, 250–251
    checking, 245

Straight line
    through origin, 298–299, 360

Substitution
    solving algebraic equations by, 211

© 2020 Marshall Cavendish Education Pte Ltd

Photo Credits

NOTES

NOTES

NOTES

NOTES

NOTES

© 2020 Marshall Cavendish Education Pte Ltd

Published by Marshall Cavendish Education
Times Centre, 1 New Industrial Road, Singapore 536196
Customer Service Hotline: (65) 6213 9688
US Office Tel: (1-914) 332 8888 | Fax: (1-914) 332 8882
E-mail: cs@mceducation.com
Website: www.mceducation.com

Distributed by
Houghton Mifflin Harcourt
125 High Street
Boston, MA 02110
Tel: 617-351-5000
Website: www.hmhco.com/programs/math-in-focus

First published 2020

ISBN 978-0-358-10191-8

Printed in Singapore

| 5 6 7 8 9 10 | 1401 | 27 26 25 24 23 |
| 4500861396 | | B C D E F |

The cover image shows a Eurasian lynx.
This medium-sized wild cat can be found in the thick forests of Siberia, and in remote, mountainous parts of Europe and Asia. Eurasian lynxes have dark spots on their fur, long, black tufts at the tips of their ears, and they have excellent hearing. They are nocturnal hunters that approach their unsuspecting prey very quietly from out of the darkness. Although their numbers had previously dropped due to hunting, they are now increasing once again.